323 Rab
Rabben, Linda,
Fierce legion of friends
    : a history of hum$ 20.00
    rights campaig

W9-BTO-964

FIERCE Legion of FRIENDS

The Quixote Center
Brentwood, Maryland

FIERCE Legion of FRIENDS

A History of Human Rights Campaigns and Campaigners

LINDA RABBEN

Published by the Quixote Center
P.O. Box 5206
Hyattsville, MD 20782, USA
http://www.quixote.org

Copyright © 2002 by Linda Rabben
All rights reserved. No part of this publication may be reproduced,
stored in a retrieval system or transmitted in any form or by any means,
electronic, mechanical, photocopying, recording or otherwise without the
prior permission of the author.

Printed in the United States of America
ISBN 0-19714152-0-X
Library of Congress Control Number 2001118918

Book design by Lisa Roth

Portions of Chapter 9 appeared in somewhat different form in *Amnesty
Now* and *Agni 54*.

In Memory of My Grandfather, Gustav Golove, 1866-1953
And in Honor of Human Rights Defenders around the World:

A Toast to Freedom,
From a Friend of a Friend

"It requires no small labour to open the eyes of either the public or of individuals, but when that is accomplished, you are not yet got a third of the way. The real difficulty remains in getting people to apply the principles which they have admitted and of which they are now so fully convinced." *Lord Shelbourne, c. 1800.*

"Power concedes nothing without a demand. It never did, and it never will." *Frederick Douglass, 1857*

Ironic points of light
Flash out wherever the Just
Exchange their messages:
May I, composed like them
Of Eros and of dust,
Beleaguered by the same
Negation and despair,
Show an affirming flame.

"September 1, 1939," copyright 1940 & renewed 1968 by W.H. Auden, from W.H. AUDEN: COLLECTED POEMS by W.H. Auden. Used by permission of Random House, Inc.

CONTENTS

Illustrations *ix*

Foreword *xi*

Preface and Acknowledgments *xiii*

Introduction *1*

1. The First Human Rights Campaigns *7*

2. Campaigners and Strategies in the Late Eighteenth Century *21*

3. Nineteenth Century Antislavery: "Power Concedes Nothing without a Demand" *41*

4. The Age of Mass Movements and the "Martyrs of Chicago" *61*

5. The World of the 1890s: Lynching, Genocide, Injustice *81*

6. Sacco and Vanzetti: Agony or Triumph? *107*

7. The Scottsboro "Boys": "A Tangled, Ugly Case" *131*

8. The Rosenbergs: Sacrificing the Scapegoats *149*

9. Amnesty International: Myth and Reality *173*

10. Human Rights Campaigning since 1961 *201*

Notes *219*

Bibliography *235*

Index *245*

ILLUSTRATIONS

Cover: Sacco-Vanzetti demonstration, North End, 1919. (Courtesy of the Boston Public Library Print Department)

Frontispiece: "Affirming Flames," drawing by Linda Rabben © 2001.   *xvi*

Chapter 1: Am I Not a Man and a Brother, 1788.   *6*

Chapter 2: Olaudah Equiano, c. 1789. (Used with the permission of the Special Collections, University Library, University of California, Riverside)   *20*

Chapter 3: Am I Not a Man and a Brother/A Woman and a Sister. (Boston Athenaeum)   *40*

Chapter 4: Handbill for Haymarket Rally, May 4, 1886.   *60*

Chapter 5: *Coup de L'Eponge*. (© Agence Roger-Viollet)   *80*

Chapter 6: "A Boston Sunset," *Labor Age*, 1927. (Courtesy of the Library of Congress)   *106*

Chapter 7: Scottsboro petition (Courtesy of the Library of Congress)   *130*

Chapter 8: "No Hemos Olvidado a los Rosenberg," by Angel Bracho and Celia Calderon, 1953. (Reprinted with permission from *The Rosenbergs: Collected Visions of Artists and Writers*, edited by Rob Okun © 1988)   *148*

Chapter 9: Peter Benenson lighting candle. (© 1981 Amnesty International)   *172*

Chapter 10: Romaria da Terra, 1986. (Photo by Linda Rabben)   *200*

FOREWORD

This book is about my spiritual and political ancestors, and possibly yours as well. The people whose stories are told in these pages were deeply concerned about injustices like the slave trade, anti-Semitism, racism and political prosecutions. They deplored human rights abuses and took action, no matter what the economic, racial or ethnic status of the victims. They never let their own relative powerlessness stop them. They joined with like-minded justice seekers, signed petitions, wrote letters, called meetings, formed alliances, participated in boycotts, joined in public demonstrations. And they made the world a better place.

Many books describe the works and leadership of those who led crusades for justice, peace or human rights. Many authors, for example, have celebrated William Lloyd Garrison, Sojourner Truth and Harriet Tubman. But who were the people they led? Who came to antislavery meetings, read the *Liberator*, ran the underground railroad, signed petitions and joined in public protests?

For the first time, this book focuses on such people. It is the history of human rights *campaigns and campaigners* over the past 200 years, rather than the history of a few leaders. It describes the roles of the rank-and-file, the folks at the grassroots, the extraordinary works of ordinary citizens who acted for social change.

The Quixote Center is proud to publish this book. We have been working with great people like those described in this book for a quarter-century, and we want to celebrate their unsung contributions to the work of justice. Like those on whose shoulders we stand, our Quixote friends dream "impossible dreams" of justice and human rights for our nation, for the world at large and—because we grew from the Catholic social-justice tradition—for the Roman Catholic Church itself. These crusaders let injustice move their hearts and interrupt their lives. They stand publicly with people or advocate causes that others judge unworthy, radical or unsavory.

Quixote collaborators have written countless letters to legislators and newspapers in the past twenty-five years. They have called for—among other things—the ratification of the Equal Rights Amendment, a death penalty moratorium and debt cancellation for countries in the Global South. In the 1980s, they pressed for an end to military aid to El Salvador and the Nicaraguan "Contras," and in the 1990s, they defended the return of Jean Bertrand Aristide as the duly elected president of Haiti.

In the 1980s, tens of thousands responded to Reagan's "Contra" war in Nicaragua by filling cargo containers with humanitarian aid, which we shipped to the victims of that war. Many still give generously for all types of economic development in Nicaragua, just as thousands of people give what they can for literacy programs and reforestation in Haiti. Thousands more signed ads in *The New York Times*, publicly aligning themselves with the call for basic reforms in the Roman Catholic Church, such as ordination of women, an end to mandatory clerical celibacy, gay and lesbian rights, and acceptance of artificial contraception. On many occasions, our constituents circulate petitions, call meetings, form local action groups and join all manner of public demonstrations. These actions are the essence of social change.

This book celebrates great people who let injustices bother them and move them to action, who take public stands for justice and refuse to let the powerful become repressive. They are the ones who, in the words of the Scriptures, "bring good news to the poor, give sight to the blind, set the captives free" and work for the day of Jubilee.

Let their stories and their courage seep into your bones as you read. You may find yourself becoming more firmly a part of today's "fierce legion of friends."

Maureen Fiedler, S.L.
Co-Director, The Quixote Center
August 2001

PREFACE AND ACKNOWLEDGMENTS

When I was studying history in high school and college, I often daydreamed about going back to the past in person. In recent years, while reading historical novels or biographies, I have tried to imagine what it would be like to talk and live with people in the time before my birth. Or I wonder what they would think of the present and how they would experience it. Spending time in other cultures as an anthropologist has not lessened the intensity of my desire for *la récherce du temps perdu*. This wish to go back, to touch the unrecoverable, must be a common feeling and a common motivation for reading and writing about the past. A historian friend admits as much.

The idea of a history of human rights campaigns came to me after a decade of work with Amnesty International. From the late 1980s on, I worked on Brazilian human rights cases for Amnesty, as a researcher at the International Secretariat in London and a volunteer Brazil expert for AIUSA. Through this work I met and collaborated with courageous human rights activists from many countries whom I admired intensely.

In the midst of these activities, I often wondered where the idea for Amnesty International came from, and how and why the organization's strategies developed as they did. I started to read about the history of the human rights movement, but the studies available did not answer my questions about Amnesty's ancestry and evolution. Amnesty's "creation myth," commemorated with its "toast to freedom" at every annual meeting, explained little. I felt a need to discover what came before Amnesty.

In reading about famous campaigns and cases, I encountered a rich, sometimes tragic and inspiring history of groups and individuals who crusaded for generations with courage and persistence for the dignity of all people. The lineage of the modern human rights movement went back further than I had expected; it included cases and individuals I knew little about or had never heard of before. Despite the distance of time and space, I had the delightful experience of meeting kindred spirits. May they breathe again in these pages.

Skilled scholars and researchers led me across disciplinary boundaries. Adam Hochschild, David Kertzer, Gerda Lerner, Dorothy Thompson, Howard Zinn in particular and many others have written fascinating, meticulously researched accounts about campaigns and campaigners of the past 200 years. Andrew Blane and Priscilla Ellsworth did a great service by collecting oral histories of the organization's pioneers in the mid-1980s. The work of all these people inspired me.

Many colleagues gave encouragement and useful suggestions. J.R. Oldfield of Southampton University in England responded with kindness to an e-mail message from a stranger and helped me frame the chapters on the antislavery movement. Howard Zinn encouraged me to go ahead at an early stage and read the completed manuscript. Michael Meeropol and Rob Okun made helpful suggestions and provided useful information. Maureen Fiedler, S.L., was always ready to hear about the latest chapter and was the book's first reader. She helped me in many ways—spiritual and practical—at all stages of the project.

Amnesty veterans William Schulz, Patti Whaley, Larry Cox and Morton Winston found time to help. Harry Rubenstein, social history curator at the National Museum of American History, opened up the world of material culture to me. Terence Turner of Cornell University helped at several critical moments. Thomas Holloway of the University of California (Davis) read a chapter and made astute comments.

The Human Rights Centre of Essex University (U.K.) welcomed me as a visiting fellow and gave me the opportunity to make a presentation about the book. Canon John Nurser, a fellow of the Centre, was a knowledgeable and kind reader who made many useful comments about the Amnesty chapter.

I am grateful to Ted Nace for his enthusiastic response to the book, which led him to give crucial moral support and assistance. I also thank Andrew Blane for reading and commenting on the manuscript. Peter B. Collins, Merrill Leffler and Mary Anderson gave useful practical advice. And I thank Emily Alman, David Alman and William Rueben for graciously agreeing to be interviewed. For them, *a luta continua*, even into their ninth decade.

Facilitating the primary research were librarians and archivists at the University of Maryland Library, the Library of Congress, the National Archives, Friends Historical Library, the British Library, the International Institute of Social History, Houghton Library, Harvard Law School Library, Boston University Library, Boston Public Library, New York Public Library, the Schomburg Collection, Anti-Slavery International, the Columbia University Oral History Research Office, the Wisconsin State Historical Society, the National Museum of American History and the British Public Records Office. All of the librarians I encountered deserve recognition for their patience, skill and dedication.

I also thank Amnesty International, the Harvard Law School Library, the Houghton Library of Harvard University, the Wisconsin State Historical Society, the Columbia University Oral History Collection, the British Library and the Friends Historical Library for granting permission to quote from documents in their collections.

Special thanks go to the publisher of this book, the Quixote Center, a unique nongovernmental organization with which I have been associated since 1996. The Center's co-directors have given me moral and intellectual support over the years, as well as financial support that helped make the book's publication possible. I am proud and grateful to be associated with the Center, its important work and its "impossible dreams."

I am also grateful to the Special Initiatives Fund of Amnesty International USA, the Ted Nace Fund and other contributors for their financial assistance. Their names are listed at the back of the book.

Designer Lisa Roth, copy editor Rea Howarth, proofreader Jerry Pederson, and Beth Ponticello, Art/Media Director of the Center for Educational Design and Communication, contributed their high standards and skills to the making of the book.

Generous friends—Moyra Ashford, Vilma Barban, Patricia Bell, Donna Hurwitz, Margrit Oyens, Leif Skoogfors and Patti Whaley—helped more than they might have realized. My family also gave substantive help. Last but not least, I am grateful to Patchouli for her steadfast companionship, sweetness and affection.

"Affirming Flames"

INTRODUCTION

At this very moment, across the world thousands of people are writing letters and sending faxes, telegrams and e-mail messages to government officials in other countries. They are politely asking that a political prisoner be released, a torture victim receive medical attention, a "disappeared" person be found, a threatened activist receive protection.

They are folding the paper, feeding the fax into the machine, clicking the "send" icon, putting the stamp on the envelope, walking to the mailbox, waiting in line at the post office. They are waiting for an answer. They are writing again, to another government official in another country. They are receiving a letter with a foreign stamp. They are reading the excuse, the denial, the sad news, the happy news. They are writing again.

A man is squinting at the light as he walks out of prison. A woman is being carried on a stretcher to a hospital. A child is crying at a funeral. A body is being exhumed. A killer is finally being indicted.

A man is being arrested for criticizing the president. Two soldiers are executing a fourteen-year-old boy. Five paramilitaries are raping someone's grandmother. A journalist is receiving a threatening phone call.

In another country, concerned individuals are writing again. Where did they get the idea they could change things by writing letters?

To find the answer to this question, we must go back more than 200 years, to a quiet road in rural England. It is 1785. As Thomas Clarkson, aged twenty-five, rides his horse on the road, he is thinking about slavery. He is thinking so hard that he forgets to guide the horse. The horse stops. Like Saint Paul on the road to Damascus, Clarkson has a vision. He thinks, "It is time some person should see these calamities to the end," and he decides to dedicate the rest of his life to the abolition of slavery.

Clarkson spent most of the next sixty years campaigning. In 1807 Britain ended the slave trade in its dominions, and in 1833, it ended slavery. Shortly before Clarkson's death in 1846, he was still working to end slavery in the United States and other countries.

Clarkson was not alone. Between the time he made his vow in 1785 and the end of his life, thousands of people joined him in the great international movement to abolish slavery. Against apparently overwhelming odds, they succeeded. But nobody who started the crusade in the late Eighteenth Century lived long enough to see the abolition of slavery in Brazil, the last western country to end it, in 1888. It took the concentrated efforts of generations of people, including the slaves themselves, to abolish slavery. And more than a hundred years later, in 2001, slavery had not entirely disappeared, although the international trading system that supported it has changed considerably. Anti-Slavery International, founded by Clarkson and others, is still campaigning against it.

The international abolitionist movement of the late Eighteenth to late Nineteenth Centuries provides the template for almost every social movement of the past 200 years. Its tactics, strategies and structures first developed in Britain and North America but spread throughout the world, changing in response to local conditions as they went. By the mid-Twentieth Century, mass movements of protest, mobilization, revolution or reform had far surpassed the abolitionist movement in magnitude and consequence.

At the same time, people across the world continued to focus on individuals whose cases seemed to exemplify the struggles of the mass movements. These "causes célèbres," as they were called, advanced the larger movements by attracting and mobilizing thousands of new adherents. Recognizing this, the managers of the great movements took up individual cases to increase their organizations' power and advance their causes. Sometimes the members of the movements pressured the leaders to campaign on such cases. The individuals who became emblematic figures did not always benefit, however. Their causes were often lost, and they are remembered today (if remembered at all) as martyrs.

The tragic fact is that many human rights campaigns failed to achieve their objectives. In highly publicized cases, from the Haymarket Affair in the 1880s to Sacco and Vanzetti in the 1920s and the Rosenbergs in the 1950s, activists set up defense committees, published appeals, raised funds, organized demonstrations, lobbied legislators and governors, worked for years—only to watch helplessly as the state imprisoned or executed its opponents. Often they were accused of heinous crimes, and supporters devoted considerable time, effort and funds to trying to disprove charges they believed were unfounded. In many instances they could not marshal sufficient resources or public support to overturn the verdict. The inevitable end to this oft-repeated ritual was the desperate, last-minute appeal for commutation of the death sentence, followed by the silent mass march to the cemetery. To this day, legal scholars and historians are still arguing about the guilt of the defendants in these cases.

Despite the movements' failures, their experiences can teach us much. The stories of these campaigns and campaigners poignantly remind us of the challenges, triumphs and difficulties of changing human societies.

For those who are still writing letters, waiting for answers and writing again, the histories of past campaigns can provide inspiration when hope of change and justice seems lost. Gross violations of basic human rights continue to happen every day, and they are part of the political systems of many countries, including our own. But a certain number of people over the past 200 years have been saved from terrible suffering, or had their suffering relieved, by the determined actions of strangers who acted out of principle and conscience.

In a letter to a supporter in 1924, Nicola Sacco, an anarchist condemned to death for robbery and murder, expressed his gratitude "towards all this fierce legion of friends and comrades." Many of those active in the struggle to save Sacco and his comrade Bartolomeo Vanzetti from execution expressed their "fierceness" through demonstrations, petitions and other nonviolent actions over a seven-year period. Thousands of people organized defense committees, raised funds, visited or wrote to the prisoners, lobbied legislators and governors, published articles, pamphlets, newsletters and books in many countries. Despite their determination and devotion, the State of Massachusetts executed Sacco and Vanzetti in 1927.

Fifty years later, at age eighty-six, Katherine Anne Porter still remembered vividly the final vigil at the prison gates.

> . . . the crowd was enormous and in the dim light silent, almost motionless, like crowds seen in a dream. . . . This was not a mob. . . . It was a silent, intent assembly of citizens—of anxious people come to bear witness and to protest against the terrible wrong about to be committed, not only against the two men about to die, but against all of us, against our common humanity and our shared will to avert what we believed to be not merely a failure in the use of the instrument of the law, an injustice committed through mere human weakness and misunderstanding, but a blindly arrogant, self-righteous determination not to be moved by any arguments, the obstinate assumption of the infallibility of a handful of men intoxicated with the vanity of power and gone mad with wounded self-importance.

For Katherine Anne Porter, her inability to save Sacco and Vanzetti was shattering. But for many others, the long effort was a formative experience. They went on to work on other campaigns, organize other groups and take other actions. Thus they were following the example of people many had never heard of and probably knew nothing about. Even today, thousands of human rights activists around the world carry on their activities with little sense of their heritage.

Because it crosses many geographic and chronological boundaries, the history of human rights campaigns has received scant attention from scholars. I have not found any published history of human rights campaigning, though many accounts of specific campaigns and cases treat each one as if it were *sui generis*.

Recent histories of the human rights movement carefully trace the intellectual roots of human rights and survey modern social movements. However, they often do not examine the specific campaigns through which the human rights movement expanded and evolved. Much of the research for this book involved gleaning brief descriptions of campaigns, their strategies and organizations from a wide range of sources focusing on other matters. It was necessary to search campaign organizations' records and campaigners' papers to obtain more detailed information about the actual conduct and strategies of campaigns.

In such files I found Emma Goldman's anguished letters about Sacco and Vanzetti, the minutes of the "Committee for Effecting the Abolition of the Slave Trade" from 1787 to 1819, handbills advertising protest demonstrations in 1886 Chicago and 1932 New York, letters to the U.S. Justice Department from black mothers of lynching victims, the scrupulous financial records of the Sacco-Vanzetti Defense Committee in Boston and many other artifacts that document the history of human rights campaigns.

Many of the campaigners remain unknown faces in the "fierce legion." Japanese railway workers demonstrating for Sacco and Vanzetti in 1927, Danish seamen sending donations to nine anarchists sentenced to death for the "Haymarket massacre" in 1886, African-American domestic workers signing a petition for the Scottsboro Boys in 1932, British housewives boycotting West Indian sugar in 1795—these were the kinds of people who comprised what came to be known as the international human rights movement. In this book I try to reconstruct their history by recounting the stories of the campaigns in which they participated, from the late Eighteenth Century to the founding of Amnesty International in 1961.

Frequently the campaigns focused on people accused of serious criminal offenses, including murder. I have not tried to make a case for the innocence of the people on whose behalf human rights campaigners worked. In many cases, that would be impossible. Instead I have sought to tell the stories of the campaigns themselves and the people who made them.

I looked at campaigns rather than broad social movements, such as the U.S. civil rights movement or the South African antiapartheid movement, for several reasons. First, campaigns have not received sufficient attention from scholars, despite their importance in the evolution of the larger social movements. Second, I particularly wanted to discover where Amnesty International and its distinctive strategies and structures came from. Campaigns focusing on individuals, using letter writing and petitioning techniques, carried out by local groups and supervised by central coordinating bodies, are Amnesty's direct ancestors. Their history is both instructive and intrinsically interesting.

Why stop at Amnesty's creation in 1961? After all, campaigns continue up to the present, and they are likely to go on into the foreseeable future. But with the founding of Amnesty International, human rights campaigning moved to a new level of intensity and effectiveness. Amnesty quickly became a permanent, international, membership organization that aims to free prisoners of conscience and end torture and the death penalty everywhere. Instead of reacting to one or another *cause célèbre*, Amnesty focused on "forgotten prisoners" around the world. Thus its originators created something new while building on a long tradition of public advocacy. By starting a grassroots organization and identifying it as part of an international movement, they sought to ensure that Amnesty would embody the universality of human rights. In the process, the international human rights movement came of age. Its recent history is the subject of many other books, articles and reports.

The human rights movement now is a many-headed creature. Diverse, dynamic, global but decentralized, it operates on every level: local, regional, national, international. It is much, much more than Amnesty International. For the contemporary human rights movement, Amnesty may have been the alpha, but it is by no means the omega.

Amnesty did not come out of nowhere. Its strategies and structure grew out of many sources. Its focus on individuals, its campaign style, its concentration on civil and political rights and its determinedly apolitical stance— all these characteristics emerged in reaction and response to a long history of social activism as well as recent movements and contemporary political conditions. To understand where Amnesty came from, we must go back not just to Thomas Clarkson on his horse, but even further, to mid-Eighteenth Century England.

Wedgwood designed and produced this emblem of the antislavery cause in 1788; it was reproduced in many forms and in many places for seventy-five years.

Chapter 1

THE FIRST HUMAN RIGHTS CAMPAIGNS

W hen was the first human rights campaign? The answer depends on the definition of *human, rights* and *campaign*. The idea that people unlike ourselves are in fact human is by no means universal. For as long as human beings have been talking (for about 50,000 to 125,000 years in *Homo sapiens'* 2 to 6 million-year history), they have been calling their particular group "we, the people" and treating the "other" as less than human. The acceptance of all humans as equal members of the same species is very recent.

The idea of rights also has a brief history. In many human societies, and certainly during the 10,000-year history of civilization, only a tiny minority has been able to claim or exercise any rights. The idea of "human rights" as the possession of all human beings has developed during the past 500 years or so, though its roots may be found in classical Greek and Roman thought and in the major religious traditions of the past five millennia. Establishing human rights as a universally accepted concept is still a work in progress.

"Campaign" dates from the early Seventeenth Century, when it was a military term, meaning "the time during which an army is in the field." It began to be used figuratively in English in 1770, at about the time when the first modern human rights campaigns were starting. (Election campaigns seem to have come later.)

Perhaps the very first "human rights campaigns"—the slave rebellions of the Roman Empire—were indeed military. Some historians believe that the first nonviolent campaign was the personal crusade of Fray Bartolomé de las Casas, a Spanish monk who defended the humanity of the New World's indigenous people in the Sixteenth Century. As a result of his efforts, popes and bishops issued several pronouncements affirming indigenous people's right to live without being enslaved, persecuted or slaughtered. But las Casas' initiative was not a campaign (in the sense of a movement), because he waged it alone, inside the church and the Spanish royal court. Neither he nor his executor could find a publisher for his treatises on justice for the Indians. At that time none of the conditions existed for a campaign in the modern sense of the word.

What are these conditions? The campaigns described in this book share the following characteristics:

- Dedicated and persistent organizers;
- Public participation;
- Involvement of influential intellectuals;
- Committed financial backers;
- Sustained attention of a relatively free press;
- A general sense of the universality of human rights.

It was not until the Eighteenth Century, and in only a few places, that these conditions came into being. My research shows that the first modern human rights campaigns began with John Wilkes' crusade for freedom of expression in Britain in the 1760s, followed by organized efforts by Quakers and others in Britain, North America and Europe to end the slave trade during the 1780s and 1790s.

WHY BRITAIN?

In the Eighteenth Century, Britain was arguably the world's freest nation. Millions of Indians, Chinese, Russians and others toiled without hope as serfs or slaves, while British white males enjoyed and exercised rights of which nine-tenths of the world's population had no knowledge or experience. According to historian Seymour Drescher, "To be enlightened was to be impressed with the vastness of unfreedom."

Britain also became the greatest slave-trading nation the world had ever seen in the early Eighteenth Century. Some Britons took pride in their prowess as traders of slaves and other goods; but many believed that "the air of this island is too free to tolerate slavery on our shores." They sang the following lyrics, written by James Thomson in 1740, with great conviction: "Rule Britannia, Britannia rule the waves; Britons never never *never* will be slaves!" Although they benefited from the slave system, most Britons did not want to see human beings sold like cattle in their markets.

Even so, some thousands of slaves, imported from Africa and other places, lived and worked in Britain—mostly in cities or as household servants on rural estates—during the Eighteenth Century. Estimates of their numbers vary widely, from 3,000 to 40,000, and it is not known how many died as slaves and how many were freed. "Freedom" for blacks in Britain generally meant living in abject poverty, begging in the streets.

Living and working conditions were wretched for most people. Rural life was almost feudal, and the vast majority of Britons were poor and landless. During the late Eighteenth Century, and especially during the Napoleonic Wars, wages fell and many people suffered from a drop in the standard of living. The population rose rapidly and towns grew in a disorganized fashion. Apprenticeship, the dominant form of job training, was brutal; workdays, even for children, lasted from 5 a.m. to 8 p.m. in mills and on the farm. According to a social historian, "Food and living conditions were only too often disgusting and inadequate." Reformers constantly compared the condition of the British working classes—the vast majority of the population—to that of slaves on West Indian plantations.

The privileged, literate few subscribed to the ideology of the "Great Chain of Being," according to which social inequality was eternal and unchanging. White, property-owning males reigned at the top of the human heap, with the world's slaves securely chained at the bottom. In his *Essay on Man* (1733-34), the British poet Alexander Pope triumphantly wrote: "The truth is clear, / Whatever is, is right." Slavery and the slave trade seemed to be immutable parts of this "natural order."

Events and changing ideas belied Pope's complacency, however. Social, political, technological and economic innovations, built on the profits of slave and free labor, were transforming the Anglo-American world. In time, the Industrial Revolution would change the whole world, for better or for worse.

Among the innovators who made the Industrial Revolution were people called "Dissenters," members of Christian sects who refused to sign a loyalty oath to the established Anglican church. British Quakers, Baptists, Methodists, Presbyterians, Unitarians and others were barred from public office and the universities unless they abjured their faith. "Though Dissent was no longer illegal, it was far from being socially acceptable," wrote historian Dorothy Marshall. Some Dissenters emigrated to the American colonies or left their sects for the Church of England; others led prosperous lives as merchants, mill owners, physicians, lawyers and clergymen; still others lived in poverty. Because they were shut out of mainstream society, some Dissenters supported radical political and social movements to change it.

THE IMPORTANCE OF INFORMATION

One of the factors spurring change was "the ease and speed with which news, people and goods could be conveyed from place to place, bringing into closer contact town and country, the provinces and London," Marshall wrote. Technological improvements meant that people could exchange ideas more easily. The press as we know it emerged in Britain, where the first daily newspaper was published in London in 1702.

Printed periodicals had begun in Europe in the Fifteenth Century, but their circulation was restricted to merchants, financiers and the nobility.

Most of the news was commercial, though it also included political gossip. In April 1493, a pamphlet about Columbus' "discovery" of America was printed in Spain, and hundreds of copies circulated in Rome, Antwerp, Basel and Florence, but it took about three years for this news to reach Britain. Censorship and repression by the authorities, as well as widespread illiteracy and taxation of publications, greatly limited the dissemination of news in Europe until the Nineteenth Century.

Nonetheless, a "Republic of Letters," composed of intellectuals, scientists, artists and clerics, did exchange news and ideas from the Renaissance on. For example, Galileo and Descartes knew of each other's work through correspondence with a friar. The *Journal des Savants* in France and the *Philosophical Transactions* of the Royal Society in England both began publication in 1665.

The British Civil War of the 1640s was the occasion for the explosive development of periodicals, pamphlets and books, which later slackened because the authorities regained control of the press. The word "newspaper" began to be used in Britain around 1670, when a few periodicals were appearing weekly.

According to Anthony Smith, from the early Eighteenth Century on, the American colonies "presented all the classic preconditions for the rapid growth of a newspaper industry": a literate population of skilled workers, fast-growing cities and a reliable postal service. Postmasters were often printers. Along with other colonists, they fought the imposition of the stamp tax, which was levied on newspapers as well as on tea. Newspapers helped build sentiment for revolution in North America for a decade before the first shot was fired.

Thousands of copies of newspapers were printed daily in Britain by the late Eighteenth Century, but readers far outnumbered buyers. Because of taxation, licensing requirements and a chronic shortage of paper, periodical prices were high in Britain. The paper shortage continued until wood pulp replaced rags as the basis of newsprint in the mid-Nineteenth Century. Crammed with tiny type, newspaper pages were almost illegible by modern standards. In addition, about half of the British population was illiterate. So coffeehouses and taverns became public reading rooms, offering dozens of papers for customers to read aloud and discuss. In this way, 5,000 copies of a newspaper might be read by 100,000 or more people. At this time, "the public" was emerging as a social and political force for politicians to reckon with, and newspapers, in the provinces and new towns as well as in London, began to play a crucial role in creating, influencing and mobilizing public opinion.

In Eighteenth Century Britain, the press "still labored under a series of frustrating restrictions which . . . made every editor and writer live in permanent fear of fines, imprisonment and the humiliation of the pillory,"

Smith wrote. But repeated battles with the government, including John Wilkes' crusade for freedom of expression, did increase the power and influence of the press during this period.

UNLIKELY HERO

An ugly, bumptious jokester, Member of Parliament and alleged pornographer, John Wilkes was one of the Eighteenth Century's most brilliant politicians. According to his biographer, Audrey Williamson, "Wilkes always tended to be virtuous by accident." In 1762 he secretly started a newspaper, *The North Briton*, which he used to advance his political career. A year later, in issue Number 45, he attacked the king's opening speech to Parliament. Since criticizing the king was a crime, the government prosecuted Wilkes for "seditious libel" and, using a warrant with no name on it, threw him in the Tower of London. Police searched his house and seized his personal papers and books, as well as letters he wrote from prison.

The House of Commons ordered that Number 45 of *The North Briton* be burnt by the public hangman, but "the mob managed to soak the faggots so that they would not burn," Williamson wrote. The cry "Wilkes and Liberty" echoed through the streets of London.

Wilkes appealed to the King's Bench (the high court) and won his release on the grounds that general warrants, without the accused's name, were illegal. He also claimed parliamentary immunity, and his constituents backed him. Nevertheless, the House of Commons expelled him. Wilkes was repeatedly re-elected to Parliament and repeatedly expelled. From 1768 to 1770, he spent two years in prison for libel. While he was there, he ran for Parliament and won, but the candidate who lost the election was seated in the House. The public protested. Williamson wrote:

> Petitions from various parts of the country supported the demand for Wilkes' release and the removal of Luttrell from his seat in the House of Commons. The campaign was personally stimulated by Wilkes' followers. . . . Eighteen counties in all [out of forty] sent petitions. . . . Throughout the country . . . the Wilkes issue and its parliamentary and libertarian implications had taken hold of the public imagination.

A brilliant propagandist, Wilkes used the government's ham-handed repression to assert freedom of expression. Immediately after his arrest in 1763, "He published an account of the events of his arrest, his accusations of those who had confined him and, in what was considered an appalling breach of political etiquette, had the correspondence between the Secretaries of State and himself printed on a flysheet and dispersed throughout London," wrote historian John Brewer. This account was reprinted in newspapers throughout the country.

Casting his conflicts as "a clash between the forces guarding liberty and those working in favour of arbitrary power," Wilkes promoted himself as a symbol of freedom. He used engravings, cartoons, ballads, pamphlets and handbills to popularize his cause. To raise funds, he sold his political writings by subscription, in installments: "Each part of the book could be purchased, a few pages at a time, for a price that was certainly no higher than a halfpenny, and may have been less," Brewer wrote. One broadsheet was advertised as "printed on fine paper, fit for framing." Thus, through skillful self-promotion, Wilkes became nationally and internationally famous. While he was in prison from 1768 to 1770, he received gifts of food and clothing from as far away as Boston, South Carolina and Hamburg.

In 1769, some 55,000 people signed petitions calling for Wilkes' release, and when he left prison in 1770, parades, illuminations and bell-ringing occurred throughout Britain and America. These demonstrations and other public events, including effigy burnings, posed serious challenges to government authority and control. For most Britons, unenfranchised and politically powerless, the streets were the only political arena. They were the much-feared "mob." Symbols, such as the number 45 and the cry, "Wilkes and Liberty," served to rally the population and threatened political order both literally and figuratively.

Brewer calls Wilkes "one of the first, if not *the* first political entrepreneur," because he pioneered many of the strategies used in later campaigns of all kinds. He published a variety of documents, raised funds from the public, sold his image on portraits, spoons, teapots, jugs, buttons, medals and other objects, organized or inspired public demonstrations, and helped change repressive laws through litigation and civil disobedience. Most significantly, he came to embody the cause of freedom of expression for which he fought. And as a symbol, he inspired the next generation of activists, who imitated his tactics if not his charisma.

CAMPAIGNING AGAINST THE SLAVE TRADE

Following Wilkes' example, the British press became bolder than it had dared to be before. To appreciate its role in ending the slave trade, we can contrast it with the press elsewhere. Newspapers were also published in France, Germany and other countries (including India), but they were more successfully suppressed and controlled by the governments there. Between 1600 and 1756, more than 800 authors, printers and booksellers were imprisoned in the French Bastille. The principal French newspaper between 1631 and 1789 was the *Gazette de France*, published by the king. Its July 17, 1789, issue did not mention the storming of the Bastille, the beginning of the revolution, which had happened three days before. During the revolution, the press became free for a few years; but later Napoleon completely controlled it, both in France and in the countries he conquered. As a result, people stopped reading the papers. Thus the influence of newspapers declined in countries where government repression was greater. Although there were campaigns to end the slave trade in France and some other countries in the late Eighteenth Century, they were less effective than the British campaign for this and other reasons.

Many newspapers in Britain opposed slavery in the late Eighteenth Century, printed advertisements of meetings protesting the slave trade and articles supporting its abolition. Nonetheless, they also printed advertisements for the recovery of runaway slaves or slave sales. Whatever their opinions of slavery, newspaper publishers needed advertising revenues to survive. They were part of a growing but still weak industry.

In contrast, the slave traders constituted one of the most powerful political, social and economic sectors of British society. It seemed that "in the world economy . . . there was no competitive alternative to slave-grown cotton or sugar," Drescher observed. Even Britons who were not personally involved in the slave trade benefited from it. "The slave trade at this time was not only buttressed by charters, treaties and an act of Parliament, it was the foundation of many very respectable merchants' fortunes," Marshall wrote. "Highly respectable" defenders of the slave trade included not only West Indian plantation owners living in England, but also merchants, lawyers, annuitants, creditors and heirs, Dale Porter wrote. The philosopher John Locke, who wrote against the slave trade, invested in it. Quaker merchants were among the most successful slave traders, even though their denomination condemned the trade. Marshall wrote, "The West Indian planters . . . always one of the best organized of the parliamentary lobbies, would be hard hit by any interference with their labor supply, and would resist [abolition] tooth and nail." In the 1784-90 Parliament, forty-five members of the House of Commons—almost forty percent of the body—constituted a powerful proslavery bloc. Many nobles and the royal family, the most powerful people in Britain, also supported the slave trade. For twenty years they could—and did—defeat any attempt to end slavery in the House of Lords.

Such were the forces arrayed in favor of slavery and the slave trade. Anchored by the "Great Chain of Being," the institution of human bondage and the international trading system that supplied it seemed unassailable. Nevertheless, David Brion Davis pointed out:

> . . . profound social changes, particularly those connected with the rise of new classes and new economic interests in Britain and America, created an audience hospitable to antislavery ideology. This ideology emerged from a convergence of complex religious, intellectual and literary trends—trends which are by no means reducible

to the economic interests of particular classes, but which must be understood as part of a larger transformation of attitudes toward labor, property and individual responsibility.

Opposition to the slave trade came from several social groups. Dissenters and some members of the established church had been questioning the rightness of slavery on moral and religious grounds for most of the century. Intellectuals in Britain, France and other slave-trading countries had been writing against it for decades. They cited Montesquieu, who updated Christian notions of natural law in his concept of natural rights. In *L'Esprit des Lois* (1748), he maintained that every individual is self-governing, and therefore individual rights are inalienable. The word "inalienable," a legal term meaning "cannot be sold, transferred or given away," found its way into the U.S. Declaration of Independence. The success of the American Revolution, fought in the name of political and economic freedom and self-determination, profoundly affected people in many countries in the late Eighteenth Century. They were electrified by the best-selling writings of Tom Paine, who was involved in the American and French Revolutions.

Economists such as Adam Smith and Adam Ferguson saw slavery as backward and inefficient. John Locke believed that "society is composed of discrete, self-governing individuals, whose true humanity lay in the proprietorship of their persons." Large numbers of educated people in Britain and America read and were influenced by the works of these writers.

The devout absorbed antislavery sentiments in religious pamphlets and books by dissenting and Anglican clergy, including John Wesley, John Woolman and James Ramsey. They "were sure that their reform proposals would win out only after they had converted the state and its citizens. Abolitionists did not wish to do away with the existing social order," Edith Hurwitz wrote. Instead, they saw themselves as "guardians of the moral order." Religious belief was the basis of much antislavery activity. To the abolitionists, Howard Temperley wrote:

> Slavery, quite simply, was wrong. It was wrong because it violated specific biblical injunctions, because it brought suffering to its victims, and because its baneful presence perverted the normal workings of whatever social system contained it. . . . the idea that what they were engaged in was essentially a religious struggle, was one with which they were entirely familiar.

The Quakers based their opposition to slavery on the Golden Rule, as well as on their opposition to war, through which slaves were captured. They believed that any society upholding such an evil system was bound to incur the wrath of God.

The majority of the British population did not share these concerns, however. And in any case, only a small proportion had the opportunity to be politically active. During most of the Eighteenth Century, opposition to slavery and the slave trade was restricted to a tiny minority.

THE ROLE OF THE QUAKERS

The strongest opponents of slavery were members of the Religious Society of Friends, the Quakers, who numbered only about 20,000 in late Eighteenth-century Britain. But the Friends did not come easily to antislavery. Although a North American Quaker meeting passed a resolution against slavery as early as 1688, most Friends did not want to take a stand on the matter throughout most of the Eighteenth Century. In fact, some influential Quakers were slave traders or benefited from the trade.

Early in the century, Friends who vocally opposed slavery were expelled from the Society. For example, in the 1730s, Benjamin Lay carried out theatrical actions to express his opposition to slavery. Roger Bruns described one of his exploits:

> Attired in full military regalia at a meeting in Burlington [New Jersey], the obstreperous Lay knifed a bladder of pokeberry juice, showering unsuspecting and startled Quakers with the red 'blood' of the slaves. . . . While attired in sackcloth, on several occasions [Lay] sprawled in the snow and rain in front of Quaker meeting houses to dramatize the plight of the Negroes.

Such actions did not endear him to other Friends, who "disowned" him. Lay retired to live like a hermit in a cave outside Philadelphia, sallying forth from time to time to converse with Benjamin Franklin and other abolitionists.

By midcentury, however, Quakers were changing their minds about slavery. John Woolman, a much-loved Quaker preacher who traveled extensively in America and Britain, urged Friends to divest themselves of slaves, tried not to use slave-produced products and would not accept travel expenses from Quaker slave owners. His gentle persuasion seems to have affected many Friends.

Although some American meetings expelled slave traders in the 1750s, British Quakers were the first to condemn the slave trade and slavery officially (in 1758 and 1761). Looking to the London Yearly Meeting for guidance and counsel, the American meetings followed London's example in the 1770s. All Friends' meetings in the American colonies decided to excommunicate slave-owning members in 1776.

In the mid- to late 1770s, the American Quakers began leading their British counterparts toward more public efforts to oppose slavery. In 1775 they were instrumental in founding the first antislavery society in

America, the Society for the Relief of Free Negroes Unlawfully Held in Bondage, in Pennsylvania. The London Meeting for Sufferings followed suit by establishing a twenty-three-man committee to promote the end of the slave trade in 1783. (Women were not allowed to participate in this and many other antislavery initiatives, but they took part in the 1787-94 campaign in other ways.)

THE FIRST CAMPAIGNER

From the 1750s to the 1780s, Anthony Benezet was "the most prolific and influential propagandist against slavery in the Eighteenth Century," Bruns wrote. An American Quaker, Benezet gathered information, compiled statistics, wrote pamphlets and articles, distributed literature in the colonies and Europe, wrote to heads of state, religious leaders and politicians, organized petition campaigns and tried to persuade Quakers to work against slavery. For years, wrote Bruns, "Benezet deluged the London Meeting for Sufferings with a seemingly inexhaustible stream of tracts, pamphlets and letters detailing the evils of slavery and appealing for English Friends to arouse public opinion against the institution." He collaborated with Quaker and other sympathizers in America, including Benjamin Rush, Thomas Paine, William Livingston and Benjamin Franklin. In 1772 he initiated a twelve-year correspondence with Granville Sharp, an Anglican antislavery activist in Britain. Sharp had already found an antislavery pamphlet by Benezet in a London bookshop five years before and had it reprinted. Another British activist, Thomas Clarkson, used Benezet's writings as sources for his own antislavery books. Benezet also corresponded with abolitionists David Barclay and Richard Shackleton in Britain and Abbé Raynal in France.

One of the members of the London Meeting for Sufferings' antislavery committee was William Dillwyn, who had attended Anthony Benezet's school for black children in Philadelphia. According to Judith Jennings, Dillwyn and five other committee members met privately in 1783, "to consider what steps could by them be taken for the Relief and Liberation of the Negro Slaves in the West Indies, and the Discouragement of the Slave Trade on the Coast of Africa." They continued their association with the larger committee but tried to act independently, "without submitting written materials to the central Quaker organization for review," Jennings wrote. Soon this unauthorized subcommittee was placing weekly antislavery articles in newspapers in a dozen cities throughout Britain. By the end of the year, ten different articles were circulating.

Meanwhile, the twenty-three-man committee published 2,000 copies of a pamphlet "respectfully recommended to the serious consideration of the Legislature of Great-Britain by the people called Quakers." They also sent to Parliament the first-ever petition against the slave trade, signed by more than 250 Quakers. The London Yearly Meeting's lobbyists delivered the petition and the pamphlet to sympathetic Members of Parliament.

In their pamphlet, the Quakers use both the secular discourse of natural law and natural rights and sacred language to make their case against slavery:

> The abolition of this iniquitous practice is not only required by the calls of justice and humanity, but is also consistent with sound policy. . . . Blessed be the God and Father of all our mercies, who hath made of one blood all nations of men, we now live under a dispensation essentially different from that of the law. . . . All distinctions of name and country, so far as they relate to the social duties, are now abolished. We are taught by our blessed Redeemer to look upon all men, even our enemies, as neighbours and brethren, and to do unto them as we would they should do unto us.

This work was clearly intended to persuade not only Quakers but politicians. It concludes with policy recommendations:

> The expectation of many, who are anxiously concerned for the suppression of this national evil is now, under Providence, fixed upon the wise and humane interposition of the legislature; to whom, with dutiful submission, we earnestly recommend the serious consideration of this important subject; with a pleasing hope, that the result will be, a prohibition of this traffick in future, and an extension of such relief to those who already groan in bondage, as justice and mercy may dictate, and their particular situations may admit.

Neither the petition nor the pamphlet had any apparent effect on the intended audience. No Member of Parliament introduced a bill to end the slave trade in 1783 or for several years after. India, not the West Indies, was the focus of parliamentary debates in the mid-1780s. But the Quakers' modest efforts did demonstrate the Society of Friends' organizational strength as "an international pressure group," in Davis' words—as well as their intellectual coherence, quiet determination and political flexibility.

Unlike some other dissenting groups, the Friends were willing to collaborate with other religious denominations in what we would call ecumenical coalitions. Their international networks included Baptists, Anglicans and the Methodist leader John Wesley, who wrote an antislavery tract in 1774. Although they used special forms of address ("thee" and "thou") among themselves, wore plain clothing and refused to flatter or bow to anyone, they tried to persuade other denominations by using common forms of language and secular or broadly Christian arguments. They did not claim a monopoly on salvation or proselytize among other groups. Because they believed that the "inner light" of spirituality dwelt in every person, they acknowledged the equality of all in the sight of God—a belief that buttresses the concept of universal human rights. As a result, they could see African slaves as human beings who should be free. They also had been influenced by Enlightenment philosophers such as Locke and Montesquieu. In a pamphlet published in 1784, committee member Joseph Woods wrote, "No right exists . . . to alienate from another his liberty . . . and therefore every purchase of a slave is in contradiction to the original inherent rights of mankind." Firm in their convictions and ready to act, they were well prepared to take a leading role in the antislavery cause.

COLONIAL PIONEERS

Meanwhile, in the American colonies, Quakers already had been leading antislavery efforts for about a decade. In 1774, 3,000 Quakers signed a petition calling for emancipation of all slaves in New Jersey. William Dillwyn, Benezet's former student and later member of the London Meeting's antislavery committee, lived in New Jersey at the time. In 1783, after Dillwyn had moved to London, Benezet wrote to him and others, urging them to attack the slave trade. They imitated the American Quakers' tactics by sending their own petition to Parliament.

The Pennsylvania Legislature voted to end slavery within its borders in 1780, "when Anthony Benezet personally and successfully solicited 'every member of the government' on behalf of an act for gradual emancipation, the first of its kind in America," Friends historian Thomas Drake writes. The Quakers petitioned one state legislature after another to end slavery and the slave trade. By the end of the Eighteenth Century, all the Northern states had outlawed slavery or the importation of slaves. And although the Quakers did not succeed in the national Congress, the United States did ban slavery in its Northwest Territory in 1787. A year later, the Constitution's framers acknowledged the necessity to end the slave trade by putting off its abolition for twenty years, until 1808. Abolition of slavery in the North was so gradual, however, that some slaves born in 1799 were still in bondage thirty years later. One example is Sojourner Truth, born a slave in New York near the end of the Eighteenth Century but not freed until 1828.

British Quakers were following all these developments. But in more than three years of quiet lobbying, they had managed to persuade only two or three Parliament members to support their cause. By 1787 it had become clear that the Quakers would have to change their tactics to gain their objective. What Drescher called the "first major public campaign in any country for a philanthropic cause" was about to begin.

*Olaudah Equiano freed himself from slavery and became one of the earliest abolitionists.
This portrait is from his autobiography, first published in 1789.*

Chapter 2

CAMPAIGNERS AND STRATEGIES IN THE LATE EIGHTEENTH CENTURY

What does the abolition of the slave trade mean more or less in effect than liberty and equality? What more or less than the rights of man? And what is liberty and equality, and what the rights of man, but the foolish fundamental principles of this new philosophy? –The Earl of Abingdon, 1792

The Quakers were not the only forces that took to the field. Anglicans, Dissenters, Deists, secular intellectuals and former slaves also campaigned against slavery and the slave trade during the second half of the Eighteenth Century. A handful attained prominence through their courageous and persistent work over many years.

In 1774, John Wesley, the founder of Methodism, published *Thoughts on Slavery*, in which he cited Benezet's writings. His clear opposition to slavery inspired other Dissenters. A decade later, Methodists in the United States threatened to expel members who had been slaveholders for more than two years. American Baptists also condemned human bondage. In 1785, the Baptist General Committee of Virginia declared hereditary slavery "contrary to the word of God," and in 1790 the same committee called slavery a "violent deprivation of the rights of nature, and inconsistent with republican government," Donald Mathews wrote. In a 1772 letter, Anthony Benezet recommended that Granville Sharp contact London Presbyterians, who "would be well pleased to see an End put to the Slave-Trade, and many, to slavery itself."

THE RESCUER

By 1772, Granville Sharp had already been working against slavery for several years. The twelfth child of the Anglican Archdeacon of Northumberland, Sharp was apprenticed to a Quaker merchant at age fifteen because his father could not afford to send him to university. Later he worked as a clerk in the Ordnance Office at the Tower of London. In 1765, when he was thirty, he had an encounter that changed his life.

One day, when Sharp was visiting his brother's surgery, he almost fell over an injured slave, Jonathan Strong, who was waiting in a long line for medical attention. His owner, a West Indian plantation proprietor living in England, had beaten Strong so savagely that the twenty-year-old slave was going blind. According to Sharp's biographer, Edward Lascelles, Strong had been "turned adrift into the streets to die." Sharp and his brother cared for Strong and found him a job. Two years later, his former owner saw Strong in the street and had him kidnapped and taken to prison. He then sold Strong and was going to ship him to the West Indies. Strong managed to send a letter to Sharp, who went to the prison "and in a few minutes heard enough to start him on the crusade which ended in the abolition of the slave trade," Lascelles wrote.

Sharp obtained Strong's release, but the owner brought suit against the Sharp brothers. When the renowned barrister William Blackstone withdrew from the case, Granville Sharp decided to defend himself in court. Lascelles wrote, "He had never opened a law book in his life . . . but he embarked at once on this stupendous piece of work, and for the next two years devoted his leisure to the study of constitutional law."

Sharp's legal research so impressed the owner's lawyers that they defaulted from the case. In 1769, he published his brief as a tract, "The Injustice of Tolerating Slavery in England." Meanwhile, his brother was supporting Wilkes in his campaign for freedom of expression.

Sharp became well known as a defender of slaves and worked on several cases similar to Strong's. Among the most dramatic was the case of Thomas Lewis in 1770. Like Strong, Lewis was abducted by his former owner and put on a ship bound for the West Indies. A neighbor who had heard Lewis' cries sent a message to Sharp, who rushed to a magistrate for a writ of habeas corpus. According to the great antislavery campaigner Thomas Clarkson:

> The vessel on board which a poor African had been dragged and confined had reached the Downs, and had actually got under weigh for the West Indies. In two or three hours she would have been out of sight; but just at the critical moment the writ of habeas corpus arrived on board. The officer, who served it on the captain, saw the miserable African chained to the mainmast, bathed in tears, and casting a last mournful look on the land of freedom, which was fast receding from his sight. The captain, receiving the writ, became outrageous; but knowing the serious consequences of resisting the law of the land, he gave up his prisoner, whom the officer carried safe, but now crying for joy, to the shore.

Finding no evidence that the plaintiff actually owned Lewis, Lord Mansfield, England's chief justice, set him free, but he refused to rule on the larger question of the legality of slavery in Britain. Mansfield was a slave owner, as were some of his relatives and friends. He feared the economic consequences if 700,000 slaves in the British Empire should be freed as a result of his decision.

Two years later, Sharp brought before Mansfield another slavery case that he hoped would set a precedent. Like Lewis, James Somerset had been abducted and placed on a ship to the West Indies. This time, Leo D'Anjou wrote, Lord Mansfield found that "English law did not allow the master to seize his servant to be sold abroad." His decision did not outlaw slavery in Britain, though many people believed it did. Human bondage continued in Britain until Parliament passed a law emancipating slaves throughout the British Empire in 1833.

The Somerset case was extensively covered in the newspapers, and the court's public galleries were filled with former slaves and Sharp's supporters. Although it did not bring the result Sharp had hoped for, the Somerset case did make slavery and the slave trade public issues. It also spurred the formation of various organizations, including societies of former slaves, to work on behalf of blacks in Britain.

For example, in October 1772, the secretary of a "Black Society" wrote to the editor of a London newspaper, the *Public Ledger*, expressing concern for the welfare of a black maidservant who had been declared chattel on the death of her master. The society asked the editor to bring the case to public attention. This letter, one of the few extant documents of black groups in London, could be interpreted as evidence that grassroots organizations of freed slaves were also conducting human rights campaigns at the time.

Sharp quit the Ordnance Office during the American Revolution because of his sympathy for American independence. From that time on, his brothers financially supported his antislavery crusade. He had already expanded his activities beyond rescuing and assisting slaves. In 1772, he canvassed Anglican bishops and archbishops. "A very great majority of them . . . gave me reason to hope that they would publicly oppose any further encouragement of the Slave-Trade had it come before them in the House of Lords," he found. By 1779, almost all of Britain's bishops had assured Sharp that they would oppose the slave trade.

Clarkson said Sharp

> . . . is to be distinguished from those who preceded him by this particular, that, whereas these were only writers he was both a writer and an actor in the cause. In fact, he was the first labourer in it in England. By the words 'actor' and 'labourer,' I mean that he determined upon a plan of action in behalf of the oppressed Africans, to the accomplishment of which he devoted a considerable portion of his time, talents and substance.

Among Sharp's accomplishments were writing a 350-page tract, *The Law of Retribution*, that cited biblical precedents against slavery; corresponding with antislavery campaigners in Britain, America and Europe; leading delegations to Parliament and chairing the committee that coordinated the 1787-92 campaign against slavery.

Throughout his years as an activist, Sharp stayed true to his initial conviction that slavery was evil. "I thought (and I ever shall think) it to be my duty to expose the monstrous impiety and cruelty . . . not only of the Slave Trade but of Slavery itself. . . and . . . to assert that no authority on earth can ever render such enormous iniquity legal." Granville Sharp was living proof of John Stuart Mill's contention, "One person with a belief is a social power equal to ninety-nine who have only interests."

THE EMBATTLED ADVOCATE

One of Sharp's allies was a Scotch clergyman, James Ramsey. First trained as a doctor, Ramsey worked on slave ships and then settled in St. Kitts as an Anglican minister. After twenty years in the West Indies, he and his family returned to England. In 1784 he published *An Essay on the Treatment and Conversion of African Slaves in the British Sugar Colonies*. His biographer, Folarin Shyllon, called it "a damning indictment and exposé of British West Indian slavery."

The book showed the influence of Enlightenment philosophy. Ramsey condemned slavery not only on religious grounds but as a violation of natural law:

> The prime design of society is the extension of the operation of law, and the equal treatment and protection of the citizens. Slavery, therefore, being the negation of law, cannot arise from law, or be compatible with it. As far as slavery prevails in any community, so far must that community be defective in answering the purposes of society. . . . Slavery . . . is an unnatural state of oppression on the one side, and of suffering on the other; and needs only to be laid or exposed in its native colors, to command the abhorrence and opposition of every man of feeling and sentiment.

Because Ramsey was an eyewitness to the brutality of slavery, it was difficult to cast doubts on his accuracy and credibility. Reviews of his book in literary periodicals were overwhelmingly positive. So the planters waged "a campaign of vituperation and vilification" that went on for years, Shyllon writes. Ramsey replied to his critics with a series of pamphlets. He also received death threats, suffered public harassment and fended off challenges to duels.

Ramsey felt less isolated when he met Granville Sharp and Thomas Clarkson through his publisher, James Phillips, who also was a member of the London committee that coordinated the anti-slave-trade campaign.

Even before his book was published, he cultivated relationships with important politicians, including William Pitt, the prime minister, and William Wilberforce, who later spearheaded the slave-trade abolition bill in the House of Commons. Ramsey succeeded in converting Pitt to the antislavery cause. After his first meeting with Pitt, Shyllon writes, "Ramsey started to bombard Wilberforce with letters and memoranda dealing with every aspect of slavery and the slave trade, urging, explaining and advising." In 1788 he testified against slavery before the Privy Council and met regularly with Pitt, who was lending his support to the anti-slave-trade forces in Parliament.

He also knew the leading black campaigner against slavery, Olaudah Equiano, who wrote a pamphlet supporting Ramsey's portrayal of slavery in 1788.

For all of Ramsey's behind-the-scenes influence, he had difficulty fending off the planters' unceasing attacks. His health failed under the strain, and he died in 1789. One of the planters bragged that he had killed Ramsey.

An indication of Ramsey's importance as a campaigner may be seen in a speech that the Duke of Clarence (later King William IV) made to the House of Lords four years after his death. The duke, who supported the slave trade, took the trouble to repeat the slanders on Ramsey that the planters had spread from 1784 on. Ramsey's book clearly continued to be a powerful weapon against slavery.

THE AFRICAN

Olaudah Equiano, who wrote in defense of Ramsey, is the most remarkable figure among the campaigners. According to *The Interesting Narrative of the Life of Olaudah Equiano, Written by Himself,* he was born in West Africa in 1745 and kidnapped into slavery at the age of eleven. He traveled widely as a Quaker sea captain's slave. After buying his freedom in 1766, he continued his travels as a seaman, reaching the Arctic at one point. Finally he settled in England.

Equiano became an antislavery activist in the 1770s, when he heard about John Annis, a slave brought to Britain from St. Kitts. In 1774, despite the Somerset decision, the owner shipped Annis back to the West Indies and ordered him to be tortured to death. Equiano had hired a lawyer to help Annis, but the lawyer took his money and did nothing. When he heard that Annis had died, Equiano went into a depression. In 1783, Equiano told Sharp about the slave ship *Zong,* whose captain had thrown more than 100 slaves overboard when supplies ran low. The ship's owners then tried to collect insurance money for their lost "property." Sharp went to court to try to stop the owners from collecting compensation. There is no record of whether he succeeded.

Later Equiano became a propagandist and speaker for the anti-slave-trade movement. He also worked for a project to settle former slaves in Sierra Leone in the mid-1780s, but he was fired after denouncing corruption in the project. Many of the former slaves who participated in this resettlement scheme were veterans of the American Revolution, having fought on the British side in exchange for their freedom. They were evacuated to London, only to find that the British government had no intention of making good on its promises of pensions and other assistance. Most of those who went to Sierra Leone soon died there.

Equiano and eight other former slaves founded the Sons of Africa, one of many black societies in London. A white observer noted in 1788: "London abounds with an incredible number of black men who have clubs to support those who are out of place"—that is, mutual aid societies. The Sons of Africa went beyond this by publishing letters endorsing the anti-slave-trade movement in newspapers, attending parliamentary hearings, lobbying politicians and collaborating in other public activities. It may be seen as a very early example of a human rights group.

On his own, Equiano presented a petition against the slave trade to Queen Charlotte. He also helped another Son of Africa, Ottobah Cuguano, write *Thoughts and Sentiments on the Evil and Wicked Traffic of the Slavery and Commerce of the Human Species*, published in 1787. Cuguano was the first writer in England to declare that slaves had the moral duty and right to resist enslavement. Using a writ of habeas corpus obtained by Granville Sharp, Equiano, Cuguano and another black leader, William Green, fulfilled this obligation by rescuing Henry Demane as he was about to be shipped to the West Indies.

Equiano published his *Interesting Narrative* in 1789. It sold thousands of copies, especially in northern England, was published in the U.S., Holland, Russia and France and went through seventeen editions in thirty years. As a result, when he died in 1797, Equiano left his family a sizable inheritance. In the context of Eighteenth Century British society, this was a considerable achievement.

Equiano linked disparate sectors of the antislavery movement, from the black community of London to Quaker and non-Quaker campaigners, politicians and the public. Though not a community leader in the modern sense, he capably represented the former slaves to the larger society through his manifold activities. Other blacks in Britain, without his advantages, also worked to end slavery. Although it formally existed until 1833, Peter Fryer wrote,

. . . in practical terms the institution of slavery, in Britain itself, largely withered away between the 1740s and the 1790s. And it did so as a result of the slaves' own resistance . . . by running away. . . . Individual acts of resistance, multiplied many times over, became self-emancipation: a gradual, cumulative and irreversible achievement which constituted the first victory of the abolitionist movement in Britain.

THE IDEOLOGUE

The nascent movement against slavery and the slave trade in the 1770s and 1780s developed amidst an international ferment of political ideas and initiatives. The American Revolution galvanized intellectuals on both sides of the Atlantic. Foremost among them was Thomas Paine, who mixed science and philosophy and published the results in language accessible to anyone who could read.

Like many of his readers, Paine was largely self-taught. His father was Quaker, his mother Anglican. As a young man, he converted to Methodism before abandoning organized religion. In the 1750s he attended popular-science lectures in London. "The men and women who attended the lectures . . . were mainly self-educated shopkeepers and artisans, many of whom leaned toward unorthodox religious views, and religious Dissenters, with strong leanings toward political radicalism," writes Paine's biographer, John Keane. They wanted to believe in "a universal law of benevolence, binding together human beings for the sake of their happiness and freedom."

Paine became a low-level civil servant in a provincial town and continued his political education in debating societies, where he polished his writing and speaking skills. In late 1774 he migrated to America. Soon after his arrival he published his first article, denouncing slavery, and within a few months was editing a new magazine in Philadelphia. Less than a year later he published *Common Sense*, which provided the platform for the revolution. It was translated into Polish, French, German and other languages. Paine said 120,000 copies were printed in three months.

Some of Paine's ideas were far ahead of their time. According to Keane, he

. . . considered all individuals of all countries as potential citizens. As citizens, he argued, they were entitled to enjoy certain rights but also were bound to honor certain duties within a worldwide framework of constitutional governments that maximized civil and political freedom and guaranteed social justice. . . . Citizenship for him implied the global abolition of despotism and injustice.

Paine spent time in France before and during the revolution there. In reply to Edmund Burke's *Reflections on the Revolution in France,* he published *The Rights of Man* in 1791. It was an instant international bestseller—the first edition sold out in three days, and Paine later estimated that more than 400,000 copies had sold in ten years. Because it was written in straightforward, idiomatic English, literati complained about its "uncouth" language.

The Rights of Man provided a utopian program for the Nineteenth Century and beyond. In it, Paine "argued that the best antidote to war is the formation of an international confederation of nationally independent and peacefully interacting civil societies that keeps an eye on the international system of nation-states, taming their bellicose urges," Keane wrote.

At first the British government did not ban the book or prosecute Paine. Instead, Keane wrote, they paid for a defamation campaign, making him "the first major publicist in modern times to be savaged by a government muckraking campaign waged publicly through the press." The second part of *The Rights of Man* came out in 1792 and sold about 200,000 copies in a year. Again, the government responded by carrying out an underground smear campaign against him and tried to remove the book from circulation without actually banning it. Keane found, "The government carefully sponsored meetings throughout the country to proselytize against Paine . . . [and] laundered payments to publishers in an attempt to flood the minds of the reading public with anti-Paine propaganda."

A royal proclamation in May 1792 inveighing against "wicked and seditious writings" triggered a nationwide antisedition campaign. According to Keane:

> Government spies were assigned to the popular societies to monitor and obstruct their activities. Billstickers were imprisoned for posting notices in favor of Paineite reforms. Bookshops selling *The Rights of Man* were visited and harassed by agents of the book police, and sometimes arrested, prosecuted, fined or imprisoned.

The government went after Paine, jailing him for debt and charging him with seditious libel. In Keane's words, "Paine's daily life now resembled that of a latter-day dissident." Spies tailed him, and a new smear campaign began. In semi-hiding, he wrote a letter to the Home Secretary that concluded, "I am, Mr. Dundas, not your obedient servant, but the contrary!" After his trial for seditious libel was postponed, Paine fled to France in September 1792. He was later tried in absentia and found guilty, and his supporters rallied in the streets.

The French Revolution was at its height. The Legislative Assembly made Paine and several British anti-slave-trade activists honorary citizens of France. They also elected Paine and the Deist intellectual and scientist

Joseph Priestley to the National Convention, the revolution's governing body. Priestley wisely left France for America, but Paine, intoxicated by the revolution, remained. In 1793 he published *The Age of Reason*, against organized religion. Another international bestseller, it was translated into German, Hungarian and Portuguese.

Caught in the Reign of Terror, Paine was thrown into prison in Paris. He tried to help other prisoners, many of whom were later guillotined. Scheduled to be executed, he was spared by chance: The jailer chalked his "death number" on the wrong side of his open cell door, and Paine erased it. After his release, he tried to rescue people, including Mme. de Lafayette, from prison and obtained passports for English friends.

Paine ended his days in Greenwich Village, New York, vilified for not being a Christian but with great memories of his leading role as a radical intellectual, propagandist, revolutionary and human rights activist on two continents. Not only did he put ideas into other people's heads, he acted upon them as well.

THE "MORAL STEAM ENGINE"

One of those who received honorary French citizenship with Paine in 1792 was Thomas Clarkson. Seven years after his revelation on horseback, Clarkson was the world's most important anti-slave-trade campaigner. Few people knew this, however, because Clarkson was unassuming and worked quietly. Only as an elderly man in the 1820s and '30s did he become internationally famous as "the moral steam-engine, or the giant with one idea," as his friend Samuel Taylor Coleridge called him.

The son of a provincial schoolmaster and Anglican clergyman, Thomas Clarkson expected to follow in his father's footsteps. A brilliant student at Cambridge University, he won an academic prize with an essay on the subject, "Is it lawful to make slaves of others against their will?" His main source was Anthony Benezet's book, *Some Historical Account of Guinea* (1771).

On his way from Cambridgeshire to London in 1785, he experienced his epiphany and dedicated himself to the antislavery cause, though he knew his family would be disappointed and his worldly ambitions would remain unfulfilled. He began by revising and expanding his prize essay for publication. Through a Quaker in his hometown, he found James Phillips, a printer and member of the London Meeting of Sufferings' antislavery committee. Phillips edited and published Clarkson's essay as a book in Britain and America. He also introduced him to his Quaker colleagues. In London Clarkson met Granville Sharp, who he thought might be a distant relative.

In May 1787 Clarkson and eleven others, nine of whom were Quakers, founded the Society for Effecting the Abolition of the Slave Trade, also known as the London Committee. Clarkson became the committee's grass-roots organizer and researcher and its only full-time member. Since no one had ever filled such a role before, nobody knew what to call him, so they dubbed him the "originator."

Clarkson abridged his prize essay and Phillips printed 2,000 copies. In 1788 Clarkson set off on his first field trip for the committee. It lasted five months. After a slow start—he could find only two witnesses willing to give him information in Bristol, one of the centers of the slave trade—he traveled to Bridgewater, the town where the first antislavery petition had originated in 1783, to confer with the men who had sent it to Parliament. Then he proceeded to Liverpool, another slave-trading center, Gloucester, Worcester, Chester and Bath. In Liverpool he escaped a violent gang assault, presumably by thugs hired by slavery supporters. In Manchester, a fast-growing factory town, he found a local anti-slave-trade committee already in operation. He gave a sermon there to an audience that included more than fifty blacks. "Energetic and resourceful, Clarkson provided a vital link between London and the provinces, enabling the London Committee to tap a vast reservoir of public feeling," historian John Oldfield writes.

By the end of his five months on the road, Clarkson "had collected the names of more than 20,000 seamen in the slave trade and he knew what had become of each one," his biographer, Ellen Wilson, recounted. He drew up a questionnaire with 145 questions so others could also interview sailors. This may have been the world's first survey. The thousands of pages of information he collected on this and other trips were later submitted to parliamentary inquiries, as irrefutable evidence of the slave trade's brutality to seamen as well as to slaves.

On a later trip to southwest England, Clarkson set up anti-slave-trade committees in three cities. In Plymouth he found a diagram of the inside of a slave ship that showed how slaves were packed like sardines. This diagram became one of the campaign's most widely disseminated, powerful and effective propaganda devices.

As part of his organizing work, Clarkson corresponded with 700 people across Britain for seven years. He and the committee also kept in touch with antislavery activists abroad.

In August 1789 Clarkson went to France, just beginning its revolution, to confer with the antislavery committee there. The members of the Société des Amis des Noirs included the Marquis de Lafayette, the Comte de Mirabeau, the Duc de la Rochefoucauld and the Marquis de Cordorcet, but the committee was much less influential and effective than the London committee. Its members had no way to organize a public campaign, and they told Clarkson they were waiting for Britain to abolish the slave trade first. His attempts to persuade the National Convention, the revolution's governing body, to outlaw the slave trade were unsuccessful. He stayed in France until February 1790 and returned to Britain a supporter of the revolution.

Back in England, Clarkson rounded up witnesses to testify before Parliament. He toured northern England and managed to find twenty witnesses in four months.

The following year, anti-French sentiment rose in Britain as the revolution became more violent. After presiding at a dinner in Birmingham commemorating the second anniversary of the storming of the Bastille, the reformer and scientist Joseph Priestley returned home to find his house burned by a mob. He fled England to Pennsylvania. Also in 1791, slaves rebelled on the French island of St. Domingue. Opponents of slavery, including Clarkson, who spoke out in support of the rebellion were isolated and attacked.

At the same time, the idea of a boycott of slave-produced sugar gained ground. Clarkson promoted it in his speeches and writings, but the rest of the London committee did not agree with his position until 1795. Even so, Clarkson estimated that 300,000 people in Britain abstained from sugar at one time or another to express their opposition to the slave trade.

Clarkson kept up a heavy schedule of touring, speaking and organizing until his health broke down in the mid-1790s. He traveled some 35,000 miles in all and "became the public face of abolition," in Oldfield's words. As the anti-slave-trade campaign wound down and the war with France intensified, he moved to the Lake District to farm and became friendly with Wordsworth, Coleridge and other literary figures. In 1804, when the campaign revived, he went back on the road, gathering information, speaking and organizing once again. Parliament finally voted to end the slave trade in 1807, twenty years after the founding of the Committee for Effecting the Abolition of the Slave Trade.

In the 1820s and '30s, abolitionists campaigned hard for the abolition of slavery in the British Empire, and Clarkson, then in his sixties, went on the road yet again. Parliament passed an emancipation bill in 1833. By that time, he was going blind with cataracts. In 1839 he founded the British Anti-Slavery Society, still in existence today as Anti-Slavery International. In 1840, at the age of eighty, he spoke to the General Convention of the British and Foreign Antislavery Society. He lived until 1846, writing antislavery pamphlets and corresponding with U.S. abolitionists until the end.

William Wilberforce's sons, who felt he had slighted their father in his memoirs, attacked him in print in the 1830s, and perhaps as a result, Clarkson was largely forgotten after his death. In 1996, a plaque was unveiled in Westminster Abbey to commemorate "one of the noblest of Englishmen" and one of the most effective human rights campaigners of all time.

HOW THE CAMPAIGN WAS ORGANIZED

The Committee for Effecting the Abolition of the Slave Trade that Clarkson and his colleagues founded in May 1787 was predominantly Quaker but open to men of all denominations. The Quakers provided "decision, commitment and most important, organization," Davis wrote. Five of the twelve members had already served on the Quaker antislavery committee of 1783. They were accustomed to working together, holding regular meetings, making decisions by consensus and working hard. Their communications network, linking correspondents, local activists and traveling preachers, was unparalleled. Some Quakers (and other sympathizers) were quite wealthy and readily provided financial support to anti-slave-trade initiatives. Among the original members were two bankers, four merchants, two manufacturers and a publisher. Their political views varied, but almost all supported immediate, rather than gradual, abolition. Members included both thinkers and doers. They worked in a businesslike way, renting an office, hiring a clerk, holding regular meetings, keeping careful minutes and financial accounts. Consequently the committee was well-equipped to carry out a human rights campaign. Furthermore, they understood that they needed to mobilize public participation to achieve their goal.

This understanding was itself revolutionary. The committee had only the model of Wilkes' earlier efforts and public initiatives in the American colonies to follow. These positive examples, however, tended to be overwhelmed by frightening memories of "the mob," which had wrought havoc in London in the Gordon riots of 1780, only a few years before. (Wilkes, by then Lord Mayor of London, had ended his career as a civil libertarian by putting down those riots.) Quakers vigorously opposed violence and would only undertake initiatives that they could be sure would be peaceful.

The first thing to determine was the committee's mandate. The committee decided, after some discussion, to restrict themselves to abolishing the slave trade. Clarkson and Sharp were keen to work to abolish slavery, but the others pointed out that any attack on slavery itself constituted an attack on the institution of private property. The consensus was that the committee would be more likely to succeed if it focused only on the trade. "It appeared soon to be the sense of the committee, that to aim at the removal of both would be to aim at too much, and that by doing this we might lose all," Clarkson wrote.

The committee drew up a mission statement, defining the committee's purposes: "for procuring such information and evidence, and for distributing Clarkson's Essay and such other publications, as may lead to the abolition of the slave trade, and for directing the application of such monies, as are already, or may hereafter be collected, for the above purposes." They soon added communicating with local groups, both nationally and internationally, petitioning Parliament and lobbying its members to their list of activities.

The committee members compiled a list of contacts. By the end of 1787, they had agents or correspondents in thirty towns, including Manchester, Bristol, Sheffield and Leeds. Wherever Clarkson went on his field trips, he tried to help set up local groups. Members also cultivated links to several sympathetic parliamentarians and the prime minister.

The committee disseminated anti-slave-trade propaganda in pamphlets, books, articles and advertisements. Oldfield found, "The committee effectively ran its own publishing house, buying up copyrights, . . . commissioning new titles or simply reprinting old ones." In 1787-88, half of their expenditures went to printing. By the end of 1788, they had published fifteen titles, and their subscription list had almost 2,000 names. They also arranged to translate and send materials to other slave-trading countries, such as France, Denmark, Spain, Portugal and Holland.

Members applied their business and marketing skills to the dissemination of information. "Early efforts were concentrated on producing cheap promotional literature that could be distributed in large quantities through the committee's county agents," Oldfield writes. In its first year of operation, the committee printed 25,526 copies of reports and 51,432 copies of pamphlets. The committee also publicized its efforts and news of the American abolition movement in London and provincial newspapers. Local groups advertised their petitions, lectures and meetings in the papers, and the papers covered their activities.

PROPAGANDA PRODUCTS

Early on, the committee realized it would need to make and market artifacts to promote the cause. In 1788 committee member Josiah Wedgwood produced a medallion that became the international symbol of anti-slavery sentiment and was reproduced in many forms. The design pictured a kneeling, chained black slave with the legend, "Am I Not a Man and a Brother?" Later versions appeared with the slogan, "Am I Not a Woman and a Sister?" The design was reproduced on cameos, hairpins, teacups, sugar bowls, ribbons, pincushions and many other objects. Wedgwood sent a sample medallion to Benjamin Franklin, who distributed copies in America. Thus Wedgwood made anti-slave-trade sentiment internationally fashionable in the 1790s, and the design endured as a powerful icon for decades afterwards.

The slave ship diagram was another important vehicle of abolitionist sentiment. In 1788-89, more than 8,000 copies were produced. Thousands were distributed abroad. Other artists also contributed images. For example, George Morland painted "Execrable Human Traffic," which was exhibited at the Royal Academy in 1788. This painting and others were made into engravings that were mass-produced.

LOCAL AND NATIONAL INITIATIVES

The London committee aimed first to educate people throughout the country and then to stimulate local petition drives. According to Oldfield, "By swamping the country with books and pamphlets and, in the case of advertising and subscription lists, adjusting to the demands of a rapidly expanding consumer society," the committee created a national constituency. Local committees would spring up before or after Clarkson came to visit. Some committees that had supported Wilkes were reactivated to work on the slave trade. In places where the dissenting tradition was strong, people heard sermons against the slave trade in church or chapel.

In Exeter, for example, a banker, a draper, a grocer and several ministers set up a committee. Quakers and Unitarians collected funds by soliciting subscriptions. They organized a public meeting in the local guildhall with Clarkson as the principal speaker and the mayor presiding. At such meetings, petition texts were often adopted as resolutions, then printed in local newspapers and placed in the town hall, coffeehouses or other public places for signing.

Local committees had corresponding members who lived far from towns but kept up with the issue by subscribing to publications. Local newspapers sometimes published the subscription lists, attesting to the social respectability of subscribers and the campaign. Subscribers in Exeter in 1788 included shopkeepers, merchants, small manufacturers (weavers, tailors and dyers), doctors and lawyers. These middle-class people also frequented bookshops, where they would gossip, read newspapers that published information about the anti-slave-trade campaign and sign anti-slave-trade petitions.

THE ROLE OF WOMEN

Petition signers included town councils, electors, magistrates, freeholders, clergy and "gentlemen." Women were excluded, since it was not considered "respectable" for them to participate in public affairs. So women acted in other ways. They bought anti-slave-trade souvenirs, boycotted slave-produced sugar and wrote, published and purchased antislavery literature. According to historian Clare Midgley, Hannah More's poem, "Slavery," was written "explicitly as propaganda to aid Wilberforce at his opening of the parliamentary campaign against the slave trade in 1788." In 1789, Mary Leadbeater, an Irish Quaker, wrote a poem, "The Negro. Addressed to Edmund Burke," appealing to Burke, a leading Parliament member, to oppose slavery.

Two-hundred women were on the London Committee's subscription list in 1788. Later, women met separately to discuss the sugar boycott, and a few women made abolitionist speeches at debating societies. Appearances by women at such events were among "the earliest examples of public speaking by women in Britain outside the context of religion," Midgley writes.

THE PRINCIPAL WEAPON

Local groups sent 102 petitions with more than 60,000 signatures to Parliament in 1788. As the campaign reached its peak in 1792, groups from all over Britain sent 519 petitions, signed by 400,000 people, to Parliament. The House of Commons responded by passing a resolution endorsing the gradual ending of the slave trade. This was not sufficient for the committee, which supported immediate abolition. In any case, the House of Lords overturned the resolution the following year.

The committee was always careful to ensure that petition campaigns were timely. They coordinated their efforts with those of the members leading the fight in Parliament, especially William Wilberforce, who tended to be conservative and cautious. He believed public gatherings in the capital city would offend or alienate the House of Commons. And so, at his request, the London committee never convened a public meeting in London during all the years of the campaign.

Petitioning became the principal tool and activity of the anti-slave-trade movement. It was especially attractive to people in the fast-growing industrial towns of the Midlands, which had no representation in Parliament. In Manchester, for example, twenty percent of the male population—two-thirds of the eligible voters—signed the first petition that the local abolitionist committee circulated. Drescher noted, "The abolitionists of Manchester innovatively decided to use their subscription fund to purchase advertisements of their own petition in every major newspaper in England, calling for similar actions."

The Manchester committee's leaders came from the Unitarian community, the local Literary and Philosophical Society, the British College of Arts and Sciences and the Manchester Academy. Some of the members were involved in local politics through their service on the municipal Board of Health. Manchester was also a center of the constitutional reform movement. In 1794, when the government was repressing all political activity outside Parliament, two prominent antislavery activists and reformers from the town were tried for sedition and acquitted. But by that time, anti-slave-trade advocacy, associated with support of the French Revolution, had almost ceased in Manchester. It would start again in 1804.

The language of petitions was religious and humanitarian. The text would usually point out that slavery caused insurrections, was contrary to

British values of liberty and natural rights and constituted an impediment to progress. This rhetoric was acceptable to many middle-class people, Dissenters and Anglicans, who comprised the majority of signers.   As a result, anti-slave-trade sentiment became respectable in a relatively short time.

Slave-trade supporters paid abolitionists a powerful compliment by imitating their methods. Planters and their allies organized public meetings, conducted petition drives in slave-trading centers such as Liverpool and Bristol, provided witnesses to testify at parliamentary hearings and published pamphlets and articles supporting the trade. Though they won the first round of the battle in Parliament, their efforts did not achieve the same success as their opponents'. By 1792, public sentiment had shifted decisively, from acceptance of the slave trade as part of the natural order of things, to a sense that it violated natural law and should be ended.

The campaign expanded steadily between 1787 and 1792. Although pro-slave-trade forces in Parliament succeeded in defeating Wilberforce's bill several times, their margin of victory kept narrowing. War with France and government repression of all dissent during wartime delayed the end of the slave trade; but the sea change in public opinion portended that abolition would come when peace returned.

WHY DID THE CAMPAIGN END?

From 1794 to 1804, the government made public political activity of all kinds almost impossible. In 1795, antisedition laws known as the "Two Acts" suspended habeas corpus and banned most public meetings. Even more repressive legislation, the Seditious Societies Act in 1799, included, in Walvin's words, "savage punishments" for political activity of any kind. Reformers were tried for treason for setting up correspondence and debating societies to discuss parliamentary reform. Booksellers were prosecuted for selling Thomas Paine's *The Rights of Man*, which was banned. The London committee may have declined to actively promote the sugar boycott because they feared it "might be viewed as subversive in the reactionary climate of the period," Midgley wrote.

In the committee's minutes of August 20, 1793, is a cryptic comment, "So difficult is the situation in which we now feel ourselves. . . ." but no further explanation. Less than a year later, in May 1794, they closed the office. In 1795, they sent a letter to correspondents expressing their dismay at Parliament's lack of action on the trade, "We are reduced to the necessity of informing our friends that all our hopes from that quarter are nearly vanished." After March 1797, no further entries in the committee's "Fair Minute Book" appear for seven years. In 1804 the committee reconstituted itself and worked until Wilberforce's bill finally passed in March 1807. This second campaign focused less on grassroots organizing and more on Parliamentary lobbying. The tide of public opinion had already turned, however, and the grassroots structures were in place, waiting to be revived, when a new campaign to abolish slavery began in 1814. After two more campaigns, Parliament finally abolished slavery throughout the British Empire in 1833.

THE RESULTS

In the long run, the anti-slave-trade campaign achieved its objective of convincing Parliament to end British participation in the slave trade. Davis concluded:

> . . . from the best modern estimates, it would appear that the British abolition act was not ineffective in reducing the number of slaves transported to the New World. Although it would require more than a half-century of bribes, diplomacy and coercion for Britain to realize her objective, the act of 1807 served as a symbolic precedent that gave courage and sanction to generations of reformers in the U.S., France and Brazil.

The 1787-92 campaign had greater results than these, however. In Drescher's words, it created "an alliance which would link innumerable and disparate individuals, including people who had no direct previous role in the national political process. . . . Abolitionism institutionalized from one basic symbol a shared activity, a shared vision of the future. . . ."

Among its accomplishments was the empowerment of hundreds of thousands of unenfranchised people—city dwellers, Dissenters, women, former slaves, workers—to act outside the established political structures that refused to admit them. Sooner or later, they, too, would be demanding entry into the halls of power.

In 1792, Thomas Hardy, a skilled craftsman, antislavery activist and founder of the London Corresponding Society, which worked for parliamentary reform, pointed out, "The rights of man are not confined to this small island but are extended to the whole human race, black and white, high or low, rich or poor." Until the 1840s, "the language and imagery of slavery were infused into British radical and working-class politics," Walvin wrote.

Time and again, abolitionists, radicals and reformers made explicit comparisons between chattel slavery and abuses such as flogging, poverty, cruelty to women and children, brutal working conditions and the unrepresentative political system. Furthermore, they questioned the inevitability of injustice and pointed the way to an achievable alternative. To them, the first anti-slave-trade campaigners bequeathed the language and ideology of universal freedom and human rights.

With energy, determination and persistence, the anti-slave-trade campaigners fought against apparently overwhelming odds and won. But they did more than set a heroic example. They provided the practical model for the organizations, strategies and initiatives that propelled the great social and political movements of the following two centuries, from Chartism to antiapartheid. Echoing down the generations like folk memories, their words, ideals and accomplishments moved people around the world to action.

"Can we behold, unheeding,
 Life's holiest feelings crush'd;—
While *Woman's* heart is bleeding,
 Shall *Woman's* voice be hush'd?"

This American version of the antislavery icon, produced in 1863, acknowledges the importance of women abolitionists.

Understanding.

Chapter 3

NINETEENTH CENTURY ANTISLAVERY: "POWER CONCEDES NOTHING WITHOUT A DEMAND"

H uman bondage continued as one of the great issues of the Nineteenth Century. Once the slave trade had been legally abolished in the British Empire (1807) and prohibited into the United States (1808), slavery itself became the target of activists in all the countries that practiced or benefited from it, from Brazil to Denmark.

British antislavery organizations revived the strategies of the Eighteenth Century campaigns. These included:

- Letter writing to authorities at all levels;
- Petitioning and lobbying legislators;
- Holding mass meetings, demonstrations and marches;
- Publishing tracts, books, articles, reports and advertisements;
- Boycotting products;
- Creating and disseminaing promotional slogans and products;
- Raising funds through appeals and subscriptions.

WOMEN MOVE AHEAD

Men and women formed societies and associations that coordinated these activities. In 1823, the British Anti-Slavery Society was founded, and two years later the first women's antislavery society was organized in Birmingham. Because women were not supposed to be politically active in public, they tended to take actions that they could carry out in their homes or with other women. They spearheaded boycotts of West Indian sugar and other products made with slave labor. They wrote antislavery tracts, held women's meetings, organized money-raising fairs, and circulated and signed women's petitions. All in all, they did much of the work involved in antislavery campaigns, though their contributions were seldom acknowledged.

The final British campaign against slavery, from 1829 to 1833, had considerable popular support. Its public meetings attracted thousands.

Local and national abolitionist groups presented 5,020 petitions to Parliament in 1833. One women's petition to the House of Lords contained 179,000 signatures; another to the House of Commons had 187,000.

Thanks to all these efforts, Parliament ended slavery in the British Empire in 1833. The law mandated a five-year "apprenticeship" period for slaves, but many in the antislavery movement objected to gradual emancipation. According to Midgley, a successful campaign for immediate freedom "took place in the context of a massive growth in political activism and organization by working-class men and women involved in campaigning against the New Poor Law of 1834 and in the Chartist Movement."

CHARTIST CROSS-FERTILIZATION

Chartism was one of Nineteenth Century Britain's most important social and political movements. Predominantly working-class, its members sought a bill of rights that would guarantee universal suffrage, abolition of property qualifications for Members of Parliament, annual parliamentary sessions, the secret ballot, equalized constituencies and salaries for parliamentarians. During the 1830s and 1840s, Chartists organized huge public demonstrations and petition campaigns. In 1839, a Chartist petition with 1.3 million signatures was submitted to Parliament. In 1842, Parliament received a Chartist petition with 3.3 million signatures. The final petition of 1848 contained 5 million signatures.

Chartists (especially women) boycotted shopkeepers who refused to support pro-Chartist candidates. The movement also published newspapers and other printed materials. During the 1830s and '40s, a number of legal cases involving trade unionists became Chartist causes. The Chartists held conventions and mass demonstrations to which the authorities responded with violent repression and prosecutions for unlawful assembly and even treason. More than 300 leaders were prosecuted, and many were transported to Australia or imprisoned in Britain.

Chartist activity tended to wax and wane depending on economic conditions. During the depression of the late 1830s, historian Dorothy Thompson writes, "Chartists attempted the tactics of mass meetings, drilling, firearm training and local confrontations with authority, as well as the collection of signatures, the bringing together of the convention and the presentation of the national petition. The petition's rejection [by Parliament] had been followed by an attempted rising, and by the imprisonment of hundreds of the most active men in the movement."

In response, new organizations formed to help the families of imprisoned Chartists. One of the leaders of the 1840 Sheffield insurrection died in prison in 1842, and 50,000 people attended his public funeral. In 1842, Thompson writes, "More people were arrested and sentenced for offences concerned with speaking, agitating, rioting and demonstrating than in any other year. . . . It was the nearest thing to a general strike that the century saw."

Despite all this activity, Chartism failed to attain its objectives in the short term. "By the end of 1842 . . . every tactic had been attempted with no success," Thompson writes. Petitioning failed and as a result was abandoned as a strategy in British politics. In 1848, when revolutions were breaking out across Europe, the British government fended off public rebellion with a massive show of force.

Although Chartism survived for another ten years, its leaders moved to other causes, from cooperatives to workers' education and the women's movement. All of the Chartists' demands were later adopted—Parliament members' property qualifications were dropped in 1858, male suffrage was expanded in 1867, and the secret ballot was approved in 1872. The other reforms took much longer—women did not receive the vote until after World War I.

Chartism may have represented the aspirations of Britain's working-class majority, but the movement's inability to make an effective alliance with the middle class doomed it in the long run. Chartism's failure taught a hard lesson to human rights activists in Britain and other countries about the limitations of mass movements and the power of the forces arrayed against them. But Chartists and abolitionists did have a fruitful interchange. Chartist orators compared black slavery in the colonies to wage slavery at home. They pressured British abolitionists to support them and cultivated relationships with visiting American abolitionists such as William Lloyd Garrison and Frederick Douglass. They and middle-class Britons helped persuade the British government not to grant diplomatic recognition to the Confederacy during the U.S. Civil War. Having adopted the discourse, strategies and tactics of the antislavery movement, they passed them along to later generations of activists in Britain and beyond. Chartism's influence may have been subterranean, but it was enduring and widespread.

THE IMMEDIATIST

While Chartists and abolitionists were campaigning in Britain, the antislavery movement in the U.S. was becoming increasingly vocal and radical. William Lloyd Garrison started one of the first abolitionist newspapers, *The Liberator*, in 1831. Its subtitle was, "Our Country Is the World. Our Countrymen are Mankind." In his opening editorial, he "emphasized only his reliance on the Declaration of Independence and a nonsectarian intention to enlist all religions and parties in 'the great cause of human rights,'" his biographer, Henry Mayer, noted.

Garrison was uncompromising. In the first issue of *The Liberator*, he proclaimed, "I am in earnest—I will not equivocate—I will not retreat an inch—and I WILL BE HEARD." He believed in immediate, not gradual, emancipation; maintained a racially integrated workplace; socialized and worked with blacks at a time when whites reviled "amalgamation"; and was a feminist before the word was invented. Three-quarters of *The Liberator's* readers were free people of color, and much of the financial support for the paper came from them. Along with many blacks, he opposed colonization of freed slaves in Africa and spoke strongly for their integration as equals into American society. Throughout the Nineteenth Century, this position was unacceptable to the majority of the white population.

An indefatigable organizer, Garrison pushed abolitionists in New England and other parts of the country to set up antislavery societies. The American Anti-Slavery Society was founded in 1833. Garrison declined a job as a field agent for the Society so that he could keep publishing *The Liberator.* By 1835, there were seven state abolition societies and more than 500 local groups; in 1837, thirty-eight agents were in the field for the American Anti-Slavery Society. That year, 400,000 petitions with 1 million signatures were sent to Congress, which had passed the infamous "gag rule" to prevent them from being considered or even received.

Garrison's language was powerful, and as a result he was frequently attacked, not only verbally but physically. In 1835, Mayer wrote, "A mob in Charleston, South Carolina, had broken into the federal post office and seized several mailbags from New York containing American Anti-Slavery Society pamphlets. A crowd of 3,000 people watched the captured documents fuel a bonfire while effigies of [Society President Arthur] Tappan and Garrison cast hanging shadows over the lurid scene." Also in 1835, Garrison was almost lynched by a mob in Boston; afterwards, members of Boston's black community provided protection for him.

Garrison's colleague, Lewis Tappan, was involved in one of the earliest antislavery cases to become the subject of a campaign in the U.S. Slaves who had taken over the ship *Amistad* on the high seas were captured near Long Island in 1839 and prosecuted for piracy. The case went to the U.S. Supreme Court, which freed them in 1841. Tappan and other abolitionists set up a defense committee that raised funds, primarily from free blacks, to pay the lawyers who defended the slaves. To raise money, the committee sold portraits, painted by a black artist, of Cinque, the ship's slave leader. Blacks also contributed funds for thirty-five Amistad slaves to return home to Africa with three missionaries and two black teachers.

In the 1840s and '50s Garrison and other abolitionists took up a series of cases involving fugitive slaves. For example, in 1842 a court ordered George Latimer, a runaway slave living in Boston, to be returned to his owner in Virginia. During court proceedings to decide Latimer's fate, Garrison published 5,000 copies of a news sheet on the case three times per week. A defense committee organized to petition Congress for Latimer's release. Black Bostonians were especially involved in the case, holding many meetings in churches to protest his imprisonment. Abolitionists threatened to rescue him from jail. Under all this pressure, Latimer's owner offered to sell him, and the Boston sheriff freed him. The next year, after receiving petitions signed by 65,000 people, the Massachusetts legislature passed a personal liberty law to prevent runaway slaves from being returned to their owners. Former President John Quincy Adams, then a U.S. Congress member, introduced the petition in Congress as part of his long-running campaign against the gag rule. Garrison made a speech in which he urged slaves to flee North, where abolitionists would protect them. This was one of many reasons why supporters of slavery hated Garrison and would have liked to see him jailed, if not killed. Southern Congressional members introduced legislation to outlaw abolitionist organizations but never succeeded in passing it.

FROM OPPOSITION TO RESISTANCE

In 1850 Congress passed the Fugitive Slave Act to implement the provision in the U.S. Constitution authorizing the return of runaway slaves to their owners. This law did much to make the abolitionists respected, if not loved, in the North. In the 1830s and '40s, anti-black riots had broken out in New York, Philadelphia, Hartford and other cities as white workers felt threatened by blacks who they feared would take their jobs. But whites recoiled when they began witnessing runaway slaves being seized, imprisoned and sent South. Prominent abolitionists declared they would resist the new law at huge demonstrations in eastern and midwestern cities. Local officials in Chicago and New York stated they would not assist in capturing or transporting fugitive slaves. At a mass meeting in Boston in October 1850, Frederick Douglass prophesied, "We must be prepared should this law be put into operation to see the streets of Boston running with blood." The next day, slave catchers came for two prominent runaways, the abolitionist campaigners William and Ellen Craft, who fled to England.

In early 1851, the escaped slave Frederick Jenkins was arrested in Boston. A group of blacks rescued him from the courtroom and sent him to Montreal. Eight men were indicted for the daring rescue, but none was convicted. Also in 1851, Thomas Sims was marched in chains through Boston streets to be sent back to his owner in Georgia after a rescue attempt failed. Later that year, William McHenry, known as "Jerry," was rescued from a Syracuse prison, and local blacks helped him escape to Canada. Until the Civil War, abolitionists in western New York celebrated "Jerry Rescue Day" every year. Mayer wrote about another fugitive case, in Pennsylvania, in which "several dozen Quakers . . . who had refused to aid the marshals were indicted for treason . . . but the grave charge could not be sustained and all the proceedings were quashed."

The most celebrated fugitive-slave case of the 1850s happened in Boston in 1854. Anthony Burns, a twenty-year-old runaway, was arrested at the request of his Virginia owner and brought before a federal court. Abolitionists tried to rescue him but failed. During the attempt, a policeman guarding the courthouse was killed. Like Thomas Sims, Anthony Burns was marched by federal troops to Boston harbor, where a federal ship waited to transport him to Virginia. Historian James Stewart describes the scene:

> Nearly 50,000 people jammed into the street leading from the courthouse to the wharf, where a ship awaited Anthony Burns. The police, unable to disperse the crowd, contained it on the sidewalks by standing on the curbs in close ranks, side by side, with their arms interlocked. Marines, meanwhile, formed into a mounted cortege, and deputy marshals assembled on foot around Burns. They attempted to manacle him but thought again when Burns swore that he would fight if they tried it. . . . The procession began moving forward to loud cries of 'Shame! Shame!' Flagstaffs on public buildings carried the Stars and Stripes at half mast or upside down, shopkeepers draped their storefronts in black, and people hung out of upper windows, jeering and spitting at the passing soldiers. . . . the crowd surged through the police cordon toward Burns, and the Marines charged with swords drawn, seriously wounding several people. With order restored, the troops broke into raucous choruses of 'Carry Me Back to Old Virginny' as they moved Burns onto the ship.

Back in Virginia, Burns was tortured and abused for a month, then sold to a slaver. Abolitionists purchased him with funds raised from whites and blacks in Boston. Burns became an antislavery speaker, wrote an autobiography and used the proceeds to go to Oberlin College. He became a pastor in Indianapolis but moved to Canada when Indiana passed a law forbidding the entry of free blacks. In 1862 he died in Ontario at the age of twenty-eight. Some of the abolitionists who had tried to rescue him were indicted, but no jury in Boston would convict them.

The Burns case was notable for the involvement of prominent intellectuals, including some who had not been closely associated with abolitionism before. Ralph Waldo Emerson, who had kept aloof from the movement, "began to involve himself in such unaccustomed activities as political organizing, local committee work, petitioning the governor and raising funds," Burns chronicler Albert Von Frank wrote. Emerson's friend, Henry David Thoreau, had published *Civil Disobedience* in 1849 and declared himself an abolitionist in 1851. He was enraged by what happened to Anthony Burns. "My thoughts are murder to the state," he wrote.

Soon after Burns' forced march through the streets, Garrison accepted an invitation to make a July Fourth speech. There he publicly burned the U.S. Constitution, the Fugitive Slave Act and court documents related to the Burns case.

FEARLESS SISTERS

Garrison helped bring to prominence Angelina and Sarah Grimké, South Carolina sisters who became important abolitionist speakers. They were not the first women to speak publicly against slavery; the very first was Maria Stewart, a black woman born free in Connecticut in 1803, who made antislavery speeches in Boston in 1832. She moved to New York after male abolitionists in Boston expressed strong disapproval of her actions. In New York she was active in black women's organizations and became a schoolteacher, but her public speaking career was over.

In the mid-1830s, as abolitionism was gaining both support and opprobrium in the North and the South, Angelina Grimké wrote a letter to Garrison, whom she did not know, expressing her heartfelt opposition to slavery. At the time she and her sister Sarah were living quietly in Philadelphia as Quakers. Without asking her permission, Garrison published Angelina's letter in *The Liberator*. Her conservative Quaker community was appalled by her action and pressured her to retract or alter her letter, but she refused. Soon she was corresponding with women abolitionists in Massachusetts and working with the Philadelphia Female Anti-Slavery Society. Other society members included Lucretia Mott, a Quaker mother of six; Lydia White and Sydney Ann Lewis, who ran "free produce" stores that sold no slave-produced goods; Marguerite and Sarah Forten, daughters of the black shipbuilder James Forten, who financed Garrison's *Liberator*; Harriet Purvis, wife of black community leader Robert Purvis; and Sarah and Grace Douglass, black Quakers with whom Angelina sat on a segregated bench at meeting for worship.

Angelina and Sarah began by publishing antislavery tracts. In the "Appeal to the Christian Women of the Southern States," Angelina urged southern white women to take action against slavery. "First you can read on this subject. Second you can pray over this subject. Third you can speak on this subject. Fourth you can act on this subject," she wrote. She urged women to free their slaves and pay them wages, to teach slaves to read (which was illegal in most southern states) and to petition state legislatures to end slavery. The Philadelphia Quakers were displeased, but Angelina refused to be intimidated. She and Sarah became the first women abolitionist agents in the United States, working without pay for the American Anti-Slavery Society.

In late 1836 the sisters attended a two-week training session for agents along with thirty-eight men, two of whom were black. Garrison and Arthur Tappan also attended. The training was conducted by Theodore Weld, who later married Angelina.

Sarah and Angelina Grimké made their debut as antislavery speakers by lecturing in a church to an audience of 300 women. This was a truly shocking act because they broke a biblical taboo by speaking from the pulpit. It should be noted, however, that women preachers were not completely unprecedented. Quaker and Methodist women had been accepted as preachers in the Eighteenth Century, and during the "Second Great Awakening," the religious revival of the 1820s, many women gave testimonies in camp meetings and churches. Still, the sisters were severely criticized, even reviled, for their public appearances, as well as for their support for women's rights.

Abolitionists of both sexes were hated and assaulted during the 1830s. Historian Gerda Lerner wrote:

> Every effort was made to deny them a hearing, frighten their audiences away and keep free Negroes from attending their meetings. . . . [The press] prepared the ground for violence with a barrage of distorted interpretations of abolitionist views or outright lies. At their meetings hecklers abounded, sometimes drummers or other kinds of noisemakers invaded the hall and kept up a steady racket. Frequently the speakers were pelted with rotten eggs and vegetables; at times they were hit with bricks, sticks or other handy weapons. Occasionally they were tarred, feathered and ridden out of town on a rail.

The sisters encountered violence on several occasions during their 1837 tour, which lasted twenty-three weeks and included at least eighty-eight meetings in sixty-seven towns where more than 40,000 people heard them. The most spectacular incident occurred in Philadelphia, where abolitionists had just finished building Pennsylvania Hall because they had had so much difficulty in finding venues where they could meet. Angelina spoke there as rocks came crashing through the windows and a mob seethed outside. The mayor asked the abolitionists to prevent blacks from attending the evening meeting, but they refused. Lerner wrote, "The women were determined not to give in to intimidation. When they left the hall they walked arm in arm, a white woman with a colored woman," while hecklers threw stones at them. Later that night the mob burned Pennsylvania Hall to the ground. This was the last time for many years that Angelina, who had married Theodore Weld two days before, would speak in public.

According to Lerner, the sisters did not quit antislavery work, though they were hobbled by "ill health, poverty and domestic problems," as they lived typical women's lives in the Nineteenth Century. They continued writing, doing research and serving on committees. In their later years, the sisters and Theodore Weld taught and administered cooperative schools for abolitionists' children. Determined to fight racism as well as slavery, they socialized with blacks and welcomed into their family the children their brother had fathered by a slave in South Carolina. Their two black nephews, Archibald and Francis Grimké, became eminent men in their time.

SOCIETIES AND PETITIONS

Through their public speaking, the Grimké sisters inspired the formation of many antislavery societies. In 1837, the peak year of the American abolitionist movement, more than a thousand such societies had some 100,000 members. The local societies sponsored public meetings that featured guest speakers furnished by state and national organizations. There they would sell tracts and pamphlets and circulate petitions.

The pamphlets may have been less effective than the petitions because they did not necessarily lead to any further action. The petitions, on the other hand, "served to give the ordinary person a sense of participation in the democratic process and provided a means for those outside the political structure [women, blacks] to make their weight felt," Lerner wrote. In her words, petitions provided "a most effective way of reaching community and neighborhood with a simple, brief message and garnering immediate results in the form of signatures. It enabled the local societies to measure their appeal in a tangible way, utilize antislavery literature as a direct means of influencing sympathizers and win new adherents. It also made it possible to overcome sectarianism and isolation."

Since the U.S. Congress was refusing, through its gag rule, to receive or consider petitions, the antislavery petition campaign became a campaign for free speech. Lerner noted that many signed the petitions "to protest the denial of the right to petition," rather than slavery itself.

American women seem to have gotten the idea to petition from British women abolitionists, who urged the Americans to adopt a method they had found effective. "Women took to petitioning with enthusiasm and perseverance, possibly because it was the only means of political expression open to them at the time," Lerner observed. The local societies organized around petition drives. Soon they were carrying out what one woman abolitionist called "that most odious of all tasks": gathering signatures.

SUBVERTING THE "NATURAL" ORDER

In speaking publicly, publishing tracts, organizing local groups and leading petition drives, the Grimké sisters and other women abolitionists found themselves defending the right of women to participate in public life. Men of the cloth attacked them with particular ferocity. In 1837, a Congregational minister in Massachusetts accused women activists of causing "the alienation of the sexes, the subversions of the distinguishing excellence and benign influence of woman in society, the destruction of the domestic constitution, the prostration of all decency and order, the reign of wild anarchy and shameless vice," according to Yellin and Van Horne.

In "Letters on the Equality of the Sexes," Sarah Grimké made a tart reply, "All I ask our brethren is, that they will take their feet from off our necks, and permit us to stand upright on that ground which God designed us to occupy."

Conflict over the role of women in abolitionism reached a climax in 1840, when British abolitionists convened an international antislavery convention in London and refused to allow women representatives from the U.S. to participate. Garrison and black abolitionist Charles Remond left the floor and sat in the gallery with the women. Eight years later, women abolitionists convened the world's first feminist meeting in Seneca Falls, New York, and began their long fight for women's equality. (Frederick Douglass was one of a handful of men participating.) In their campaigns for suffrage and other human rights, they would use the strategies and tactics they had learned during their years in the antislavery movement.

Many feminists continued working on black and women's rights. In her speeches Sojourner Truth, a former slave, proclaimed her equality as both a woman and an African-American. For many years she earned her living by lecturing and selling photographs of herself, a grandmotherly figure wearing a shawl, holding her knitting, seated on a chair next to a table with a vase full of flowers. But what she spoke of was her hard work as a slave and a free woman struggling to maintain her family. Thus Sojourner Truth became an icon of black womanhood while challenging conventional notions of woman's role. After the Civil War, when black men but not black women gained the right to vote, she said: "I feel that I have a right to have just as much as a man. . . . if colored men get their rights and not colored women theirs, the colored men will be masters over the women, and it will be just as bad as before."

SELF-EMANCIPATION

Among blacks' most important contributions to the antislavery movement were their activities as public speakers. From the 1830s until the Civil War, some two dozen speakers, including Frederick Douglass, Sojourner Truth, William Wells Brown, Charles Remond, Frances Ellen Watkins and the Crafts, embodied for their audiences the suffering of slaves and the courage of those who escaped slavery. Many of the speakers made extended tours of Britain, where they "abolitionized sentiment of the British rank and file" and middle-class people, writes Benjamin Quarles.

In 1842, soon after he began his public career, Douglass spoke at a series of meetings on behalf of the escaped slave George Latimer. Then he and Garrison raised funds to buy Latimer's freedom. Douglass also used his own life story to convince audiences of the evils of slavery and the equality of blacks. His speeches, books and newspaper made him the most famous and admired African-American of the Nineteenth Century. Throughout his long life, he dedicated himself to fighting for human rights. In supporting women's rights in 1848, he said: "We cannot be deterred from an expression of our approbation of any movement, however humble, to improve and elevate the character of any members of the human family. . . . All good causes are mutually beneficial." At the end of the century, when he was in his seventies, he was speaking out against lynching and encouraging the next generation of black activists to continue the work he had begun almost fifty years before.

Many other former slaves and free people of color were not only active but instrumental in the antislavery movement. James Forten, a prosperous shipbuilder in Philadelphia, lent funds to Garrison to start *The Liberator*. Blacks raised funds to send Garrison to Britain in 1833; individuals contributed fifty cents to five dollars, and groups gave four to 124 dollars. Blacks joined and supported state and national antislavery societies. According to Quarles, one donor to the American Anti-Slavery Society was "a colored woman who makes her subsistence by selling apples in the streets [of New York]." A wealthy black lumberyard owner, William Whipper, donated $1,000 a year to the society for thirteen years.

Because white abolitionists sometimes condescended to or discriminated against them, people of color organized their own antislavery societies, petition drives and meetings, as well as self-help associations, literary societies, temperance associations and other groups. When whites treated them as equals or made sacrifices for the cause, blacks were quick to offer help. For example, after a white editor, Elijah Lovejoy, was killed by a mob in Alton, Illinois, for publishing abolitionist articles, blacks in other places held memorial services for him and raised funds for his widow.

Blacks also undertook symbolic actions to challenge racism in the North. Jezer, et al., describe how they "sat in the white sections of railroad cars, waited to be served at white tables and tried to integrate steamboats. Blacks and whites walked down the street, arm in arm, male and female, or they sat down to eat together. Often these actions brought the practitioners violent reprisals and they usually maintained their nonresistance. Frederick Douglass . . . participated in a great many of these direct actions."

A SECRET CAMPAIGN

Perhaps the most effective activity that blacks undertook was their secret work for the Underground Railroad, the loosely organized network that helped thousands of slaves escape to the northern states and Canada. It is difficult to ascertain when the Railroad started operating, but by the 1830s, the border state of Ohio had more than 100 "conductors" or "stationmasters," including John Brown. The foremost worker was Harriet Tubman. After escaping from slavery in Maryland in 1849, she returned South fifteen times, conducting about 300 people to freedom. Had she been caught, she would have been hanged. Free people of color and escaped slaves hid people in their houses, helped them stow away on boats and trains, drove them in wagons and showed them how to "follow the drinking gourd" North. Well-known black abolitionists, including William Wells Brown, Frederick Douglass, William Whipper and Lewis Hayden, participated in the Underground Railroad, but most of the workers were anonymous—known only as "a friend of a friend."

From the 1830s on, black communities set up vigilance committees that "aided the fugitives in a variety of ways—boarding and lodging them for a few days, purchasing clothing and medicine for them, providing them with small sums of money, informing them as to their legal rights and giving them legal protection from kidnappers," Quarles wrote. Similar groups existed in Philadelphia, New York, Detroit, Cleveland and other cities. Blacks also helped escaped slaves find work and get settled in the North. When Frederick Douglass escaped from slavery in 1838, he received help only from blacks, not from whites. David Ruggles, the secretary and general agent of the New York Vigilance Committee, sheltered him for two weeks. The Philadelphia Vigilance Committee started as an integrated organization, but over time black leaders like Robert Purvis and William Still managed it. This committee helped about 300 slaves a year.

Funds for the vigilance committees came from local black and white communities and women's groups in the U.S. and Britain. Black churches raised funds, the committees held social events, black women organized fairs, and abolitionists passed the hat at their meetings. Because most supporters were poor, the committees often ran short of cash.

People who helped slaves escape did so at their peril. Black and white "conductors" were jailed, sometimes for years, and free people of color were sometimes sold into slavery for aiding slaves. In the 1850s, a Methodist preacher named Samuel Green in Dorchester County, Maryland, was sentenced to ten years in prison for possessing a copy of *Uncle Tom's Cabin*, but the real reason for the harsh penalty was his work for the Underground Railroad.

Both before and after the passage of the Fugitive Slave Act of 1850, James Horton wrote, "No African American was safe from slavery," and every white person was a potential enemy to blacks. Escaping became even more difficult and dangerous after 1850. To reach freedom, slaves had to go all the way to Canada. The law was draconian, denying slaves due process and the right to testify in court and making it possible for professional slave catchers to kidnap people without a warrant. Aiding runaways became a federal crime. Abolitionists met in Boston in October 1850 to declare that they would resist the law, and according to Mayer, "Huge rallies against the law took place from the eastern seaboard to the Great Lakes." The numbers of escaping slaves increased during the 1850s; as many as 40,000 reached Canada by the beginning of the Civil War. Without the assistance of thousands of unknown people on the Underground Railroad, this massive flight would not have been possible.

"THEY ARE TRAMPLING OUT THE VINTAGE WHERE THE GRAPES OF WRATH ARE STORED"

Violent efforts to end slavery went on throughout its long history. Slaves rose up in rebellion with some frequency. Several revolts in the South during the 1820s and '30s led to harshly repressive laws against everything from teaching slaves to read and write to passing information that might help them escape. A few black intellectuals in the North, such as David Walker, supported violent resistance to slavery, but most opponents eschewed violence. Garrison and his faction declared themselves "nonresisters," by which they meant nonviolent resisters who would not participate in the political process, which they regarded as rigged in favor of slavery. Others were more pragmatic. Eventually the American Anti-Slavery Society split over tactics and ideology, leading black abolitionists to organize their own groups and some white abolitionists (such as Theodore Weld and the Grimké sisters) to withdraw from the movement for a time.

In the 1850s, large-scale violence over slavery erupted in "bloody Kansas." Out of this maelstrom emerged John Brown, who made his reputation in the territory as a killer of proslavery settlers.

Before he launched his ill-fated raid on Harper's Ferry in 1859, Brown consulted with prominent abolitionists and sought their financial and moral support. Apparently he received some funds from wealthy backers in the Northeast, but Douglass and Garrison told him his plan to seize weapons from a federal arsenal and distribute them to slaves in Virginia could not succeed.

With a small group of black and white followers, including three of his sons, Brown attacked Harper's Ferry on October 16, 1859. He was captured, wounded but alive, and sentenced to hang. In court he made a statement, expressing his willingness to die for the cause, that electrified the public. Broadsides of the speech were widely distributed.

The raid on Harper's Ferry "shocked the entire country and produced an emotional furor without precedent in the nation's experience," Mayer writes. Many whites condemned Brown's action and dismissed him as a mad fanatic, but abolitionists like Henry David Thoreau considered him a hero. Blacks reacted strongly. They held prayer and sympathy meetings throughout the North. They wore black armbands or fasted on the day of Brown's execution. When the train bearing his body reached Philadelphia, writes Mayer, "the train station overflowed with black people, singing hymns and seeking to comfort the martyr's widow." They contributed money to a relief fund for his family and bought his portrait to hang in a place of honor in their homes.

In exile on the island of Jersey, the French poet Victor Hugo sent a letter protesting Brown's execution to the editor of the *London News*:

> Such things [as Brown's execution] cannot be done with impunity in the face of the civilized world. The universal conscience of humanity is an ever-watchful eye. Let the judges . . . and the slave-holding jurors, and the whole population of Virginia, ponder it well: they are watched! They are not alone in the world. At this moment, America attracts the eyes of Europe.

A longtime opponent of the death penalty, Hugo was also one of the Nineteenth Century's most revered writers, often called the conscience of his age. When he took notice of a case, others followed his pointing finger. His sentiments echoed around the world. With his letter to the editor, a landmark in the history of human rights, Hugo made the death of John Brown an international *cause célèbre*.

SYMBOLS, IMAGES, ICONS

The image of John Brown, who had the face of an Old Testament prophet, was one of many representations that antislavery campaigners used to promote their cause. Portraits of Frederick Douglass, Cinque (the leader of the *Amistad* mutiny), Sojourner Truth and other antislavery figures hung in thousands of homes. The "Am I Not a Man and a Brother" design and its companion, "Am I Not a Woman and a Sister," circulated for more than seventy years in Britain and the United States. These emblems appeared on cameos, combs, coins, medals, china, handicrafts and stationery and were widely reproduced in books, newspapers and broadsides. Women would make goods with the design and sell them at antislavery fairs to raise funds for the cause. A beseeching woman slave pictured kneeling in chains on a sugar bowl encouraged women to abstain from buying West Indian sugar.

Thomas Clarkson's slave ship diagram was another long-lived symbol of abolitionism, wordlessly portraying the horrors of slavery. Abolitionists purchased and saved illustrations of Pennsylvania Hall and Prudence Crandall's Connecticut school for black girls, both of which antiblack mobs burned to the ground. Theodore Weld published an antislavery almanac, which contained weather and crop information interspersed with antislavery propaganda, including speeches, important dates in the history of abolitionism, runaway slave advertisements, even jokes. Escaped-slave speakers sold copies of their autobiographies during their speaking tours. A Massachusetts sea captain, arrested in Florida for aiding fugitive slaves, was chained, pilloried and branded on the hand with the letters SS (slave stealer). Yellin wrote, "Back home, he went on the antislavery lecture circuit, recounting his harrowing experience and displaying his 'branded hand,' which was daguerrotyped by Southworth and Hawes." Using such a variety of material objects, from photographs to embroidered pincushions, abolitionists both disseminated their ideals and financed their activities in the U.S. and Britain.

THE SPIRITUAL BASIS OF THE ANTISLAVERY MOVEMENT

Underlying the abolitionists' actions were strong religious convictions. From the Quakers to Sojourner Truth, they regarded slavery as a sin and an abomination and framed their arguments against it in biblical language. Garrison cited the Bible frequently in *The Liberator*, modeled himself after the prophets and saw himself as doing God's work. Like many others, he believed God would punish the United States with destruction if slavery continued unchallenged.

The associations and societies that the abolitionists formed had their roots in religious bodies such as Bible societies. The Quakers' "Meeting for Sufferings" originated to aid Friends who were persecuted by governments but eventually turned to broader social concerns.

The leaders of the antislavery movement in Britain not only were Quakers but also Dissenters, women and others whose rights were limited by British law. "If all were equal before God, then all could equally do God's task. Antislavery was God's work and women took up its challenge with great enthusiasm," Hurwitz writes. In the U.S., women began to speak out in the context of the great religious revivals of the early Nineteenth Century. Unable to separate their religious from their political beliefs, Angelina and Sarah Grimké felt compelled by conscience to express their convictions publicly, in both religious and secular venues.

A British Quaker, Elizabeth Heyrick, called for immediate, not gradual, abolition as early as 1824, almost a decade before Garrison began promoting "immediatism." In her first pamphlet on the subject, she called liberty "a sacred unalienable right" and said immediate emancipation was necessary for moral reasons. According to Midgley, "Heyrick's conversion to immediate emancipation followed her conversion to Quakerism, and her post-conversion obsession with sinfulness and self-denial can be linked to her call to people to renounce the sin of slavery and deny themselves slave-grown products." Her pamphlet went through three editions and was favorably reviewed in religious periodicals. Gradually male abolitionists began quoting her in their pamphlets. It seems clear from this and other examples that religious belief and rhetoric made many converts to the ideals of human rights.

Many of the antislavery campaigners worked simultaneously on other causes, from prison reform to temperance. "Although formally distinct from each other, the evangelical organizations propagated the same world-view, tapped the same financial resources and had many of the same men on their boards of directors," William Rogers wrote. For white abolition-ists, "the antislavery cause was a benevolent and evangelical mission bound to an array of religious concerns. They opposed a broad range of sins— slavery, violence of any kind, gambling and the drinking of alcohol. For them slavery was the worst example of a general evil that robbed humans of their free will," Horton writes. While also profoundly influenced by reli-gious values, blacks had even more powerful and immediate reasons to work against slavery. Their lives and the lives of their families were at stake.

Frederick Douglass expressed their concerns in both religious and prac-tical terms:

> The whole history of the progress of human liberty shows that all concessions yet made to her august claims have been born of strug-gle. . . . If there is no struggle there is no progress. Those who profess to favor freedom and yet deprecate agitation, are men who want crops without plowing up the ground. They want rain with-out thunder and lightning. They want the ocean without the awful roar of its many waters. The struggle may be a moral one, or it may be a physical one; or it may be both moral or physical, but it must be a struggle. Power concedes nothing without a demand. It never did and it never will.

INTERNATIONAL ABOLITIONISM

The British and American abolition movements were far more grassroots than those in other countries. In France, abolitionists never succeeded in creating a mass movement against slavery. The Société Française pour l'Abo-lition de l'Esclavage, founded in 1834 with about fifty members, was "drawn almost exclusively from the intellectual and political elite of Paris." Accord-ing to Serge Daget, no public antislavery meetings were held in France between 1814 and 1848, when slavery was abolished, and so "abolitionist ideas were not disseminated by word of mouth." Parisian workers signed two antislavery petitions in the 1840s, but "the masses were fairly lacking in religious feeling, and with moral feelings impaired by grinding poverty they had other things to think about than working for the blacks," Daget writes. Reactionary or monarchist regimes after the Napoleonic Wars were not interested in promoting freedom for anyone. Slavery seems to have ended in France and its empire as a result of British governmental and non-governmental pressure and the British example.

In Brazil, the established Catholic Church "*never* raised its voice . . . in favor of emancipation," according to Joaquim Nabuco, the country's most renowned antislavery campaigner. Secular antislavery societies formed there only after 1850, when the British succeeded in pressuring the Brazilian government to stop the importation of slaves. As Nabuco pointed out, "In England the struggle against slavery was a religious and humanitarian movement. . . . By contrast, abolitionism in Brazil [was] above all a *political* movement. . . ."

Heavily influenced by positivism and social Darwinism, Brazil's elite intellectuals considered the country "backward" because of its reliance on slave labor. They cited Montesquieu on natural rights, but their vision of an ideal society was quite undemocratic. Free labor would be incorporated "into a hierarchical society, where each one recognizes his place and feels himself part of a whole," writes historian Celia Azevedo.

Brazilian slavery was already in the process of being very gradually abolished by a series of laws passed from the 1850s onward; but without the abolitionists' efforts and the successful importation of free labor, it could have lasted well into the Twentieth Century. Afro-Brazilian journalists, poets and lawyers founded the small abolitionist movement, along with elite white politicians. They formed societies, wrote, spoke and intensively agitated for emancipation from the late 1860s until abolition in 1888. Nabuco was elected the first president of the Brazilian Antislavery Society in 1880. According to Azevedo, he imported immediatism into Brazil, and abolitionism became "the first national mass movement that raised the issues of freedom and social justice" in the 1880s.

Since the vast majority of Brazil's population was poor and illiterate (and twenty percent were slaves), an organized mass movement against slavery developed slowly. Abolitionism "took off" as a movement around 1882. Historian Robert Conrad observed, "Antislavery clubs and societies eventually appeared in even the smallest Brazilian towns, and near the end of the struggle the movement even invaded the countryside and the plantations. . . . representatives of every class and profession eventually became involved in abolitionism. . . ." A demonstration of 10,000 people in Rio de Janeiro celebrated the abolition of slavery by the northern province of Ceará in 1884. Abolitionists in Rio and other cities went from street to street, trying to convince owners to free their slaves. Under this pressure, the slave population of Rio decreased from 32,000 in 1880 to 7,500 in 1887.

In the mid-1880s, a Brazilian underground railroad began operating. Abolitionists provided runaways with escorts, forged manumission papers, hiding places and train tickets. A group of abolitionists formed a secret society that sent agents to the plantations to incite the slaves to flee. "Urged on by the abolitionists, captives suddenly began to leave plantations in large numbers" in 1886 and 1887, Conrad writes. Simultaneously, the importation of free laborers from Europe made it possible to replace the slaves who fled. In addition, the army refused to act as slave catchers, and the Brazilian slave system collapsed. The Princess Regent signed an emancipation law on May 13, 1888.

About two years after emancipation in Brazil—one of the largest Catholic countries and the last to end slavery in the Western Hemisphere—Pope Leo XIII explicitly condemned slavery in the encyclical *Rerum Novarum*. This encyclical later inspired several generations of Catholics to work for human rights and social justice around the world.

Whatever the differences among abolitionist movements in various countries, activists learned from and exchanged ideas with one another, adopted similar strategies and tactics, and created and maintained channels of communication. For example, at age nineteen, Nabuco translated articles from the British publication *Antislavery Reporter* into Portuguese so his father, a senator in the National Assembly, could quote its arguments in his speeches. Garrison and Douglass visited the aged Thomas Clarkson in Britain in the 1830s and '40s to seek his support for their positions on contested issues. Abolitionists carried on correspondence with colleagues and sympathizers in other countries for decades.

Abolitionist movements inspired or gave rise to other social movements that spread human rights values around the world. Trade unions in many countries borrowed organizational structures and strategies from antislavery and other groups. Thoreau's *Civil Disobedience* inspired Mohandas Gandhi's early struggles against racial discrimination in South Africa and his later campaigns against colonialism in India. Thus, through the practical experience of hundreds of local, national and international campaigns, a nascent global culture of human rights took root throughout the Nineteenth Century.

Attention Workingmen!

GREAT

MASS-MEETING

TO-NIGHT, at 7.30 o'clock,

AT THE

HAYMARKET, Randolph St., Bet. Desplaines and Halsted.

Good Speakers will be present to denounce the latest
atrocious act of the police, the shooting of our
fellow-workmen yesterday afternoon.

Workingmen Arm Yourselves and Appear in Full Force!

THE EXECUTIVE COMMITTEE

Achtung, Arbeiter!

Große

Massen-Versammlung

Heute Abend, ½8 Uhr, auf dem

Heumarkt, Randolph-Straße, zwischen Desplaines- u. Halsted-Str.

☞ Gute Redner werden den neuesten Schurkenstreich der Polizei,
indem sie gestern Nachmittag unsere Brüder erschoß, geißeln.

☞ Arbeiter, bewaffnet Euch und erscheint massenhaft!

Das Executiv-Comite.

This handbill announces the "indignation meeting" that triggered the Haymarket massacre of 1886. Many radical workers in Chicago were German—thus the bilingual text.

Chapter 4

THE AGE OF MASS MOVEMENTS AND THE "MARTYRS OF CHICAGO"

In the 1860s, as slavery declined or ended in the Americas and feudalism ended in Japan and Russia, reformers in many societies turned their attention to groups, such as women and industrial workers, that were beginning to organize politically. Many abolitionists withdrew from activism at this time, but some made the transition from antislavery to other movements. One of the most important campaigners of the period was Wendell Phillips, a great public speaker who influenced several generations of activists. Phillips began as an abolitionist but in his later years turned to labor issues.

THE GOLDEN VOICED AGITATOR

As a young man, Phillips began speaking out against slavery after the death of Elijah Lovejoy, the abolitionist editor, in 1837. In the 1840s he called for the racial integration of railroads and public schools in Massachusetts. The Fugitive Slave Act appalled him. A declared resister of the Act, he joined in the unsuccessful campaign to secure the release of Thomas Sims in 1851.

In 1854 Phillips was personally involved in the Anthony Burns case, promising Burns that he would gain his freedom. He raised the money to buy Burns from a Virginia slave trader after the escaped slave's forced return to his owner. Later he helped Burns enter Oberlin College and advised him while he was there.

Soon after the Burns case, Phillips began a twenty-five-year career as a professional speaker. For nine months out of the year he would travel throughout the North and West, giving speeches. Stewart pointed out, "Expanding networks of roads, railways, canals and telegraph lines meant swifter, cheaper and wider distribution of all kinds of information" and ensured that Phillips' speeches would be published throughout the country the day after he made them. "A huge reading public now formed the popular orator's second audience, participating in lectures at one remove while scanning their newspapers," Stewart wrote.

After John Brown's execution, Phillips expressed strong support for Brown's actions and helped turn the tide of Northern public opinion in his favor. Phillips traveled to Philadelphia, where he met Brown's widow and accompanied her and Brown's coffin to her home in North Elba, New York. He was the only well-known abolitionist (including those who had secretly funded Brown's raid) to speak at Brown's funeral. During a subsequent speaking tour he portrayed Brown as a transcendent figure who had struck a blow for freedom, morality and justice.

Phillips' uncompromising stands earned him many enemies. Before and after the outbreak of the Civil War, he was so hated that he traveled with a bodyguard.

Emancipation of the slaves was only part of Phillips' agenda. He insisted "that no truly free society could maintain itself unless government power secured liberty for everyone," and he developed "sweeping programs for a reconstructed America, where federal law would prevent racial exploitation from ever again restricting individual freedom," according to Stewart. In his opposition to racism and segregation he was well ahead of his time.

PHILLIPS TURNS TO FREE LABOR

Once the war was over, Phillips linked the rights of freed slaves to all workers' rights. He was one of the first American reformers to advocate the eight-hour workday, in 1864. "Shut a man up to work ten, eleven or sixteen hours a day, and he comes out the fag end of a man, with neither the brains nor the heart to discharge the duties of citizenship," he said in a famous speech. He may have invented the slogan of the eight-hour movement when he said in 1865, "It is a fair division to give [the worker] eight hours for labor, eight hours for sleep and eight hours for his own—his own to use as he pleases."

In 1869 Phillips spoke before the Massachusetts legislature to support women's suffrage in state elections and laws banning discrimination against women. He also called for a commission to investigate conditions in factories in the state. He worked hard for passage of the Fifteenth Amendment but recognized that the struggle for equal rights for blacks was far from finished.

Phillips began speaking against the concentration of wealth in the 1870s. "I am fully convinced that hitherto legislation has leaned too much—leaned most unfairly—to the side of capital. . . . The law should do all it can to give the masses more leisure, a more complete education, better opportunities and a fair share of the profits," he said. He called the labor movement "the last noble protest of the American people against the power of incorporated wealth." Phillips even supported the Paris Commune in

1870, though he added that American workers should not follow its violent example but should acquire power through the ballot.

Phillips was one of the organizers of the Labor Reform Convention held in Worcester, Massachusetts, in 1870 and wrote in its platform, "We affirm as a fundamental principle that labor, the creator of wealth, is entitled to all it creates." That year he ran for governor of Massachusetts on the Labor Reform Party ticket and received twelve percent of the vote.

One of the precursors of the Social Gospel movement, Phillips was willing to join forces with socialists in preaching the overthrow of monopoly capitalism—but he did so on religious grounds. He compared workers' uprisings to slave insurrections and called them "the righteous and honorable resistance of a heartbroken and poverty-stricken people to a despotism which flaunts its insolence and cruel rule." In a famous address at Harvard University in 1881, he said, "Dynamite and daggers are necessary and proper substitutes for Faneuil Hall and the *Daily Advertiser*."

Perhaps if Phillips had lived to see the Haymarket case of 1886-87, in which eight anarchists were sentenced to death for conspiracy, he might again have called—as the anarchists did—for "dynamite and daggers" to defend workers' rights.

At age seventy-two, a year before his death in 1884, Phillips wrote to an old comrade, "Let it not be said that the old Abolitionist stopped with the negro [sic] and was never able to see that the same principle he had advocated at such cost claimed his utmost attention to protect all labor, white and black, and to further the discussion of every claim of downtrodden humanity."

Phillips' eloquence, courage and dedication to social and economic justice influenced the next generation of reformers and activists. Henry George, who wrote *Progress and Poverty* and campaigned for a single tax on land; Henry Demarest Lloyd, a crusading journalist who wrote *Wealth against Commonwealth*; and Eugene V. Debs, the great American labor leader and Socialist candidate for President—all cited him as an inspiration.

A CAMPAIGN CULTURE

As a traveling orator, Phillips was not unique. The lyceum and Chautauqua movements provided venues and opportunities for public speakers to communicate directly with large audiences throughout the U.S. Other forms of public discourse also developed considerably during the second half of the Nineteenth Century. The most important were the election campaign and the advertising campaign.

Most early election campaigns in the U.S. were local. Agents canvassed, shook hands, "buttonholed" voters, plied them with food and drink and bribed them. Before 1850, "office seekers made few personal appearances, for it was not usually considered proper to ask for support," Robert Dinkin writes. But as the press expanded and communication and transportation improved, campaigns became increasingly elaborate. A foreign observer compared U.S. election parades in 1832 to Latin American religious processions. In 1840, John Quincy Adams commented, "One of the most remarkable peculiarities of the present time is that the principal leaders are traveling about . . . holding forth, like Methodist preachers, hour after hour, to assembled multitudes under the canopy of heaven." The camp meetings of the Second Great Awakening of the 1820s and abolitionist campaigning in the 1830s had paved the way for this development of electioneering.

The new, "army-style" campaign after 1850 featured huge torchlight parades, floats, banners, flags, portraits of the candidates, rallies, barbeques, tree plantings, songs and slogans. Broadsides, pamphlets and campaign biographies became important vehicles for publicizing the candidates. These events and publications required large amounts of money, which candidates raised through solicitations, public dinners, admission charges and subscriptions. When civil service laws banned political contributions by public employees, the candidates went to the private sector for support.

Another feature of the "army-style" campaign was the organization of voters into neighborhood political clubs. These clubs had uniformed companies of young men who marched in parades and other events. Parades with brass bands and marchers attracted huge crowds. Fireworks and torchlight processions were dramatic and ritualistic occasions that became important forms of popular outdoor entertainment. Other political events included picnics, clambakes and mass meetings.

Speeches at these events were long and elaborately rhetorical. "People of that day, enthusiastic about politics and used to hearing lengthy sermons, listened intently to an orator's discourse, which might go on for two to three hours," Dinkin writes. Some candidates went on long tours, covering thousands of miles, while others spoke only from their front porches. Presidential candidates generally did not campaign extensively until the late Nineteenth Century. The hoopla was considered to be beneath their dignity.

Various objects promoted candidates: ribbons, handkerchiefs, bandannas, medals, tokens, painted or printed portraits, banners, posters. Buttons and badges were distributed in large quantities starting in 1896. These objects became common in many kinds of public campaigns.

BEYOND BARNUM

The development of campaign advertising accompanied the evolution of a complex capitalist economy in the United States and other industrializing countries. Modern advertising emerged in the 1880s, as products became more standardized, technological changes made packaging possible and attractive, and assembly-line techniques vastly increased production. Manufacturers sought to control the prices of their products by creating constant, predictable demand for them. This they accomplished through advertising. During the late Nineteenth Century, writes Susan Strasser, "the goal of advertising shifted from an emphasis on providing information to an attempt to influence buyers by any means possible."

Advertisers used a variety of methods to promote their products. Billboards, posters, electric signs and streetcar advertisements appeared after 1880. As the business of advertising became more complex, manufacturers began to hire advertising agencies to market their products for them. These agencies "used language that described market competition as war and the market as a battlefield," Strasser noted. Reviving the original meaning of the word, they conducted full-blown *campaigns*, planning and coordinating different forms of advertising for different audiences and areas.

As advertising became more sophisticated, political organizations and candidates applied its techniques and strategies to their campaigns. The U.S. government first used advertising to recruit soldiers for the Civil War. Later, civic organizations placed advertisements in newspapers to promote their causes. And the organizations that sprang up to coordinate human rights campaigns also used advertising to publicize their concerns. A few years after P.T. Barnum pioneered the use of handbills to advertise patent medicines, organizations such as political parties, labor unions and mutual-aid societies were disseminating their messages from Chicago to Tokyo in the same way.

SPREADING THE NEWS

Newspapers were the principal sources of information about elections and the major vehicles of advertising campaigns. By 1890 there were 12,000 newspapers in the United States, up from 2,300 in 1850. They published political cartoons, polls, editorials, articles and advertisements that reached millions of readers.

Technological developments increased the availability and influence of newspapers. The telegraph made rapid, long-distance transmission of news possible. Wire services such as Reuters, Havas and Associated Press began disseminating news around the world in the 1840s and '50s. By 1860, fast presses could produce 20,000 papers an hour. In 1866, wood pulp became the basis of newsprint, ending the chronic paper shortage that had limited the size of newspapers. Sunday papers grew considerably and became the most popular reading matter available in both the U.S. and Britain. They were often sensationalistic and slanted to attract the credulous, uneducated and newly literate.

Pioneering publishers Joseph Pulitzer and William Randolph Hearst sought to gain readers by promoting stunts, such as Nellie Bly's trip around the world in seventy-two days, or crusades, like the Spanish-American War. According to Mitchell Stephens, in the 1880s and '90s, the most successful papers mixed sensationalism, populist politics and crusades, but the tabloids that appeared later "disdained the progressive crusades that had been an integral part of the 'new journalism.'" Newspaper editorial lines were often harsh and reactionary, reflecting the opinions and interests of the owners and advertisers, but readers seemed unconcerned, as long as the stories held their interest.

In Europe, after the revolutionary convulsions of 1848, "The newspaper was the carrier of insurrection, and established the basis for political activity for the rest of the century," Smith wrote. Karl Marx started out as a journalist, agitating for press freedom in the Rhineland. Forced into exile in London in 1850, he edited the foreign edition of the *Rheinische Zeitung* and wrote commentaries for American newspapers. His collaborator Frederich Engels was a newspaper editor who applied his journalistic skills to writing *The Condition of the Working Class in England*, an early example of an exposé. British newspapers dramatically increased their circulation to the poor and working classes after the stamp tax was abolished in 1855.

Special trains started running in 1876 to distribute the London dailies throughout the country. In 1880 London had eighteen daily newspapers, and there were forty-four religious papers, thirty-five temperance papers, thirty-three humor publications, twenty-four fashion papers and twenty-one sports papers in Britain. In 1900, Paris had 139 daily newspapers. British and European newspapers were class-based and generally linked to political parties, sometimes receiving secret subsidies from them. Journalists were former politicians; politicians were former journalists.

But journalists exposed situations and evils that politicians did not want to touch. The late Nineteenth-Century muckrakers investigated political corruption, poverty, organized crime and lawbreaking by the rich and powerful. They sometimes played crucial roles in publicizing the *causes célèbres* that became the subjects of human rights campaigns.

These trends in the European and American press spread to Japan, India, Brazil and many other countries, whose journalists and publishers readily imitated or adopted foreign models and styles. Thus developed an international mass audience for news. Anyone who could read could become part of it. From that audience, both international public opinion and international social movements began to emerge.

A JAPANESE HUMAN RIGHTS CAMPAIGN

A few years after the U.S. Civil War ended, on the other side of the world, Japan underwent a comprehensive social, political and economic revolution called the Meiji Restoration. In the mid-1860s emerging elites overthrew the Japanese feudal regime. They took over the government and abolished the samurai class. Merchants and farmers began expressing themselves politically. The new government tried to control the pace and nature of change but had to respond to pressures from below to create a somewhat more democratic society.

The government hired European and American experts to design Japanese versions of modern political and economic institutions, such as the police, judiciary, armed forces, railroads, postal system, education, banking—even baseball. Members of the Japanese elite went abroad to study and returned home with new ideas that they were determined to put into practice.

Both the government and private individuals promoted western ideas. Even before the Restoration, Japan had a higher literacy rate than many European countries, and the new government sponsored a universal literacy campaign. It also set up reading rooms where ordinary people could read newspapers. Meanwhile, intellectuals established educational and political societies to study western texts such as John Stuart Mill's *On Liberty*, Samuel Smiles' *Self-Help* and Rousseau's *Social Contract*. During the 1870s hundreds of these societies sprang up in villages and small towns—more than 300 in the provinces around Tokyo alone, and hundreds more in other regions.

According to Stephen Vlastos, journalists, lawyers and intellectuals, "dressed dramatically in black capes and broad-brimmed hats," traveled throughout the country as lecturers, promoting western ideas. "Some highly committed members toured villages and market towns; traveling by ricksha, horseback and even on foot, they lectured at temples, schools, storehouses and wayside shrines, wherever they could assemble a crowd," Vlastos writes.

From 1870 on, a human rights movement of former samurai, merchants, farmers, peasants and intellectuals developed with astonishing rapidity. It was called *jiyu minken undo*, or the People's Rights Movement. The movement's main purpose was to call for constitutional representative government. Vlastos writes,

> Espousing liberty, equality and the right to elect government officials, the people's rights movement brought together at various times former Restoration leaders and intellectuals, urbanites and villagers, *shizoku* [former samurai] and wealthy commoners and,

finally, radicals and impoverished farmers—all who shared an interest in opposing oligarchic rule.

In 1874, several movement leaders published the "Memorial on the Establishment of a Representative Assembly," in which they paraphrased the American revolutionary watchword, "Taxation without representation is tyranny."

> The people who have the duty to pay taxes to the government concurrently possess the rights to be informed of the affairs of the government and to approve or reject such governmental matters. This is the principle universally accepted in the world, which requires no further elaboration on our part.

During this period, newspapers grew rapidly: By 1883 there were 199 newspapers throughout Japan, and in 1890 there were 716. Followers of the People's Rights Movement used newspapers to disseminate their ideas. For example, in 1879, "Sakurai Shizuka, a commoner farmer of moderate means from Chiba, published an appeal in which he denounced the oligarchy's failure to institute representative government and invited prefectural assembly delegates and concerned citizens throughout the country to join forces in a new campaign," Vlastos recounted. The appeal was published in a Tokyo daily, and Sakurai Shizuka disseminated thousands of copies through the mail.

As the People's Rights Movement broadened its base, the government reacted in 1875 and 1876 by imposing repressive press laws that restricted political criticism and set up a censorship apparatus. More than 200 editors and reporters were fined or imprisoned between 1876 and 1881.

In 1880, People's Rights Movement leaders founded the Association for Establishment of a National Assembly. The association's principal activity was circulating a petition calling for a national assembly. "During 1880 more than 240,000 persons signed similar petitions," Mikiso Hane notes. The government refused to accept the petitions and imposed the Law of Public Meetings, restricting gatherings and associations. More than 400 meetings were broken up in 1881 and 1882.

In 1881 the government tried to co-opt the People's Rights Movement by issuing an imperial proclamation of its intention to promulgate a constitution and establish a national assembly by 1890. The movement split, and political parties overshadowed the local societies and associations. Imitating Montesquieu, the new Liberal Party's statement of principles declared, "Liberty is the natural state of man and the preservation of liberty is man's great duty." When the government promulgated the constitution in 1889, however, it gave the Japanese people only "very limited rights and freedom," Hane writes. Nonetheless, the work of the People's

Rights Movement did lead to creation of the structures of representative government in Japan.

Thus the concepts and campaign strategies that animated abolitionism, Chartism and other Nineteenth-Century human rights movements spread even to societies with no previous tradition of political mobilization or free circulation of ideas. Using new technologies such as the press, the telegraph, steamships and railways, popular movements in many countries adopted and applied universalistic ideals imported from geographically and socially remote points of origin.

THE AGE OF LABOR

As industrialization spread throughout the world, the labor movement also grew. The great revolutionary convulsions of 1830, 1848 and 1870 alarmed European governments and the economic, political and social elites they defended. The related movements of Chartism, republicanism and unionism gathered mass support and posed serious threats to monarchical and oligarchical regimes in many countries. Governments imposed a variety of measures to suppress or co-opt opposition and prevent challenges to their rule. Nevertheless, the second half of the Nineteenth Century saw the unstoppable efflorescence of mass movements of workers. Through strikes, uprisings, demonstrations and other highly organized forms of mobilization, workers challenged and sometimes changed the status quo.

Some intellectuals, clergy, artists and politicians contributed ideas, words and funds to workers' movements. They also made links between the privileged sectors of society and the organizations and individuals that led the movements. Their participation helped broaden support and sympathy for causes that might otherwise have been lost, as well as for causes that really were lost. Each *cause célèbre* gained additional adherents in more parts of the world, helping build and consolidate what eventually became the international human rights movement. In the Nineteenth Century, however, this movement was still inchoate, unarticulated and unrecognized.

The Haymarket Affair stands as a landmark in the history of international campaigning on behalf of workers. The desperate struggle to commute the death sentences of eight Chicago anarchists, and later to pardon three of them, mobilized workers' organizations around the world and galvanized several generations of activists. It may have led to the founding of the American Federation of Labor, the rise of progressive and reform movements and the careers of Emma Goldman and other giant figures of the Left. It may also have delayed the institution of the eight-hour day in the U.S. for fifty years and spurred powerful forces that fiercely and effectively resisted all kinds of social change for three generations. Like several other cases recounted in this history, the Haymarket was more tragedy than triumph.

THE LABOR MOVEMENT EMERGES IN CHICAGO

In the 1870s and early '80s, American workers repeatedly clashed with police, army troops and hired strikebreakers. Strikes in 1876 and 1877 were so violent and widespread that many feared a revolutionary uprising in the United States. In highly industrialized Chicago, twenty-five to fifty workers were reported killed, 200 were injured and 400 were arrested in 1877. Cavalry troops broke up the railroad strike that year, and anti-labor vigilante groups were active in Chicago. Remembering the Paris Commune of 1870, newspapers whipped up anti-Communist hysteria. Wendell Phillips reacted to such charges in 1879, "Of all the cants that are canted in this canting world, the cant of our American hypocrites bewailing European Communism is the most disgusting." Owned by some of America's most powerful industrialists, the Chicago press was also virulently antilabor.

Labor conflicts increased over the next decade. In 1886, 1,400 strikes involved 500,000 U.S. workers. Among the best-organized workers in Chicago were the anarchists. According to Paul Avrich, they "engaged in a wide range of activities. Immense street parades were arranged, dotted with placards and banners." These parades imitated and rivaled those of "army-style" election campaigns. The Chicago anarchists also called giant "indignation meetings" to protest violence against workers elsewhere, such as "the dispersal of a public meeting by the London police and the arrest of William Morris and J.L. Mahon of the Socialist League," Avrich wrote. They knew about such faraway incidents from mainstream, labor and anarchist newspapers.

The Chicago anarchists sent speakers on tours, sponsored social events such as picnics and dances, managed organizations, printed and distributed thousands of pamphlets, and published newspapers and books. At their public meetings, they called for workers to arm themselves. Albert Parsons, one of their most effective leaders, declared, "Every man must lay by a part of his wages, buy a Colt's navy revolver and learn how to make and use dynamite." At a march to the Chicago Board of Trade on its opening day in 1885, Parsons called for workers to "agitate, organize, revolt."

Parsons' wife, Lucy, was even more radical than her husband. In 1885 she published "Dynamite! The Only Voice the Oppressors of the People Can Understand" in the *Denver Labor Enquirer*. Both she and her husband had been active in the labor movement since the early 1870s.

FROM RALLY TO RIOT

On May 1, 1886, at the climax of a national campaign for the eight-hour workday, 80,000 workers marched in downtown Chicago. There was no violence. But on May 3, police broke up a strike at the McCormick Reaper Works, wounding and killing an unknown number of workers. Enraged, Parsons and his comrades called an "indignation meeting" for the next evening, May 4, in Haymarket Square. They spread word of the meeting with a handbill in German and English, but only a few hundred people came. As one of the speakers, Samuel Fielden, was concluding his remarks, police attacked the crowd. Suddenly someone (whose identity was never determined) threw a crude bomb, killing a policeman. In the melée that followed, six more police were killed, probably by one another's bullets. It is unknown how many workers died.

Police immediately rounded up every anarchist they could find (without warrants) and held dozens incommunicado. Thirty-one were indicted for conspiracy to commit murder, and eight were tried; two others were kept in jail until the trial ended. The eight defendants "were the backbone of the local anarchist movement—its most effective organizers, the editors of its journals, its ablest speakers and writers. The police had long been awaiting the opportunity to silence them," Avrich writes. Most had been nowhere near the meeting at Haymarket Square on May 4.

Six of the accused were workers of German ancestry. Albert Parsons was the only one of old American stock. Samuel Fielden, the son of a Chartist who had immigrated to the U.S., was a Methodist lay preacher as a youth. He later became a union organizer. A distant relative of his had been a Member of Parliament who introduced the bill establishing a ten-hour workday, which the House of Commons passed in 1847.

The press response to the "Haymarket Riot" was hysterical. One Chicago paper called for the "extermination" of anarchists. *The Washington Post* called them "a horde of foreigners, representing almost the lowest stratum found in humanity's formation." Another paper referred to them as "a few long-haired, wild-eyed, bad-smelling, atheistic, reckless foreign wretches, who never did an honest hour's work in their lives, but who, driven half crazy with years of oppression and mad with envy of the rich, think to level society and its distinctions with a few bombs."

Although the trial took place only six weeks after the riot, the press had convicted the anarchists well before they came to trial. During this period, two of Chicago's most respectable socialists organized a legal defense committee, which, according to Henry David, "was very successful at raising money" to pay the defense attorneys, who included a Civil War hero. The committee sought funds from "liberally minded humanitarians of all creeds" and published its appeals in liberal and labor newspapers and magazines, Avrich writes. Some groups of workers made weekly donations of one to five dollars throughout the trial and appeals. Wealthy women sent their jewelry. Donations came from Europe, India and Japan. Altogether the committee collected $40,000, which paid all the defense's expenses.

But in the supercharged atmosphere, no lawyer could have gotten the anarchists off; all eight were sentenced to death. After the trial, David wrote, "Not a daily newspaper of standing in the entire country had a word to say in criticism of the trial or the verdict." On the street, dissenters were intimidated into silence. According to Avrich, "To voice the smallest doubt regarding the trial, the validity of the verdict or the propriety of the sentences might be construed as a token of anarchist sympathies."

Historians have severely judged the Haymarket trial. In Carl Smith's words, it was

> so unfair and irregular that it remains one of the most shameful proceedings in American history. It can be understood only in terms of the willingness of the citizens of Chicago and of the nation to accept, even to expect and demand, decisive action to preserve what they saw as social order. It was a show trial in every sense of the term, intended not only to point out to other would-be agitators their likely fate, but also to convince the public that the established system of authority was right and effective.

For both prosecution and defense, the trial was a morality play. It gave the anarchists an unrivaled opportunity to take center stage. "When they found themselves in the middle of what had become a national and international spectacle, they presented their case not so much before judge and jury, but . . . before the court of public opinion," Smith wrote. After sentencing, all eight made speeches that were "printed and reprinted, translated into many languages, made into pamphlets, serialized in the anarchist press and circulated by anarchist groups throughout the world," Avrich writes.

THE CLEMENCY CAMPAIGN

As soon as the trial ended, the defense committee went into high gear, raising funds for the appeal. It sponsored protest meetings, circulated petitions for a new trial and sold copies of Albert Parsons' Haymarket speech for ten cents a copy. For the anarchists, this was an unparalleled opportunity to propagandize the working class.

Lucy Parsons went on tour a few hours after the verdict was handed down. In seven weeks she traveled to sixteen states, addressing more than 200,000 people at universities, labor halls and other venues. A rousing speaker, she was described by a reporter as "a remarkably strong-willed and determined woman of a fair education and no ordinary ability." During her tour Parsons collected more than $5,000 for the defense. But she considered "her primary task . . . to tell the American people about anarchism," her biographer, Carolyn Ashbaugh, wrote.

In her speeches at this time she declared, "I am an anarchist and a revolutionist! . . . I propose to continue so, even if I reach the gallows also [prolonged applause]. I propose to . . . fight for justice . . . till I, too, am strangled." She also said, "Had I seen the liberties of my countrymen trodden underfoot, I would have flung the bomb myself. I would have violated no law, but would have upheld the Constitution."

As a result of such statements, she was repeatedly arrested, jailed or prevented from speaking. According to Ashbaugh, "She met roadblocks at every step of her way. Halls were closed to her at the last moment, detectives stood in every corner of the meeting halls, police kept her under constant surveillance." But Lucy Parsons' touring "brought herself and the case into the national limelight and kept them there for months. It acquainted thousands of people with radical ideas and helped to build the basis for the reform and radical movement of the 1890s," Ashbaugh writes.

The Illinois Supreme Court took six months to hand down a decision on the appeal. During this time, "public opinion underwent a perceptible shift. . . . A growing number of observers . . . concluded that the condemned men had not received impartial justice," observed Avrich. Over the objections of its leader, local chapters of the Knights of Labor, then America's largest labor organization, passed resolutions asking for mercy.

William Dean Howells, a novelist, editor and literary critic known as the dean of American letters, became uncomfortable with the death sentences. But he stood alone among literary figures in protesting the verdict. When he circulated a petition calling for clemency for the Haymarket defendants, none of his friends and colleagues would sign it. Well-known Chicago journalist Henry Demarest Lloyd also wrote and spoke against the death sentences. Other prominent individuals wrote and published articles and pamphlets on the subject. Civil War General Matthew Turnbull wrote, "Was It a Fair Trial? An Appeal to the Governor of Illinois," and in one day Lucy Parsons sold 5,000 copies at five cents each on the streets of Chicago.

Karl Marx's daughter, Eleanor Marx Aveling, and her husband visited the condemned men and spoke in their favor during a U.S. tour. The prisoners wrote their autobiographies, received visitors and corresponded with sympathizers. They were pessimistic about their chances for commutation.

After the state supreme court rejected the appeal, the clemency campaign intensified. French parliamentarians and British workers sent petitions calling for commutation of the sentences to the governor of Illinois. William Morris, George Bernard Shaw, Peter Kropotkin and Annie Besant spoke at a Haymarket rally in London. The American labor leader Samuel Gompers signed a public appeal calling the verdict "judicial murder." The

Knights of Labor split over the issue, and a few weeks later, Gompers and others founded the American Federation of Labor, which soon passed a resolution asking for mercy for the Haymarket anarchists.

"By November 1887, the number of those who questioned the justice of the verdict had reached an impressive total. No class was wholly unrepresented in this group. No longer was there an unqualified roar of condemnation of the accused. . . . The governor of Illinois was deluged with pleas asking for commutation of the death sentences," writes David.

After the U.S. Supreme Court refused to overturn the verdicts, an Amnesty Association of about 150 members sought to persuade the governor to commute the sentences to life imprisonment. The Association asked the prisoners to sign appeals for mercy; only three of the eight would do so. Lucy Parsons refused to urge her husband to sign. According to Ashbaugh, "She was determined that Albert must die a martyr in the struggle for economic emancipation."

As the execution date of November 11, 1887, approached, the Amnesty Association circulated commutation petitions among the privileged sectors of Chicago society. In less than a week, 40,000 signatures were collected. Lucy Parsons sat on the street, next to "a small wooden stand piled high with petitions," and was arrested for distributing circulars without a permit, Avrich wrote. Selling pamphlets on the streets, she was arrested when so many people surrounded her, trying to buy them, that she blocked traffic. The police told her to move along, so she "walked briskly down the street selling pamphlets as fast as she could make change. Again a large crowd gathered around her. . . . The police had harassed and chased her through the streets for two hours, but she had still sold 5,000 pamphlets, bringing in $250," Ashbaugh recounted.

Across the U.S. and Europe hundreds of demonstrations called for a reprieve. Avrich describes how "day after day, petitions, letters, telegrams, resolutions flowed in from all parts of America and the world" to the Illinois governor's office. Samuel Gompers went to Springfield to plead with the governor for mercy. At a hearing attended by hundreds, Gompers said,

> If these men are executed it would simply be an impetus to so-called revolutionary movement which no other thing on earth can give. These men would, apart from any consideration of mercy or humanity, be looked upon as martyrs. Thousands and thousands of labor men all over the world would consider that these men had been executed because they were standing up for free speech and free press. . . . Are we not strong enough, and intelligent enough to protect our lives and interests as a people without

the execution of these men? I cannot conceive what possible good results the execution of these men will have upon society.

The three prisoners who signed the request for mercy had their death sentences commuted. One killed himself in his cell. Four, including Albert Parsons, were hanged on November 11, 1887. More than 200,000 people watched the funeral procession as it moved through downtown Chicago, and 20,000 marched to suburban Waldheim Cemetery for the funeral.

According to Avrich, the press "exulted" over the executions, but they also "aroused a storm of indignation and protest." Around the world, people mourned "the Martyrs of Chicago." Workers in Havana collected $955 to send to the anarchists' families. Australian workers demonstrated. On the first anniversary of the executions, 3,000 attended a commemorative meeting at Waldheim Cemetery, and other meetings took place in Europe. In 1889, the International Socialist Conference declared May Day as a worldwide labor day to commemorate the Chicago anarchists. Ever since, May Day celebrations throughout the world (but not in the United States) have included mention of the Martyrs of Chicago.

THE SECOND CLEMENCY CAMPAIGN

Soon after the executions, the Pioneer Aid and Support Association was founded to help the men's families and pay for a monument on their graves. A collection of Albert Parsons' writings was published; police confiscated most of the copies. Police in Chicago and elsewhere harassed and arrested Lucy Parsons every time she spoke publicly, which was often. Judges usually fined her five dollars and let her go. In 1888 she toured the eastern U.S. and Britain. In later years she became a Chicago fixture, walking picket lines, selling or giving away leaflets, speaking from soapboxes, until her death at age eighty-nine in 1942.

In 1890 a campaign to free the three surviving anarchists intensified with the revival of the Amnesty Association by Henry Demarest Lloyd and others. In January 1892, Association lawyers went to the U.S. Supreme Court to request a new trial, but the petition was denied. That year Clarence Darrow joined the campaign, and "many leading citizens in Chicago became involved in the movement, feeling that the hysteria was over, and the three living victims could be released with little harm to society," Ashbaugh writes. In addition, the police officers responsible for the Haymarket attack were found to be corrupt and were fired. Thus their version of events was discredited.

A new governor came into office in 1893. John Peter Altgeld, a reformer, had escaped from poverty to become a state judge renowned for his probity and compassion. He was "deluged" with petitions, including one with 60,000 signatures, for the release of the three Haymarket prisoners,

Avrich writes. Some of Chicago's leading citizens quietly indicated their support for a pardon.

On June 25, 1893, during the Chicago World Exposition, the monument over the anarchists' grave was unveiled. One day later Governor Altgeld pardoned the three surviving anarchists and proclaimed their innocence in an 18,000-word report that scathingly attacked the police, prosecutors and judge for their handling of the case. According to Avrich, Altgeld immediately became "the most reviled man in America." This uncompromising action doomed his political career. Twenty years later, the poet Vachel Lindsay wrote an elegiac poem about Altgeld, "The Eagle That Is Forgotten," in which he asked,

THE CONSEQUENCES OF HAYMARKET

According to David, the Haymarket case led to "the first major 'red-scare' in American history, and produced a campaign of 'red-baiting' which has rarely been equaled." Congress, state legislatures and city councils passed anti-anarchist laws in the 1890s and 1900s. Anarchists were prohibited from entering the United States. American anarchists who tried to exercise freedom of speech and association were arrested and imprisoned. Antilabor laws, which broadened the definition of conspiracy to include labor organizing, also were passed. Local and federal authorities often used the Sherman Anti-Trust Act to break strikes or unions. Municipalities and states built armories to hold weapons for militias and police to use in case of uprisings and disturbances. The eight-hour movement was suppressed for many years.

On the other hand, the case impelled Samuel Gompers to break with the Knights of Labor and start the American Federation of Labor, a much more effective organization that laid the foundation of the modern American labor movement.

Henry Demarest Lloyd staked his career as a journalist on his support for clemency for the Haymarket anarchists. He told his father that "he hoped he could always be found on the side of the underdogs because they were usually right." He paid a high price for his campaign efforts: social ostracism and financial difficulty. His father-in-law, the publisher of the *Chicago Tribune*, disinherited him and never again spoke to him or his wife. Historian John Thomas wrote, "The Haymarket tragedy was the central symbolic event for Lloyd's generation of reformers, academicians and churchmen. The riot and its punitive aftermath signaled the onset of a decade of increasingly bitter confrontations."

Lloyd overcame his isolation to become part of a generation of intellectuals who created the "Social Gospel" after 1886. Through his work on the Haymarket case, he became friendly with reformers and radicals including Clarence Darrow, Samuel Gompers, William Dean Howells, Eugene V.

Debs and Jane Addams.

His 1888 lecture, "The New Conscience, or the Religion of Labor," became one of the principal texts of the Social Gospel movement. In it, Lloyd characterized the American labor movement as "a religious crusade powered by faith in an evolutionary socialism, but one whose holy writ was the Declaration of Independence and whose saints were Jefferson, Lincoln and Wendell Phillips."

GENESIS OF A RADICAL

Obsessed by the case, in 1887 an eighteen-year-old named Emma Goldman read "every line on anarchism I could get, every word about the men, their lives, their work. I read about their heroic stand while on trial and their marvelous defense. I saw a new world opening before me." The executions "crystallized my views . . . and made me an active anarchist." Thus began her career as an organizer, agitator, lecturer and author that ended with her death in 1940.

Goldman's longtime companion, Alexander Berkman, also became an anarchist after Haymarket. A fervent young believer in "propaganda of the deed," Berkman walked into manager Henry Frick's office in Pittsburgh during the 1892 Homestead Steel strike and tried to kill him. Frick recovered and Berkman spent fourteen years in prison. Goldman went to jail for advocating birth control and speaking against American participation in World War I. She earned the distinction of being called "the most dangerous woman in America."

After the war, the U.S. government deported Goldman and Berkman to the Soviet Union under laws that made it easy to get rid of anarchists, who, identified as terrorists, were still as despised as they had been in 1886. The pair found that anarchists were even more persecuted in the Soviet Union than in the U.S. and became bitter opponents of the new regime. Goldman did not find another situation in which she could act as an anarchist until the Spanish Civil War in the late 1930s. She went to Spain, met anarchist counterparts there and, in her late sixties, hurled herself into the struggle one last time.

Her biographer, Alice Wexler, wrote that for Goldman, Haymarket

> acted as a catalyst, galvanizing her imagination and propelling her directly toward the movement to which she would dedicate her life. Indeed, although the Haymarket affair intensified the popular stereotype of the anarchist as a wild-eyed terrorist and weakened existing links between anarchism and the labor movement, the Chicago events also stimulated widespread discussion of revolutionary ideas and may even have acted as a stimulus to radicalism in general.

Goldman was only one radical among the millions that Haymarket profoundly affected. For many years afterwards, workers all over the world gathered on November 11 to commemorate the executions of the Martyrs of Chicago. After World War I, Armistice Day observances replaced such commemorations, and May 1 became the date to remember Haymarket.

Echoes of Haymarket have lingered over the years. In 1927 Emma Goldman wrote a sad letter from exile in France to a comrade in America, "How little progress we have made in the last forty years . . . when such heroic men as Sacco and Vanzetti must pay the price even as their comrades did on the black Friday of 1887." In 1986, at a Haymarket centennial observance at Waldheim Cemetery, anarchists upstaged the main speaker by climbing on the martyrs' monument and placing a red and black flag on the statue of Dawn holding the fallen worker. In 1992, Brazilian newspaper reports on May Day commemorations referred to the Martyrs of Chicago as if every reader would know who they were. Altgeld may be forgotten, but the memory of Haymarket endures. So does the international labor movement that came out of the tumultuous Nineteenth Century.

The French Army crucifies Alfred Dreyfus, c. 1898; drawing by H.G. Ibels

Chapter 5

THE WORLD OF THE 1890s: LYNCHING, GENOCIDE, INJUSTICE

B y the end of the Nineteenth Century, people had been organizing and conducting human rights campaigns for more than a hundred years. It is worth repeating the kinds of activities that characterized these campaigns almost from the beginning:

- Letter writing to authorities at all levels;
- Petitioning and lobbying legislators;
- Holding mass meetings, demonstrations and marches;
- Publishing tracts, books, articles, reports and advertisements;
- Boycotting products;
- Creating and disseminating promotional slogans and products;
- Raising funds through appeals and subscriptions.

Participants included:

- Dedicated and persistent organizers;
- A literate public with some free time and disposable income;
- Influential intellectuals;
- Committed financial backers;
- A relatively free press.

Participants also shared a general sense of the universality of human rights. This sentiment allowed or even impelled them to work on behalf of people of other cultures, classes and races, who had values very different from their own or may have done things they could not approve of.

Over time, campaigners came from increasingly diverse backgrounds and regions. As workers became more literate and began organizing across the world, they interested themselves in faraway comrades who seemed to symbolize their own struggles for equality and dignity. They learned about cases in other parts of the world through the press and via improved communications technology. The Haymarket Affair may have been the first campaign to attract supporters from many countries on almost every continent. And as social groups of many kinds organized their own associations, mass movements of previously unorganized groups also formed.

These emerging groups and movements, frequently composed of the unenfranchised, the poor and the ostracized, did not have sufficient political or economic power to gain their objectives merely by strength of numbers. The unsuccessful uprisings, the Chartist movement and the failed revolutions of 1848 and 1870 proved that. Groups and movements had to find allies in more privileged sectors of society to speak for them in the corridors of power and to persuade elites of the wisdom of change in terms they could accept. They also needed broad public support for their causes.

Intellectuals and artists who sympathized with social movements, such as Harriet Beecher Stowe, Victor Hugo and William Dean Howells, sought to parlay their celebrity into moral authority by publicly advocating causes. Their participation ensured that movements would gain public attention, if not approbation. Although some of the causes may have failed, intellectuals and celebrities kept lending their talents and support to them— and continue to do so. People today may wonder why they should pay attention to movie stars, entertainers or artists who declare their support for environmental or liberation movements, but such widely publicized declarations do seem to have some effect on both public opinion and policy makers.

MARK TWAIN WEIGHS IN

One of the Nineteenth Century's most successful writers, Mark Twain (1835-1910) also was a human rights activist, especially in his later years. In the 1890s he joined the Anti-Imperialist League and publicly opposed the Spanish-American War. As the Twentieth Century began, he wrote two articles that expressed his horror at recent events. One, which he did not publish, was called "The United States of Lyncherdom." The other, which was published and republished many times, was called "King Leopold's Soliloquy." This article denounced a forced-labor regime in the Belgian Congo that led to the deaths of as many as 15 million—half the country's population—between 1880 and 1910. In both pieces, Twain denounced organized violence against people very different from himself.

Twain wrote "The United States of Lyncherdom" in 1901, after the lynching of a black man in his home state of Missouri. In the article he suggests that missionaries be brought back from China to disperse lynch mobs in the South. The Chinese should be left alone, he says, because "almost every convert runs a risk of catching our civilization. . . . We ought to think twice before we encourage a risk like that; for, *once civilized, China can never be uncivilized again* [his italics]." Perhaps Twain decided not to publish this article because he believed the public would not accept his sardonic indignation and his questioning of organized religion. Some of his more outrageous pieces, like this one, did not see the light of day until many years after his death.

Twain knew that mobs of white men, women (and even children) were lynching hundreds of black men every year in the United States. Some witnesses bought souvenir postcards picturing mutilated, burnt victims swinging from trees and sent them, with jolly greetings, to friends and relatives. An exhibition of these postcards shocked and revolted viewers in New York City almost a hundred years later. Few blacks and even fewer whites spoke out against lynching in the late Nineteenth Century.

A LONE CRUSADER

One courageous black woman, Ida Wells-Barnett, crusaded against lynching from the 1890s to the 1920s. Almost single-handedly, through unremitting efforts, she forced American society to acknowledge that lynching was a systematic practice in some parts of the country. She challenged the principal rationale for lynching: whites' belief that black men were natural rapists who sought to violate the purity and honor of white women. For a woman even to mention this subject was far more outrageous than for Twain to joke about missionaries. Slander and death threats could not stop Wells-Barnett from writing, speaking and acting against lynching. She was indomitable.

Ida B. Wells was a young journalist living and working in Memphis, Tennessee, when a friend was lynched in 1892 as a result of his business rivalry with a white grocery owner. In a furious editorial, she declared that whites lynched blacks to terrorize them and to punish enterprising blacks for their success. She quoted white newspaper stories about white women who had affairs with black men, cried rape when they were discovered and later recanted their rape accusations.

At the time her editorial was printed, Wells was out of town. She could not return to Memphis without risking her life, so she published a series of articles about lynching in *The New York Age*. The articles also circulated in Tennessee. Both black and white community leaders in Memphis condemned the lynching and Wells. White leaders were concerned about the city's reputation and a black boycott of segregated streetcars that was hurting business in the town.

In her articles, Wells urged blacks to arm themselves in self-defense against lynch mobs and called whites barbaric. In return, Memphis newspapers called Wells a harlot. Thus was her career launched. A month after her articles appeared in New York, Frederick Douglass published a piece against lynching in the elite *North American Review*. A few months later, Douglass wrote the introduction to a pamphlet Wells published on lynching and encouraged her to campaign nationally and internationally. She then became a public speaker, first to black and later to white audiences in the U.S. and Britain.

Wells went to Britain at the invitation of a British Quaker. Her biographer, Linda McMurry, commented, "In a society permeated with white supremacy, white recognition was an important step in obtaining legitimacy both in and outside the black community." Her speaking tour in Britain made her an international celebrity, thanks to favorable coverage by British newspapers. Wells spoke to Bible societies, mission associations, Friends' meetings and in public halls. Asked by a local politician why he should pay attention to such a remote issue and what good it would do, Wells replied:

> The pulpit and the press of our own country remain silent on these continued outrages and the voice of my race is stifled or ignored whenever it is lifted in America in demand for justice. It is to the religious and moral sentiment of Great Britain we now turn. These can arouse the public sentiment of Americans so necessary for the enforcement of law. The moral agencies at work in Great Britain did much for the overthrow of chattel slavery. They can in like manner pray, write, preach, talk and act against civil and industrial slavery; against the hanging, shooting and burning alive of a powerless race. America cannot and will not ignore the voice of a nation that is her superior in civilization, which makes this demand in the name of justice and humanity. . . .

At least two organizations formed in Britain to combat lynching and racism after her visit.

Wells later said she considered her British tour successful because of the attacks on her that then appeared in the Memphis papers, the *Atlanta Constitution* and *The Washington Post*. Northern newspapers were more supportive.

On her return to the U.S., Wells went to Chicago in time for the world exposition of 1893. Blacks had been excluded from the planning, and the exhibitions included depictions of antebellum plantation life that portrayed blacks as contented slaves. Wells compiled "The Reason Why the Colored American Is Not in the World's Columbian Exposition," an eighty-one-page pamphlet. Frederick Douglass wrote the introduction, and 10,000 copies were distributed during the fair. While she was in Chicago, Wells spoke at a labor conference with Henry Demarest Lloyd, Henry George and Booker T. Washington.

The following year Wells returned to Britain on a five-month tour. She aroused controversy there by accusing the Women's Christian Temperance Union of racism. This tour made Wells nationally famous in the U.S.

"The more white southerners protested, the more publicity Wells received," McMurry writes. African-Americans leapt to her defense.

Soon after, six states—North Carolina, Georgia, South Carolina, Ohio, Kentucky and Texas—passed antilynching laws, but they seem to have done little good.

Wells then toured the northern U.S. for a year. In her speeches she appealed to white editors and clergy to oppose lynching, since "it was the white people of the country who had to mold the public sentiment necessary to put a stop to lynching." Because what she had to say was so controversial, she was in great demand as a speaker.

In 1895 Wells published *A Red Record*, a 100-page pamphlet with a list of recent lynchings. She sought a Congressional investigation into lynching, but southern Democrats blocked it. As a result of her work, newspapers and periodicals covered lynching more extensively and in a more negative light.

Wells married a black Chicago lawyer, Ferdinand Barnett, and took time out to have several children, but she did not end her campaigning. Inspired by her example, black women in many cities formed "Ida B. Wells Clubs" and other associations for mutual aid. In later years she helped found the National Association for the Advancement of Colored People (NAACP) and many local organizations.

When a black postmaster was lynched in Lake City, South Carolina, in 1898, Wells-Barnett spoke at a protest meeting in Chicago, then took her baby son to Washington and lobbied in the Capitol for an antilynching bill for five weeks. Accompanied by seven Illinois congressmen and a senator, she met with President McKinley, asking him to investigate the postmaster's murder because he was a federal employee. McKinley promised action but did nothing.

After a particularly gruesome lynching in 1899, Wells-Barnett raised funds to pay a detective to investigate at the scene. She published a pamphlet, "Lynch Law in Georgia," to point out the discrepancies between white newspapers' accounts and the detective's findings. She also ran a bureau to investigate lynchings and sent out letters asking for 10,000 people to disseminate her reports and for twenty-five-cent contributions. Wells-Barnett often had difficulty finding sufficient funds to carry out her activities. A combative person, she frequently clashed with other black leaders and was forced, as one colleague commented, "to play a lone hand."

Wells-Barnett kept writing pamphlets against lynching but focused more on local issues as the years passed. In 1905 she took the controversial step of starting a kindergarten for black children in Chicago.

She also was a woman's suffragist. When the National American Women's Suffrage Association asked her not to march with the all-white Illinois delegation in a demonstration in Washington, D.C., she refused to comply. "At the beginning of the procession she was not seen. Along the route, however, she stepped out from among the spectators, was flanked by two white women, and continued to the end," recounted Mildred Thompson.

In 1909, Wells-Barnett said in a speech:

> Agitation, though helpful, will not alone stop the crime [of lynching]. Year after year statistics are published, meetings are held, resolutions are adopted and yet lynchings go on. The only certain remedy is an appeal to law. Lawbreakers must be made to know that human life is sacred and that every citizen of this country is first a citizen of the U.S. and secondly a citizen of the state in which he belongs.

After a lynching in Cairo, Illinois, in 1909, Wells-Barnett went personally to the scene to investigate the role of the sheriff in the incident. (Illinois had passed a law holding sheriffs responsible for lynchings.) She took evidence of the sheriff's negligence to the state capital. McMurry observes: "In the end her lone voice prevailed over those of prominent whites. . . . Apparently her effort did halt lynching of prisoners in Illinois."

In 1913, McMurry wrote, Wells-Barnett

> led a successful campaign to prevent the passage of a law segregating public transportation in Illinois. . . . That same year . . . she [and other activists] fought bills in Congress that would have prohibited interracial marriage in the District of Columbia. In 1915 they also led the battle against segregation of social activities at Chicago's integrated Wendell Phillips High School and instigated a letter-writing campaign against a proposed national immigration law that would have excluded Africans.

After riots against blacks in East St. Louis in 1917, Wells-Barnett went to the town, arriving "in time to accompany a group of black women under military escort as they returned to their homes to get some of the belongings left behind in the flight from the white mobs," wrote McMurry. As a result of her activities during World War I, the FBI and the Military Intelligence Division put her and her husband under surveillance as "pro-German." Threatened by the Secret Service when she protested the execution of thirteen black soldiers for mutiny in 1917, she replied, "I would consider it an honor to spend whatever years are necessary in prison as the one member of the race who protested."

Wells-Barnett was selected as a nongovernmental delegate to the Versailles peace conference after World War I, but could not go because the U.S. government refused to issue her a passport. In an "Address to the Country and the World," she declared, "Every denial or violation of justice, humanity and democracy has become a matter for correction and abrogation on a world basis by a World Court" and called for international attention to the "utterly undemocratic conditions under which every person of color is forced to live in this country." For statements like these, far ahead of her time, she was considered unacceptably radical, an extremist, and her influence declined.

But Wells-Barnett continued to act. When twelve blacks were sentenced to death after a race riot in Arkansas in 1919, she went to meet with the prisoners' wives and mothers and sneaked into jail to see the prisoners. She published a pamphlet on the case, and the NAACP took it up. The condemned men were freed in 1925.

Wells-Barnett kept protesting and lobbying until her death in 1930. Throughout the 1930s, Congress repeatedly failed to pass the federal antilynching bill for which she had campaigned. Lynch mobs continued to kill scores of blacks every year until after World War II. In U.S. Justice Department files from the 1920s and '30s are letters, often written in pencil, from lynch victims' mothers, appealing for justice. Stapled to them are form letters, "The Department . . . regrets to inform you that it would have no authority to take any action with respect to the matters to which you refer." A photograph in the Justice Department files of the 1930s shows a large, handmade poster tacked to the side of a barn. On the poster is a cartoon of a black man hanging from a gallows. Underneath are the words, "I voted yesterday."

Despite Ida Wells-Barnett's dedication, fearlessness and persistence, she could not end lynching by herself. It would take a mass movement in the 1950s and '60s to secure the basic rights to life, liberty and equal protection of the law that were guaranteed to African-Americans by the U.S. Constitution. But through her determined work, the peerless Wells-Barnett pointed the way.

AND IN AFRICA . . .

In "King Leopold's Soliloquy," published as a pamphlet in 1905, Mark Twain brought a horrible crime—genocide in the Belgian Congo—to public attention in America. "Twain Calls Leopold Slayer of 15 Million," said the headline in the *New York World*. But he was by no means the first American to expose what King Leopold of the Belgians, who personally owned the colony, was doing in Africa. In 1890, a black lawyer and clergyman, George Washington Williams, went to the Congo and discovered that Belgians were committing many abuses, including buying and selling slaves, in the colony. Williams published two pamphlets about what he had seen and wrote to the U.S. Secretary of State, accusing Leopold of "crimes against humanity." This phrase was not in general use at the time.

King Leopold, a master of public relations, orchestrated a campaign to discredit Williams, who died of tuberculosis in 1891 at age forty-one. For awhile, the Belgians' forced labor regime, characterized by kidnapping, killing, beating and mutilation of men, women and children on a massive scale, went unreported in Europe and America.

In the mid-1890s, a black American missionary, William Sheppard, published articles in church periodicals denouncing Belgian atrocities, such as amputating the hands of Congolese, including children, who refused or failed to gather rubber and ivory. His reports attracted little attention, but soon other missionaries and travelers began publishing attacks on "the Congo's rubber terror." A Swedish missionary, E.V. Sjöblom, published an exposé of Leopold's regime in a Swedish newspaper in 1896, and it was reprinted in other European countries. In 1897, Sjöblom spoke to a public meeting in London about the situation in the Congo.

Leopold forestalled criticism by setting up a "Commission for the Protection of the Natives" that met twice. As other events, including the Dreyfus Affair and the Boer War, filled the front pages, the Congo faded from view.

Meanwhile, E.D. Morel, a young shipping company employee in Liverpool, figured out by checking shipping manifests that rubber and ivory arriving in England from the Congo were being produced by slave labor. He refused to keep his findings to himself, despite his employer's efforts to buy him off. In 1901 he quit his job and started writing about the Congo full-time. Backed by a Liverpool businessman, he founded and edited *The West African Mail*. Without experience as a social crusader or strong religious convictions, Morel nonetheless had a "prodigious capacity for indignation," wrote Adam Hochschild, who called him "the greatest British investigative journalist of his time."

Morel did not work alone. In Parliament, Sir Charles Dilke spoke out about the Congo. The Anti-Slavery Society and the Aboriginal Protection Society also denounced the situation. But Morel went further by describing the systematic nature of the Belgian atrocities, based on the Congo regime's organization and control by one man, King Leopold, who was completely unaccountable for his actions.

Morel was not allowed to enter the Congo, but missionaries and returning officials leaked information to him. By 1903 he had made the Congo a political issue in Britain. That year the House of Commons passed a resolution urging that the Congo's "natives should be governed with humanity." The British Foreign Office then sent Roger Casement, its consul in the Congo, into the interior for three months to investigate Morel's charges. According to Hochschild, Casement's final report was "in the language that Amnesty and similar groups would later make their own: formal and sober, assessing the reliability of various witnesses, filled with references to laws and statistics, and accompanied by appendices and depositions." Because Casement gave interviews to the press, the Foreign Office had to publish the report.

One Belgian newspaper, which was linked to Congo business interests, replied that people with missing hands "were unfortunate individuals, suffering from cancer in the hands, whose hands thus had to be cut off as a simple surgical operation."

Morel and Casement met and decided to found an organization to work on the Congo issue. They "discussed ways and means and drew up a rough plan of campaign," Hochschild writes. In 1904 the Congo Reform Association (CRA) was organized. Morel enlisted prominent individuals, including William Wilberforce's great-grandson, to participate. The association's first meeting in Liverpool attracted a thousand people. Because he was still in the foreign service, Casement raised funds secretly for the association.

Morel, who ran the Congo Reform Association for a decade, was a tireless worker, a skilled public speaker and propagandist, and a brilliant fundraiser. He obtained funds from prominent Quakers in Liverpool and kept costs down by working from his home. At mass meetings he was careful to include on the podium Members of Parliament from the three major parties, clergy from the Anglican and dissenting churches and respected elite figures. He would show slides of Congolese whose hands had been severed; the slides were reproduced in the press and seen by millions. His contacts with the press were excellent, and he frequently wrote for the London *Times*, the most prestigious newspaper in the English-speaking world. He fed information to Belgian papers and distributed it internationally via wire services.

Morel also kept in touch with European and American journalists and writers, including Anatole France, Nobel Prize winner Bjornstjerne Bjornson and Mark Twain. In 1906 he wrote to Twain, "Those wretched people out there have no one but us after all. And they have the right to live."

Local groups of the Congo Reform Association throughout Britain "organized their members to send funds, to write to their representatives in Parliament and to produce an unending flow of letters to local newspapers," Hochschild writes. A ladies' branch sent two representatives to the CRA's executive committee meetings. By 1910 the CRA had branches in Germany, France, Norway, Switzerland and other European countries. Public meetings on the Congo were held as far away as Australia and New Zealand.

Two Baptist missionaries, John and Alice Harris, who had worked in the Congo, traveled full-time for the association. During their first two years, they spoke publicly 600 times. Another important contributor to the work was Hezekiah Shanu, a Nigerian businessman in the Congo who sent information to Morel. Because he was a British subject, Congo authorities did not arrest him but harassed him mercilessly, until he killed himself in 1905.

Leopold waged an elaborate and expensive counter-campaign, complete with books, pamphlets and professional lobbyists. He also bribed reporters and editors to write and print favorable articles. When Twain published "King Leopold's Soliloquy," Leopold replied with a forty-seven-page pamphlet, "An Answer to Mark Twain."

In 1904 Morel visited the United States. He met with President Roosevelt in the White House and traveled with Twain, speaking in several cities. An American CRA was founded; G. Stanley Hall, president of Clark University, was its first leader. The Harrises addressed more than 200 public meetings in forty-nine cities. Petitions signed by governors, university professors and presidents, bishops and newspaper editors arrived at the State Department. Hochschild notes, "Although Morel had vocal individual supporters throughout Europe, only in the U.S. did the cause of Congo reform become the full-scale crusade it was in England."

Leopold reacted by hiring an American lawyer as a lobbyist and paid him the enormous sum of $500,000 for one year's work. When the king dropped him, the lawyer sold his story to the *New York American*. "King Leopold's Amazing Attempt to Influence Our Congress Exposed" ran for a week and included atrocity photos. In it, the lawyer revealed that he had bribed a staff member of the Senate Foreign Relations Committee to keep reformers from testifying or gaining access to committee members. As a result, the U.S. changed its Congo policy. Thereafter the State Department joined the British Foreign Office in pressuring Leopold to end his one-man rule of the territory. In 1908 the Belgian government bought the Congo from Leopold at a very high price.

When missionaries in the Congo spoke out about continued atrocities, Belgian officials started prosecuting them for "calumny." Conviction brought a sizable fine or five years in prison. William Sheppard, who had never stopped denouncing Belgian abuses, was tried under some palm trees in 1909, with the U.S. consul and vice-consul in attendance. Sheppard was acquitted, but no action was taken against the state company that had accused him.

Once the Belgian government had purchased the Congo and made some reforms, Morel found crusading more difficult. He and Arthur Conan-Doyle, the creator of Sherlock Holmes, could still draw large crowds in Edinburgh, Liverpool and Plymouth. Conan-Doyle published a book, *The Crime of the Congo*, based on information that Morel had provided, and it sold 25,000 copies in one week. But by 1910, the American CRA had collapsed. And although Morel supported British imperialism, his support for African land rights made enemies in the Foreign Office. He closed the CRA in 1913.

Acknowledging that "the wounds of the Congo will take generations to heal," Morel declared that "we have struck a blow for human justice that cannot and will not pass away."

The atrocities in the Belgian Congo may have decreased, but a government-imposed head tax perpetuated forced labor there for many years. Other colonial powers also maintained forced labor regimes. The French government suppressed a report on similar conditions in its Congo colony. From 1903 to 1906, the Germans massacred the Herero people in Southwest Africa, but there was no international protest. In 1975, after the Congo became independent, a Belgian diplomat tried to gain access to his government's Congo files for a commission of inquiry, but he was told the files were secret and he could not see them. For eight years he fought to gain access to them. In the 1980s he published several books on the Congo, but few Belgians seem to have read them. In the Congo itself, the people silently remembered; as Morel predicted, the scars have not completely healed. At the beginning of the Twenty-First Century, civil war and atrocities were convulsing the country.

Morel spent six months in jail in 1917 for sending antiwar literature to neutral countries. In 1922 he was elected to Parliament. He died, worn out, in his early fifties. His sometime collaborator, Roger Casement, went to Peru to investigate atrocities against the Putumayo Indians by a British company. He was knighted for his services to the British Empire. During World War I, however, he spied for the Germans in exchange for arms for the Irish independence struggle. Despite an international clemency campaign, he was executed for treason in 1916.

Within a few years, the Congo genocide, the Congo Reform Association and E.D. Morel were forgotten. But the campaign "kept alive a tradition, a way of seeing the world, a human capacity for outrage at pain inflicted on another human being, no matter whether that pain is inflicted on someone of another color, in another country, at another end of the earth," writes Hochschild. Using the proven strategies of earlier campaigns and taking advantage of improved communications and international interest, the Congo campaign passed the means to express that outrage to the next generation of activists.

"TRUTH IS ON THE MARCH, AND NOTHING CAN STOP IT"

Perhaps the French did not pay much attention to the Congo campaign because they were embroiled in a much more intense and immediate struggle, the Dreyfus Affair, which roiled France from 1894 to 1906.

Captain Alfred Dreyfus was the one of the first Jews to be appointed to the French General Staff, the high command of the army. Dreyfus came from an assimilated, upper-middle-class family in Alsace, which France lost to Germany in the war of 1870. He moved to Paris and married the daughter of a wealthy Jewish family there. His fellow officers found him to be patriotic, intelligent, obedient, reserved and somewhat arrogant.

In 1894, an army intelligence officer received a letter (thereafter known as the *bordereau*) stolen from a wastebasket in the German Embassy. The letter indicated that a French officer was handing secret information to the Germany military attaché. The intelligence officer jumped to the conclusion that Dreyfus had written it because his handwriting was somewhat similar to the handwriting in the letter. His superior assumed that Dreyfus was capable of treason because he was Jewish.

Such anti-Semitism was not uncommon among Europeans in the late Nineteenth Century. The *Civilitá Cattolica*, a Jesuit newspaper in Rome, expressed a typical sentiment in 1897: "The Jew was created by God to serve as a spy, whatever treason is in preparation. . . . Not only in France, but in Germany, Austria and Italy as well, the Jews are to be excluded from the nation." Jews had been "emancipated" (given some political and economic rights) in France in 1791; but in other European countries they were deprived of certain rights until the 1830s. In the Papal States of Italy they were forced to live in ghettoes until 1870, and in Russia they were still restricted to the "Pale of Settlement" in the 1890s.

In 1894 France was just emerging from a decade-long scandal, involving three Jewish bankers and many non-Jews, over the financing of the Panama Canal. But other matters, such as an unsuccessful coup attempt by monarchists, the assassination of President Carnot by an anarchist, Socialist gains in Parliamentary elections and violent labor conflicts, were of immediate concern. The country's relations were more tense with England than with Germany, and it was peacetime. There seemed to be no particular reason for an espionage case to bring France to the verge of civil war.

Dreyfus' account of his arrest reads like a Kafkaesque nightmare. He was called to the Ministry of War one morning for a "general inspection." Without explanation, a commandant ordered him to write some sentences and stood over him, interrupting from time to time with hostile remarks.

> As soon as the dictation was over, Commandant du Paty arose and, placing his hand on my shoulder, cried out in a loud voice: "In the name of the law, I arrest you; you are accused of the crime of high treason." A thunderbolt falling at my feet would not have produced in me a more violent emotion; I blurted out disconnected sentences, protesting against so infamous an accusation, which nothing in my life could have given rise to.

Next, M. Cochefert and his secretary threw themselves on me and searched me. I did not offer the slightest resistance, but cried to them, "Take my keys, open everything in my house; I am innocent." Then I added, "Show me at least the proofs of the infamous act you pretend I have committed." They answered that the accusations were overwhelming, but refused to state what they were or who had made them.

The army conducted the Dreyfus investigation and court martial in a particularly dubious fashion. Intelligence officers fabricated documents and committed perjury on the witness stand. Unable to present conclusive proof of Dreyfus' guilt or even a motive for his alleged treason, they invented "secret" evidence that they failed to show to the defense, as required by law. Dreyfus was convicted and sentenced to life imprisonment in exile. He was then subjected to a public degradation ceremony, during which a warrant officer tore off Dreyfus' epaulets and broke his ceremonial sword over his knee, while Dreyfus repeatedly protested his innocence to fellow officers. Mobs outside howled, "Death to the Jews!"

Dreyfus then was shipped to Devil's Island off the coast of French Guiana in February 1895. Unlike other prisoners, he was kept under close watch and not allowed to move freely about the island or to associate with anyone. As many as thirteen guards kept him under twenty-four-hour surveillance. The weather was suffocatingly hot most of the time. He seems to have contracted malaria and was often ill. The food was so vile that he sometimes could not eat. Though often tempted to kill himself, he decided to stay alive to restore his family's honor. The correspondence between Dreyfus and his wife poignantly shows how they struggled to maintain their courage and support each other. He acted like a prisoner of war, determined not to betray his country (and his faith in it); but grief and despair frequently overwhelmed him. In France he was apparently forgotten.

Dreyfus' family decided that his brother Mathieu should abandon his business to campaign on behalf of Alfred. Mathieu later explained:

> I understood my task in this way. . . . I should start a personal propaganda campaign in all the circles I could reach, untiringly, and without allowing myself to be discouraged by anything; I should recruit people, then ask these recruits, and all our friends, to work within their own circles, to make propaganda, and finally to search out the culprit.

Mathieu did not want to take any public initiatives. He seemed to believe that he should act—that he would be more effective—working privately. Did he disdain seeking public support? Or did he believe that no one would help? Even French Jews shied away from the family. Léon Blum, much later the premier of France, observed, "A great misfortune had fallen on Israel. They accepted it without a word of protest, in the hope that time and silence would wipe out its effects."

Mathieu and other family members tried to convert friends and colleagues to the cause. For example, in 1897 Lucien Herr, a librarian at the Sorbonne, told his friends Léon Blum and Georges Clemenceau that Dreyfus was innocent. Herr had heard about the case in 1894 from his colleague Lucien Lévy-Bruhl, Dreyfus' cousin. Herr also read articles by Bernard Lazare, a Jewish literary critic Mathieu had asked to write about the case. Blum had heard about Dreyfus years earlier but did not become emotionally involved in the case until Herr spoke to him about it. This story says something about the interconnectedness of the Paris elite, as well as Mathieu's understanding of how to use social networks to gain support for his brother. From 1895 to 1897, his "campaign" took place privately, among individuals.

Eventually one of Alfred's jailers, who believed him innocent, told Mathieu, "Your brother's cause must be defended before public opinion." After all, anti-Semitic, monarchist and right-wing newspapers had been attacking Dreyfus from the beginning. So Mathieu changed his tactics.

Mathieu planted a false story in a London newspaper that Alfred had escaped from Devil's Island. The French government immediately denied the report, and the denial made headlines. The case catapulted back into public consciousness.

For Alfred Dreyfus, the consequences were severe. Every night for forty-five nights, his jailers shackled his ankles to his bedstead so he could not move. He had no idea why he was being tortured in this way. Apparently the army believed that a shadowy Jewish "syndicate" was preparing to rescue him.

During the fifty months he was on Devil's Island, Dreyfus received no information about what was happening in France. His wife's letters were heavily censored, delayed or never delivered. Months of waiting to receive them caused him considerable extra anguish.

As the months and years of 1895, 1896 and 1897 passed, the Dreyfus case took astonishing twists and turns. A high-ranking officer in the War Ministry, Lt. Col. Georges Picquart, discovered evidence indicating that the real traitor was a Major Esterhazy; but when he tried to bring this to his superiors' attention, he was told to do nothing. He was then sent on a dangerous assignment to North Africa, apparently in hopes he would be killed. He left a note for his lawyer to be opened in the event of his death. Picquart's lawyer leaked the information to a Parliament member. Mathieu Dreyfus found out the perpetrator's identity from another source—a man to whom Esterhazy owed money and who recognized his handwriting when the *bordereau* was reproduced in a newspaper. Esterhazy was court-martialed—and acquitted. Then Picquart was arrested. These two events aroused international indignation.

While all this was going on, newspapers in Paris and the provinces were publishing hundreds of articles, many of them filled with lies and distortions, about the case. Robert Hoffman wrote:

> Newspapers, which were always widely read and influential, now were the public's chief source of information, misinformation and polemic in the Affair, especially because of the secrecy or obscurity of many of the relevant facts. Acrimony and invective were commonplace, as was the wide repetition of tales based on gossip, invention and both calculated and careless leaks by nearly everyone with access to genuine information.

Anti-Semitic papers were particularly active in spreading falsehoods and slanders about Dreyfus, his family and his defenders. Aiming at ordinary people and workers, "they pandered to their lowest instincts. Their columns were filled day by day with expressions of passion and prejudice, the polemics reaching levels of violence which would be inconceivable today. The difficulty of bringing libel actions under the Press Law of 1881 gave them almost total immunity," Eric Cahm wrote. Some of these papers had huge audiences: *Le Petit Journal* had a daily circulation of 995,000, and *La Croix*, a Catholic newspaper, had a daily circulation of almost 191,000. In contrast, the daily circulation of *Le Figaro*, which supported Dreyfus, was only 30,000. Because *Le Figaro* and some other small papers were highly respected, newspapers with bigger circulation republished their articles, however.

Newspaper cartoonists illustrated both sides' views with strong caricatures of the leading figures in the Affair. Photographs and postcards also were used for propaganda purposes. The world's first professional filmmaker, Georges Mêliès, made eleven short films reenacting scenes from the Affair in 1899, "but fighting in the audience forced withdrawal of the films from public exhibition," Hoffman wrote. No more films were made in France about the Affair until the 1920s. The playwright Romain Rolland wrote *The Wolves* about the Affair, and Henrik Ibsen's *An Enemy of the People* was taken as an allegory of the Affair. Anatole France wrote a satirical novel based on the case; it was serialized in 1897-98.

DREYFUSARDS AND ANTI-DREYFUSARDS

In late 1896, Bernard Lazare published a pamphlet defending Dreyfus and insisting he was being persecuted because he was Jewish. Mathieu had 3,500 copies printed and distributed to all Parliament members and other prominent people. This was the moment when the pro-Dreyfus campaign became public. In mid-1897 a prominent senator declared in Parliament that he believed Dreyfus innocent. By the end of 1897, there were perhaps 300 Dreyfusards in France, mostly professors and intellectuals. Early in 1898, after Esterhazy's acquittal, they began a public campaign for "revision," the overturning of Dreyfus' court martial and a new trial. The government tried to ignore it, claiming the verdict was final. The premier told Parliament, "There is no Dreyfus affair."

The Affair reached an unprecedented level of intensity with novelist Emile Zola's publication of "*J'Accuse*" in Clemenceau's newspaper, *L'Aurore*, on January 13, 1898. The paper sold more than 200,000 copies that day. Zola's deliberately libelous article named the generals and officers he believed responsible for the cover-up and fraud. "*J'Accuse*" was thus an act of civil disobedience, and it "electrified France. Around this manifesto gathered the disparate energies that became a coherent Dreyfusist movement," wrote a Dreyfus biographer, Frederick Brown.

Zola, who was not Jewish, was prosecuted for slandering the army and convicted. He was actually relieved by the verdict—he had been sure he would be lynched in the street if acquitted. To avoid prison, he fled to England and stayed away for a year. In 1902 Zola died of carbon monoxide poisoning at home in Paris. Hundreds of thousands attended his funeral. At the time the death was ruled accidental; but in the 1930s an anti-Dreyfus worker confessed on his deathbed that while working in Zola's home, he had blocked the flue of a heater to kill him.

Immediately after the publication of "*J'Accuse*," the anti-Semitic movement went into action. Anti-Jewish riots erupted in thirty provincial towns. In Algeria, then a French colony, a full-scale pogrom took place—scores of Jews were killed and their houses burned. Four thousand people attended a public meeting in Paris to protest "insulters of the army." In a preview of the 1930s, anti-Semitic leader Jules Guérin went about Paris accompanied by a phalanx of butchers armed with cudgels and iron bars.

"*J'Accuse*" polarized public opinion. People who had never before become involved in politics found themselves taking sides. According to Cahm, the Affair "witnessed the birth of the modern idea of the intellectual committed as a member of a group, made up of writers, artists and those living by their intellect, who lend the backing of their reputation to the support of public causes." But most intellectuals did not believe in Dreyfus' innocence. Only about twenty-five percent of university professors in Paris were Dreyfusards. Few secondary teachers and civil servants openly supported Dreyfus because they feared losing their posts if they signed petitions. Anti-Dreyfus students were so numerous and powerful that Dreyfusard students were afraid to meet publicly. Fights even broke out in classrooms.

A revision petition that circulated the day after the publication of "*J'Accuse*" had only 1,482 signatures. Signers included writers such as Anatole France, Rostand, Maeterlinck, Sardou, Mallarmé, Gide, Apollinaire and Proust. Artist signers included Monet, Pissarro, Signac, Bonnard and Vuillard. Academics included Lévy-Bruhl, Durkheim and Réclus. But anti-Dreyfusard intellectuals tended to be older and more eminent.

Workers were slow to get involved in the case. In 1898 the General Workers Confederation published a pamphlet that said, "We the workers, constantly exploited, have no call to take part in this conflict between Jews and Christians! They are both the same, since they both dominate and exploit us." Organized workers saw the army as their enemy, since troops were used to break up strikes and kill strikers. Dreyfus was merely a bourgeois class enemy in their eyes. Some did believe that fighting injustice was a worthy activity for workers, but many were anti-Semitic. Socialists in Parliament came to regard the anti-Dreyfusards, some of whom were monarchists, as threats to the stability of the Republic. Others saw Catholic involvement in the case as threatening the separation of church and state. Dreyfusard sentiment tended to be coupled with anticlericalism.

France was a predominantly Catholic country, but there was a sizable Protestant minority. Among the anti-Dreyfusards' wilder charges was that a Jewish-Protestant-Masonic conspiracy was backing efforts to free Dreyfus. Consequently Protestants in France and abroad tended to sympathize with Dreyfus.

Thus was French society divided in 1898, over a prisoner 3,000 miles away who knew nothing about the battle being waged for and against him.

Soon after the Zola trial, Cahm wrote, Dreyfusards decided to "acquire the collective strength of an association, not simply to defend Dreyfus, but all those whose rights had been violated." Senator Ludovic Trarieux, a former justice minister, founded the Ligue des Droits de l'Homme (League of the Rights of Man) with a group of friends. In 1900 the League boasted 12,000 dues-paying members and local committees in 298 French towns and cities. It conducted a "massive campaign of public meetings with what amounted to a traveling road show of Dreyfusard celebrities, who seem to have spoken wherever a hall could be obtained for a night," Hoffman wrote. Catholic Dreyfusards founded the much smaller Comité Catholique pour la Défense du Droit (Catholic Committee for the Defense of Law), which had only 200 members, including priests, writers, lawyers, retired army officers and engineers. Some were persecuted by the Catholic Church hierarchy for publishing pro-Dreyfus materials.

On the other side, anti-Dreyfusards founded the Ligue de la Patrie Française (League of the French Homeland), led by respected writers and intellectuals. In 1899 it had about 100,000 members. Its anti-Semitism was

relatively subdued, and it focused on criticizing Parliament. According to
Hoffman, this league waged "an extensive, organized propaganda campaign" with publications and meetings.

In mid-1898, investigators discovered that an intelligence officer, Col.
Henry, had forged some of the documents used to convict Dreyfus in 1894.
Henry was arrested and committed suicide in his cell. Thousands donated
funds for his widow. By the autumn France seemed on the edge of civil
conflict. A new government came in and changed the balance of power
in Parliament. In early 1899, Parliament decided to allow a review of Dreyfus' case. A special session of the Supreme Court recommended a retrial,
and Dreyfus was sent back to France in June 1899 to stand trial again. Of
his arrival he wrote:

> The succession of emotions to which I was a prey may be imag-
> ined—bewilderment, surprise, sadness, bitter pain, at that kind of
> a return to my country. Where I had expected to find men united
> in common love of truth and justice, desirous to make amends for
> a frightful judicial error, I found only anxious faces, petty precau-
> tions, a wild disembarkation on a stormy sea in the middle of the
> night, with physical sufferings added to the trouble of my mind.
> Happily, during the long, sad months of my captivity I had been
> able to steel my will and nerves and body to an infinite capacity
> for resistance.

Dreyfus' lawyers told him what had happened since early 1895, when
he had been sent to Devil's Island.

> I learned of the long series of misdeeds and disgraceful crimes
> constituting the indictment against my innocence. I was told of
> the heroism and the great efforts of noble men; the unflinching
> struggle undertaken by that handful of men of lofty character,
> opposing their own courage and honesty to the cabals of false-
> hood and iniquity.... My illusions with regard to some of my for-
> mer chiefs were gradually dissipated, and my soul was filled with
> anguish. I was seized with an overpowering pity and sorrow for
> that army of France which I loved.

The lawyers gave him some of the official documents of his case.

> I read the Zola trial during the night that followed, without being
> able to tear myself away from it. I saw how Zola had been con-
> demned for having upheld the truth.... But as my sadness increased
> on reading of all these crimes and realizing how men are led astray
> by their passions, a deep feeling of gratitude and admiration arose
> in my heart for all the courageous men, learned or ignorant, great

or humble, who had cast themselves valiantly into the struggle. And history will record that the honor of France was in this uprising of men of every degree, of scholars hitherto buried in the silent labor of study or laboratory, of workingmen engrossed in their hard daily toil, of public officials who set the higher interests of the nation above purely selfish motives, for the supremacy of justice, liberty and truth.

In his cell in the town of Rennes, Dreyfus received thousands of letters from around the world expressing solidarity. Three-hundred journalists from the London *Times* and many other foreign papers attended his second court martial in August-September 1899. Queen Victoria also sent a representative.

By this time most observers outside France believed firmly in Dreyfus' innocence. After the publication of *"J'Accuse," The New York Times* criticized the French press, "What with clerical organs of slander like the *Croix*, furious anti-Semite papers such as the *Livre Parole* and the shrieking army-worshipping and foreign-hating *Petit Journal*, the difficulty of making the truth known in France begins to be seen."

The Jewish press in the United States covered the case extensively for their readers, who were mostly immigrants, recently escaped from anti-Semitic regimes in Eastern Europe. Jewish papers and committees organized public meetings, circulated petitions and cabled French and American officials. "They vowed not to purchase goods from France nor to visit that country," wrote historian Egal Feldman.

American lawyers followed the case, and the president of the American Bar Association criticized the French legal system in an 1898 speech. According to Feldman, Dreyfus' "ordeal drew a response rooted in [the American] heritage of social consciousness and humanitarianism as well as in inflated notions of American moral, social and legal superiority."

The U.S. press covered Zola's slander trial on a daily basis, portraying him as a hero. A decade after the Haymarket trial, the reformer Carl Schurz commented that Americans would find it hard to believe "such an undisguised, ruthless perversion of justice was possible in a high tribunal of a civilized nation calling itself a republic at the close of the Nineteenth Century."

Dreyfus was retried in a military court and, despite all the evidence to the contrary, convicted of "treason, with extenuating circumstances." Nobody was sure what those circumstances were. "Abroad, there was universal condemnation of France. In a score of cities, from Budapest to Indianapolis, popular demonstrations broke out. There were attacks on French consulates and the French flag," Cahm writes. Many called for an international boycott of the world's fair scheduled to be held in Paris in 1900. The

French government quickly offered Dreyfus a pardon, and he immediately accepted it. He published the following statement:

> The government of the Republic has restored my liberty. But that is nothing to me without honor. As from today, I shall continue to seek redress for the judicial error of which I am still the victim. I wish the whole of France to know, by a final judgment, that I am innocent; my heart will only be at peace when no Frenchman imputes to me the crime which has been committed by another.

In 1906, Dreyfus' first conviction was quashed. He received a promotion and the Legion of Honor, and later served on active duty during World War I. In 1927 he joined the worldwide call for clemency for Sacco and Vanzetti. And in 1935, as the world proceeded down the path to another war, he died at the age of seventy-six. In 1995, during the centennial of the Affair, the head of the French army's historical unit became the army's first official spokesperson to declare Dreyfus innocent. Three years later the Catholic paper *La Croix* apologized for its role in the Affair.

As a result of the Affair, the Left came to power in France for a decade after 1899. A secularization campaign led to a law separating church and state in 1905. Many Dreyfusards went on to play major roles in French politics, social justice movements, the arts, sciences and other intellectual activity.

The Republic was strengthened, but the seeds of its destruction also were planted, with the formation of far-right organizations such as Action Française. Some years after Theodor Herzl, then covering Paris for a Vienna newspaper, witnessed the crowd screaming, "Death to the Jews," at Dreyfus' degradation ceremony, he organized the first Zionist Congress. Much later, two of the leading anti-Dreyfusards were convicted for collaborating with the Nazis. In *Origins of Totalitarianism*, Hannah Arendt described the Dreyfus Affair as "a huge dress rehearsal for a performance that had to be put off for more than three decades."

The most striking feature of the Affair is the central role of the press and intellectuals. The Affair began in 1894 when the anti-Semitic paper *Libre Parole* published news of Dreyfus' arrest under the headline, "High Treason. The Jewish Traitor Alfred Dreyfus Arrested." Most people in France and elsewhere obtained information (and misinformation) about the case from the press rather than from public speakers. Pamphlets seem to have been less important because newspapers were so numerous (more than a hundred dailies in Paris alone), so readily available and so cheap. Petitions attracted relatively few signers.

The Affair obsessed France for years, and the way the newspapers covered it determined people's opinions to a great extent. People outside France had difficulty understanding how Dreyfus could have been convicted on such flimsy evidence; how the majority of the French population could have believed so firmly in his guilt for so long; and how he could have been reconvicted, even after Esterhazy admitted he had written the *bordereau*. Newspapers incited and reinforced popular prejudices and disseminated lies and distortions that kept France in a state of hysteria for six years. But they also published "*J'Accuse*" and helped pro-Dreyfus forces wage the public campaign that forced the government to deal with the case.

Some of the country's most eminent intellectuals, including lawyers, journalists, politicians, writers and artists, threw themselves into the Affair, waging a literal war of words. They came to understand that to achieve their objective, they had to fight in public, rather than behind the scenes in traditional elite fashion.

For example, the vice-president of the French Senate received word in 1897 from Picquart's lawyer that Esterhazy had written the *bordereau*. First he tried to use his influence privately with the president, the premier and the war and justice ministers. When he got nowhere with them, he leaked the information to the press and spoke out in the Senate. This was a turning point in the campaign—the first time a highly respected, non-Jewish figure publicly defended Dreyfus.

The following year, when the Supreme Court recommended a retrial, "polemical newspaper articles, pamphlets and books poured forth in a flood, and frequent public rallies with large audiences were held around the country," Hoffman wrote. In a short time the campaign became a typical one in the international style that had been developing elsewhere since the Eighteenth Century.

Unlike the first Haymarket clemency campaign, the pro-Dreyfus campaign succeeded. Two years of concentrated public action by the Dreyfusards, from 1897 to 1899, pressured the government into reopening the case, despite the strong resistance of the armed forces and significant sectors of French society. Ample evidence proving his innocence and Esterhazy's guilt did not suffice, however, to overturn his conviction or the perpetrator's acquittal. Those responsible for the cover-up and the forgeries were never punished, though they did lose political power. Dreyfus lived long enough to recover his honor and clear his name, but it seems unlikely that anything less than a massive public campaign could have saved him from slow death on Devil's Island.

Dreyfus became an emblematic figure. His letters to his wife (published in 1899) and his diary (published in 1901) moved readers throughout the world. With their publication he became a recognized campaigner on his own behalf. He also showed that in constantly proclaiming his innocence and surviving conditions meant to destroy him, he had never been merely a passive victim. His books still have the power to move anyone who has ever written a letter to a government asking for the release of a political prisoner.

One can also hear echoes of Dreyfus' account of his arrest in the first sentence of Franz Kafka's *The Trial*, "Someone must have betrayed Joseph K., for without having done anything wrong he was arrested one fine morning." The Twentieth Century has witnessed many more arrests and campaigns, but Dreyfus has held onto a special place among the innocent victims of injustice.

PROSECUTION AS PERSECUTION

Five years after Dreyfus received the Legion of Honor, another case of a Jew who was falsely accused gained international attention. In 1911, Mendel Beilis, a factory manager, was arrested for the ritual murder of a Christian boy in the Russian city of Kiev. For almost a thousand years, many Christians had believed that Jews killed children before Passover to use their blood in making matzoh or in secret rituals. But this belief, known as the blood libel, was almost moribund in the early Twentieth Century.

Although Kiev police did not believe in Beilis' guilt, they received an order "from the highest levels" (perhaps the Czar himself) to find a Jewish defendant and prosecute him at the earliest opportunity. The Czar or his officials often instigated attacks on the Jews to divert attention from the negative consequences of government policies. So the police arrested Beilis without a warrant, under an emergency law suspending civil rights, and kept him in jail under dehumanizing conditions for more than two years before trial.

A committee of prominent Jews formed to help Beilis and his family. A Jewish newspaper in London reported on the case from the beginning, and other western newspapers took it up during the trial in 1913. Protests over the indictment for ritual murder came from Germany, Britain, France, the United States, Canada and other countries. More than 200 German intellectuals and writers signed a manifesto deploring the accusation. A British petition with 240 signatures followed; signers included the Archbishop of Canterbury, the speaker of the House of Commons, Thomas Hardy and H.G. Wells. During the trial, seventy-four American Christian leaders signed a protest letter. Pro-Beilis demonstrations took place in Britain, the U.S. and Canada.

Many Russians were mortified, and the Russian government was displeased by the international coverage. In 1912 the governor of Kiev wrote to the Deputy Minister of the Interior: "As is known to Your Excellency, the Beilis case has attracted universal attention not only in Russia but abroad, and therefore the trial of this case will undoubtedly arouse great social interest, threatening to divert the attention of society from all other things." He therefore suggested scheduling the trial after the provincial elections.

The case had international political and economic repercussions. The U.S. government rebuked Russia for denying foreign Jews admission into the country or placing them under special travel restrictions, thereby breaking a commercial agreement between the two countries. Some prominent Jewish financiers refused to do business with the Russian government, thus slowing its military buildup against Austro-Hungary. (In 1914 the conflict between the two countries would trigger the First World War.)

Reporters from hundreds of newspapers covered the trial, which took place after many delays in autumn 1913. The London *Times* apologized to its readers for the absurdity of the accusation, and *The New York Times* professed itself baffled by the case.

The Rothschild family tried to help the defense by asking its contacts in the Vatican for assistance. Lord Rothschild sent copies of papal statements denying the blood libel to the Vatican Secretary of State and asked him to authenticate them. The Vatican did not cooperate, and the statements were not introduced at the trial.

Christian lawyers stepped forward to defend Beilis, showing that some Russians did not support the government's anti-Semitic policies. Russian intellectual and political figures signed a manifesto protesting the injustice of the trial. During the proceedings, twenty-five members of the St. Petersburg bar, including future prime minister Alexander Kerensky, were jailed for protesting. The government also arrested newspaper editors, censored news reports and confiscated newspapers containing critical articles about the case.

The Anglo-Jewish historian Lucien Wolf, who campaigned on behalf of Beilis, commented: "Personally I never expected much from the verdict. All that was necessary for us was to obtain the utmost publicity for the trial so as to enlighten public opinion outside Russia as to what is going on in that country." The international campaign accomplished not only this objective—it also led to Beilis' release. The jury decided that a ritual murder had taken place but split its verdict, and Beilis was acquitted.

Having suffered physical and psychological torture in prison for two-and-a-half years before his trial, Beilis took a long time to recover. He also found his international celebrity after his release difficult to cope with, as he recounted in his self-published memoir of 1926. Thousands of people came to visit him or sent him letters and telegrams. He could go nowhere without being mobbed by wellwishers.

Fleeing from fame as well as death threats by anti-Semitic gangs, Beilis and his family emigrated to Palestine in 1914. A few years later he moved to the United States, where he died, forgotten, in 1934. Even more than

Dreyfus, he stands as the archetypal Kafkaesque victim, one of the early Twentieth Century's foremost political, ethnic and religious scapegoats.

THE INTERNATIONAL AUDIENCE FOR HUMAN RIGHTS

All the campaigns described in this chapter became genuinely international in scope. Campaigners as diverse as Ida Wells-Barnett, Edward Morel and Lucien Wolf recognized the necessity of appealing to supporters around the world. Mostly they focused their efforts on countries like the United States and Britain, however, where middle- and upper-class people could be persuaded to donate funds, write letters to the editor and pressure legislators to take action. Black missionaries who broke the news of the Congo genocide by writing to their congregations in the United States helped broaden the base of that campaign. And Wells-Barnett not only lectured to British aristocrats, she sought support for her antilynching crusade from less privileged African-Americans and organized local projects to help the black community. Unlike Edward Morel, she created organizations that survived after her passing and served as the basis of later movements.

The campaign on behalf of Alfred Dreyfus began as a domestic effort, but foreign correspondents and wire services made it an international story. When Dreyfus was reconvicted in 1899, the international outcry and threats to boycott the upcoming world exposition surely helped push the French government to offer him a pardon. By boycotting French products, poor immigrants in America also became participants in the Dreyfus campaign.

Also during this period, Mohandas Gandhi, an Indian lawyer and spiritual leader, began applying ideas from Thoreau, Tolstoy and Hindu scriptures to develop the concept of civil disobedience and organize mass movements in South Africa and India. Along with other leaders of these struggles, Gandhi spent time in jail as a political prisoner. As symbols and practitioners of nonviolent resistance, he and others gained the support of western intellectuals, lawyers, clergy and politicians, who joined campaigns against colonialism and imperialism from the late Nineteenth to the mid-Twentieth Century.

Through these diverse efforts, the international constituency for human rights was taking shape. But the unparalleled catastrophe of the First World War would tear it apart.

Boston Brahmins in top hats crucify Sacco and Vanzetti, 1927.

Chapter 6

SACCO AND VANZETTI: AGONY OR TRIUMPH?

A Preparedness Day parade took place in San Francisco on July 22, 1916. The United States had not yet entered World War I, but Americans were anxiously anticipating the worst. During the parade a bomb exploded in the street and killed ten people.

The police rounded up people they believed to be anarchists. They arrested Tom Mooney, a union member they suspected of sabotaging electrical transmission towers during a recent strike; another union member named Warren Billings, Mooney's wife, a taxi driver and a union official. The trials of Mooney and Billings took place in a hysterical atmosphere. As in the Haymarket case, prosecutors suborned witnesses to perjury. Apparently the jurors also were bribed. Mooney and Billings were sentenced to death in 1917. The district attorney in the case used the conviction to boost his candidacy for governor.

Anarchists and unions tried to help Mooney. The International Workers Defense League, Emma Goldman and Alexander Berkman raised funds for his defense. Demonstrations took place at American embassies and consulates on May Day 1917, a few days before Mooney was scheduled to hang. Then President Wilson secretly telegraphed the governor of California asking for commutation of Mooney's sentence to life imprisonment or a stay of execution. Mooney's execution was delayed, and Wilson appointed a federal commission to investigate his and other union members' cases. The commission included two labor leaders, two industrialists, Felix Frankfurter (then a Harvard law professor and later a Supreme Court justice) and the Secretary of Labor. Early in 1918, the commission released its report, criticizing the Mooney prosecution. In response the presiding judge in the case called Frankfurter a Bolshevik.

President Wilson's intervention and the commission's findings aroused anger in California. The Hearst newspapers in the state campaigned against Mooney, while their competitors, Scripps-Howard, supported him. Mooney's wife toured the West, raising funds for his appeals. Mass meetings took place in other states, and the New York legislature passed a resolution asking for another stay of execution after the California Supreme Court denied his appeal. July 28, 1918, was declared "Tom Mooney Day," Estolv Ward, Mooney's biographer, wrote. "Letters and telegrams poured into the governor's office, the White House and other pressure targets." More than 6,000 people demonstrated on Mooney's behalf in San Francisco. The district attorney lost the gubernatorial primary election the next month. His attempt to build his political career on the Mooney case had failed.

Meanwhile, the U.S. Labor Department tapped the district attorney's telephone and discovered corruption in his office. A crusading editor published articles that exposed his malfeasance. In November 1918, the governor commuted Mooney's sentence to life imprisonment. The district attorney lost his bid for re-election in 1919.

Facing life in prison for a crime he evidently did not commit (though he admitted to having blown up electrical transmission towers years before), Mooney ran his own defense efforts. He wrote pardon petitions, sought support from prominent public figures, called for a boycott of the 1932 Olympics in Los Angeles, worked to place stories in the U.S. press and even instructed his supporters to retouch his photographs in his campaign literature. Mooney had a flair for publicity stunts. At his direction, a supporter rented a hearse, painted "Pardon Tom Mooney" and "California Justice Is Dead!!" on its side, drove around the California Capitol, then drove to Washington, D.C., and circled the U.S. Capitol.

Mooney's biographer, who assisted him in the 1930s, admits that he was "a difficult and demanding man, hard to work with and harsh on those who thought they knew better than he how to get him out of San Quentin." His ham-handed attempts to control his defense may have delayed his release, which did not come until 1939.

RADICALS UNDER ATTACK

Mooney was one of several radicals who ran afoul of the law before and during the First World War. But hatred and suspicion of anarchists dated back to the Haymarket Affair, thirty years earlier. Some anarchists promoted violent revolution and destruction of the state, and bombings and assassinations by supposed or declared anarchists took place in Europe and the U.S. from the 1880s to the 1930s. In the U.S., immigrants believed to be anarchists were particular targets for surveillance and arrest.

Two Italian anarchists, Joseph Ettor and Arturo Giovanitti, were indicted in Massachusetts for murder in 1912. Roberta Feuerlicht wrote: "Throughout the country and in Europe there were protest meetings, demonstrations and rallies, mostly to raise funds for the defense. An Ettor-Giovanitti Defense Committee was organized; all of its members were indicted by Massachusetts authorities." But witnesses convinced the jury that the two men were speaking at a public meeting elsewhere when the killing occurred, and they were acquitted. "It was still possible for Italian radicals to get a fair trial in Massachusetts," wrote Feuerlicht.

In 1915 union organizer Joe Hill was executed in Utah for murder. According to Feuerlicht, his case "aroused a storm of national and international interest and protest." Hill's final message, "Don't Mourn; Organize," became a rallying cry for the anarcho-syndicalist union, the Industrial Workers of the World (IWW).

When these sensational cases took place, anarchists were particularly feared and reviled. Before, during and after World War I, anarchist leaders were hounded from country to country, harassed, arrested and sometimes framed for murder and other crimes. Governments particularly targeted them for prosecution during the war, which they and other leftists strongly opposed. When Emma Goldman and Alexander Berkman spoke against the war, they were imprisoned for two years for "conspiring to interfere with the draft," a federal crime. Socialist leader Eugene V. Debs was sentenced to ten years in prison on a similar charge. Afraid of being drafted or jailed, scores of anarchists, including Nicola Sacco and Bartolomeo Vanzetti, two Italians who had been living in Massachusetts, fled from the U.S. to Mexico during the war.

Anti-radical sentiment continued after the war ended. "Wartime hatred of Germans transformed itself into peacetime horror of radicals, especially alien radicals. If only the menace of un-Americanism could be eliminated, it was widely felt, the nation would be cleansed, its difficulties and tensions mitigated," Avrich writes. But the tensions did not ease. The Bolshevik revolution alarmed the American government, which sent troops to Russia during the civil war of 1918-21. Violent strikes increased in the U.S., and anti-black riots raged in Chicago, East St. Louis and other cities. Meanwhile, anarchists apparently bombed Attorney General Mitchell Palmer's house in 1919 and mailed bombs to other government officials and prominent financiers.

In retaliation the Attorney General organized the "Palmer raids" of November 1919 and January 1920, in which the federal government rounded up thousands of radicals across the country, often without warrants, and threw them into jail. Intellectuals, attorneys and even some government officials protested the abridgement of basic civil rights during and after the raids. Nonetheless, some 800 socialists, anarchists and Communists, including Emma Goldman and Alexander Berkman, were deported under repressive wartime laws. Palmer did not succeed in his 1920 bid for a presidential nomination, but he did install J. Edgar Hoover as the director of the new Federal Bureau of Investigation. FBI files identified Sacco and Vanzetti as "radicals to be watched."

CRIMINALS OR VICTIMS?

Both men were activists, participating in strikes and organizing workers in the Boston area. Sacco was a skilled craftsman, Vanzetti a laborer. Sacco, in his late twenties, had a wife and children; Vanzetti, in his early thirties, was unmarried and boarded with Italian families. In 1920, after a series of payroll robberies in the Boston suburbs, Vanzetti was arrested and convicted of armed robbery, apparently on dubious evidence. He was being "fitted" for indictment for the murder of a payroll guard during another robbery in South Braintree, Massachusetts. Sacco was arrested for the South Braintree crime as well.

As in the Haymarket and Mooney cases, prosecutors in the Sacco-Vanzetti case sought to advance their political careers by securing convictions in highly publicized trials. Apparently they did not hesitate to concoct or tamper with evidence and suborn witnesses. The judge, Webster Thayer, openly expressed prejudice against the defendants, inside and outside the courtroom. One day on a golf course, he crowed, "Did you see what I did with those anarchistic bastards the other day?" Between 1921 and 1927 he denied eight defense motions for a new trial.

Prejudice against Italians was common in Massachusetts at the time. Although Vanzetti had an alibi backed by a dozen witnesses, the jury did not believe their testimony because they were Italian. Nor did they believe the Italian consulate employee who provided an alibi for Sacco. Both men were convicted of murder in 1921.

THE DEFENSE COMMITTEE

When Vanzetti was convicted of the first robbery, letters and donations started arriving from Italians and non-Italians in the United States. An Italian anarchist journalist, Aldino Felicani, set up the Sacco-Vanzetti Defense Committee after failing to get help from the Communist Party in Boston. The Communists said, "The Sacco-Vanzetti case is a criminal case. We are not interested in criminal cases," Feuerlicht writes. In 1920 and '21 the defense committee sponsored picnics, theatre shows and wrestling matches to raise funds.

Two-thirds of the Sacco-Vanzetti Defense Committee's support came from Italians and labor unions. The committee itself was composed mostly of Italian anarchists. Their lack of knowledge of Boston society caused them to make serious mistakes early on. They hired a friend of the prosecutor as Vanzetti's first lawyer, for example. Later Felicani developed skill in collaborating with nonanarchist sympathizers, who provided financial backing and produced a bulletin in English, which reached thousands of people around the country. Felicani also published an Italian-language bulletin about the case for five years.

Sacco and Vanzetti's first lawyer in the South Braintree case was Fred Moore, who had successfully defended Ettor and Giovanitti in 1912. Moore "saw the Sacco-Vanzetti case as political persecution, which it was, and he devoted his energies to fighting it in the streets, not the courts," Feuerlicht writes. He involved non-Italians in the defense efforts. Two young leftist journalists, Art Shields and Eugene Lyons, helped Moore write pamphlets and articles about the case for distribution to unions. According to Joughin and Morgan, their rhetoric may have alienated "more conservative elements in the labor group." The anarchists proved to be better organizers than agitators, and Felicani stayed behind the scenes.

The New England Civil Liberties Committee joined the campaign early in 1921, donating 500 dollars to the defense committee and publishing a pamphlet, "Sacco and Vanzetti: Shall There Be a Mooney Frame-Up in New England?"

Committee supporters also included a number of wealthy women, who made generous donations and acted as maternal figures to the two men, visiting and writing to them for years. Elizabeth Glendower Evans was the best known. "She was possessed of quite a good deal of money. She had been interested in the anti-capital-punishment movement and also in the conditions of prisoners and the rehabilitation of prisoners, all that sort of thing. She was a close friend of the Frankfurters, Felix and his wife," Gardner Jackson remembered.

A member of the League for Democratic Control in Boston, Mrs. Evans brought other members of the city's elite, such as Mrs. Louis Brandeis and historian Samuel Morison, into the campaign. In May 1921 she published an article on the case in *LaFollette's Magazine*, a national publication. Later she wrote a pamphlet, "Outstanding Features of the Sacco-Vanzetti Case," which included biographical sketches of both men and excerpts from their letters. It was published by the New England Civil Liberties Committee and the American Civil Liberties Union in 1924. In 1921, Mrs. Evans donated the considerable sum of $3,000 to the defense committee; another wealthy supporter, Selma Maximon, raised more than $7,000 in several cities. Vanzetti often called the society women "Comrade," a common term of address among revolutionaries.

During the first years of the campaign, the defense committee focused on raising funds, publicizing the case and building public support for a new trial. Local defense committees sprang up in cities across the United States and around the world. In 1921, the Comité Popular de Agitação Pró-Sacco e Vanzetti was founded in Rio de Janeiro, with branches in other Brazilian states. Defense committees also formed in Rome, Geneva, Amsterdam, Stockholm and Buenos Aires, among other cities. Left-wing organizations and individuals made donations ranging from ten cents to a dollar. Sixty years later, elderly Italian anarchists in Brooklyn and San

Francisco remembered collecting money to send to Felicani. "We held out-door meetings on street corners to protest against the treatment of the two men," one recalled. By September 1925 the committee had raised more than $287,000, mostly in small donations; monthly contributions aver-aged about $2,000, according to the financial report. In all, the commit-tee collected about $360,000 during seven years of fundraising.

Most U.S. supporters were poor, radical immigrants and workers, but influential people also became involved in the campaign. Roger Baldwin, a Harvard man who had recently founded the American Civil Liberties Union, worked hard on the case. Though not a member of the defense committee, Felix Frankfurter was a very visible supporter; some powerful alumni of Harvard Law School tried to have him fired from the faculty as a result. With Gardner Jackson, Felix Frankfurter's wife, Marion, co-edited *The Letters of Sacco and Vanzetti*, which later became an interna-tional bestseller.

A CAMPAIGNER'S LIFE

Gardner Jackson was the son of a Quaker banker and railroad magnate in Colorado. He seems to have been the only one in his large family to become a political radical. Feeling that his father cared too much for prop-erty and wealth, he "went the other way." Jackson did not enjoy going to church and found organized religion hypocritical.

When he attended Amherst College in Massachusetts during the First World War, he came under the influence of its president, Alexander Meikeljohn, who was much involved in a variety of social-justice causes before, during and after the war. But Jackson left Amherst early to fight in the war and never finished his degree.

On his deathbed, Jackson's father extracted a promise from the young man that he would go into business for a year. But Jackson hated the life of a stockbroker and became a cub reporter at the *Denver Times*. Then he got a job at the *Boston Globe*.

He told an interviewer from Columbia University: "One morning at break-fast my wife said to me, 'I've been reading in the papers the accounts of this trial of these two Italians going on out in Dedham. Pat, I don't think that they're getting a fair break. There's something that I detect in the reports of that trial that makes me feel that everything isn't shipshape. Will you try to find out?'"

Jackson asked Frank Sibley, the *Globe* reporter covering the case, for his opinion. "It's an outrage that's being perpetrated here," Sibley replied. So Jackson volunteered to work for the defense committee, occasionally at first, then full-time after 1926.

Jackson found Aldino Felicani and "began to do propaganda writing on the side. . . . I did leaflets, pamphlets, flyers, throwaways and propaganda business for the defense committee." He called Felicani "a very great factor in my evolution from then on and in the influence on our children as they came up." Felicani, whom Jackson described as refined, fastidious and impressive looking, "gave me the impression that here was a remarkable human being."

Asked by an interviewer how he became interested in the Sacco-Vanzetti case, Jackson recalled his Amherst days, when he "had read a series of articles in the *New Republic* on the Mooney case . . . by Felix Frankfurter. I had been very impressed and moved by these articles and what seemed to me their exposition of miscarriages of justice." An Amherst classmate, Malcolm Sharp, also had been influenced by Frankfurter's articles; many years later he would become a defense lawyer in the Rosenberg case.

In the early 1920s, Meikeljohn came under attack from conservative college trustees, and Jackson returned to Amherst to help him. Jackson organized a campaign on campus, but it failed, and Meikeljohn was fired. The story of Meikeljohn's ouster was national news. From this experience, Jackson may have learned some of the strategies he used later in Boston.

In the early days of the campaign, Jackson was only a part-time helper. The Italian members of the defense committee did most of the work. Bartolomeo Vanzetti also campaigned on his own behalf, by translating defense documents into Italian for distribution in Europe and by writing an autobiography, "The Story of a Proletarian Life." Translated into English by Eugene Lyons and with a foreword by Upton Sinclair, it was published as a pamphlet in 1924.

CHANGING STRATEGIES

By 1924 Fred Moore had spent $100,000 of the committee's funds but had little to show for his efforts. He left the case, and Roger Baldwin found a more conventional lawyer, who demanded $25,000 to take it on. In his documentary novel *Boston*, Upton Sinclair described how the funds were obtained to hire the lawyer:

> A young man by the name of Charles Garland, while a student at Harvard, had known Jack Reed, and became troubled in his conscience. Now Reed had given his life to the Russian revolution, and was buried under the Kremlin walls; while his friend Garland fell heir to a million dollars. His conscience not permitting him to accept it, he turned it over to a committee, to be expended for the benefit of labor. So there was the 'Garland Fund'; and in this emergency it was persuaded to lend $25,000 to the Sacco-Vanzetti defense, and William G. Thompson was put in charge of the case.

According to Feuerlicht, Moore and Felicani had believed they had to "organize, agitate and propagandize to let the whole world know it was a political trial. . . . Whether, in the end, this was productive or counterproductive is debatable." Thompson disagreed with Moore's strategies. "Personally conservative, Thompson felt demonstrations exacerbated the very powers that would pass judgment on his clients," recounts Feuerlicht. He "forced the canceling of a mass meeting in Boston, by threatening to withdraw from the case if it was held," Sinclair wrote. For a time the defense committee stopped campaigning publicly in Boston, but the press continued to cover the case. And around the world, the grassroots efforts continued—they had acquired a life of their own.

For several years the Sacco-Vanzetti case may have been better known in Europe than in the United States. Europeans believed it was a political case from 1921 on. That year, 8,000 attended a rally in Paris to protest the guilty verdict. The author Anatole France, who had campaigned on behalf of Alfred Dreyfus twenty-five years earlier, appealed to Americans in October 1921.

> People of the United States of America.
> Listen to the appeal of an old man of the old world who is not a foreigner, for he is a fellow citizen of all mankind.
> In one of your states, two men, Sacco and Vanzetti, have been convicted for a crime of opinion.
> It is horrible to think that human beings should pay with their lives for the exercise of that most sacred right which, no matter what party we belong to, we must all defend.
> Don't let this most iniquitous sentence be carried out. The death of Sacco and Vanzetti will make martyrs of them and cover you with shame.
> You are a great people. You ought to be a just people.
> There are crowds of intelligent men among you, men who think. I prefer to appeal to them. I say to them beware of making martyrs. That is the unforgivable crime that nothing can wipe out and that weighs on generation after generation.
> Save Sacco and Vanzetti.
> Save them for your honor, for the honor of your children and for generations yet unborn.
> Anatole France

Like so many other appeals, manifestos, petitions and letters, this one had no apparent effect. The U.S. public seemed uninterested in the case until around 1926, by which time the fear of radicals had faded considerably. Until mid-1926, American newspapers covered it only sporadically, academics ignored it and clergymen sermonized little about it. Reporters "did a poor job" of reporting the case. "Enough useful facts were not presented, and there was almost no probing into the main elements of legal controversy or social friction," Joughin and Morgan wrote.

A NEW GENERATION OF CAMPAIGNERS

As the months and years of appeals passed, intellectuals, writers and artists, including poet Edna St. Vincent Millay, critic Van Wyck Brooks, historian Samuel Eliot Morison, poet Lola Ridge, historian Arthur M. Schlesinger and novelist John Dos Passos, started writing and speaking about the case. However, writes Feueurlicht, "Most writers, clergymen and educators were silent and remained silent about the case for seven years, though some finally spoke out at the very end when publicity was hottest and Sacco and Vanzetti were doomed."

In October 1926, the *Boston Herald* published an editorial that said, "In our opinion Nicola Sacco and Bartolomeo Vanzetti ought not to be executed," and the editorial writer won a Pulitzer Prize. Other papers called for a new trial. This was the point at which the public started paying attention to the case.

Two months later, the governor of Massachusetts published an article, "Why I Believe in Capital Punishment," in a popular magazine, and public opinion seemed to follow his lead. In response, the Dean of Harvard Divinity School expressed his shock at the commonly expressed opinion "that on the whole it was better that these men die than that faith in Massachusetts institutions should be shaken by a further review of the case."

In 1926, Gardner Jackson went to Harvard as a special student and met the eminent historian, Arthur Schlesinger, Sr. "I had only attended those courses about two months when Aldino Felicani and Mary Donovan got hold of me and pleaded with me to take over the campaign of the defense committee, or to think up a campaign so that we could [get] public opinion more aroused and have some recourse other than through legal processes." He went to Schlesinger for advice. Schlesinger urged him to drop out of Harvard and "go and commit myself fully to the Sacco-Vanzetti people." His mentor told him he would have the experience of being involved in history instead of merely teaching it, as Schlesinger did.

Before 1926, Jackson later recalled:

> I wasn't committed to the defense of Sacco and Vanzetti as an active element of the defense. I was a newspaperman doing help on the side wherever I could, not identified publicly as part of the

effort to defend those two men. . . . I was utterly and totally sure of Sacco and Vanzetti's innocence. What really convinced me was Felicani, [during] my first long talk with him.

Jackson proposed a petition campaign to the defense committee.

I thought we could circulate petitions all over the country, getting as many signatures as we could. The petitions were addressed to the governor of Massachusetts. . . . I thought we ought to get such a mass of public opinion playing on the State House that the State House, as a political fact, would feel that they must have a review of the case outside of the courts. . . . I felt we could, in view of the fame of the case up to that point, and the widespread interest in it editorially all over the country and among the welfare, civic and church organizations, get hundreds of thousands of people all over the country on such petitions.

About twenty-five committee members, twenty-three of them Italians, met one night to consider Jackson's proposal. "There was complete acceptance. There was no criticism. There wasn't enough criticism actually. . . . They were very enthusiastic, with great warmth of appreciation to me for coming and saying that I would devote myself exclusively to this, to see if we couldn't accomplish something." So Jackson became the unpaid secretary of the Sacco-Vanzetti Defense Committee, living on inherited wealth while doing the work.

An important part of Jackson's job was keeping in touch with his colleagues in the press. He discovered that many of them agreed that the legal process against Sacco and Vanzetti had been unfair. One told him he could not risk losing his job by showing any sign of sympathy. But Jackson had not thought about such consequences in his own life. "It never occurred to me what it would do in terms of my own future operations. . . . I never thought a minute about it. . . . It was just something that had to be done."

He donated $50,000 to $60,000 to the campaign from his inheritance. "I was lucky in all this. I had an economic cushion. My immediate security was not involved in any way. I was able to indulge myself in the luxury of trying to do what seemed to me to be the right thing."

THE FINAL PHASES

Sacco and Vanzetti were sentenced to death in April 1927, after their final legal appeal had failed. At sentencing, Vanzetti made a long statement that included acknowledgment of international campaigners' efforts: "They all stick with us, the flower of mankind of Europe, the better writers, the greatest thinkers of Europe, have pleaded in our favor. The scientists, the greatest scientists, the greatest statesmen of Europe, have pleaded in our favor. The people of foreign nations have pleaded in our favor."

Feuerlicht wrote that the defense committee circulated petitions "all over the country and the world, getting between 750,000 and 1 million signatures according to Gardner Jackson," who recalled:

> We had tens of thousands of petitions, which we mailed all over the country, to labor unions, church groups and so on. . . . This was really a shot in the dark. I had a kind of mystical faith that it would result in a great response, a great many signatures. Almost immediately that happened. The rapidity with which the response came just overwhelmed Felicani and it certainly surprised me.

The defense committee took the petitions to the governor's office, Jackson remembered. "We pasted these petitions together and put them on a great roll on a stick. It was a huge roll, very heavy. Then Mary [Donovan] and I, with advance notice to the newspapermen and the photographers, each carrying an end of that stick, walked up the steps of the State House into the governor's office with this roll."

According to David, millions

> expressed their doubts [about the men's guilt] through Sacco-Vanzetti liberation committees and . . . in mass meetings in Paris and London, in Stockholm and Berlin, and in scores of other cities. In Buenos Aires, bakers and taxi drivers had begun a protest strike. . . . Thousands of demonstrators would attack American embassies; there would be bloody battles with the police, broken heads and bomb explosions, and Americans abroad would fear for their lives and the honor of their country.

Felix Frankfurter published a long article about Sacco and Vanzetti in the *Atlantic Monthly* in March 1927. It was quickly republished as a book, and "bookstores in Boston did not display Frankfurter's book but produced it from under the counter upon request," according to Feuerlicht. Jackson believed it "certainly had a tremendous effect in arousing intellectuals all over the world." Soon after, sixty-one American law professors asked the government to appoint a commission to review the case.

John Dos Passos wrote a pamphlet about the case, "Facing the Chair," and put an account of it in his *USA* trilogy. David recounted, "In the summer of 1927, [Heywood] Broun would write the angriest and most brilliant articles of the Sacco-Vanzetti case literature, denunciations of Massachusetts authority in the tradition of Zola's '*J'Accuse*' of the Dreyfus case." By early 1927, the defense committee had distributed or sold 200,000 copies of printed materials to the public.

Almost 30 years later, Jackson observed:

> The means of communication were so much simpler then. Radio
> was something new coming along. The day of instant communi-
> cation wasn't upon us. The press was the great means of com-
> munication. We couldn't have begun to do anything if we hadn't
> quite a good deal of important press support, and we did have lit-
> erary folk all over the place who pitched in, and this intellectual
> leadership in Europe.

After the death sentences, the Communist Party launched an international campaign for Sacco and Vanzetti and were said to have raised more
than $500,000. Jackson claimed the Communists gave the defense com-
mittee only $6,000 of that amount. The International Labor Defense, the
Communist Party's legal arm, set up its own defense committee, hired its
own lawyers, organized its own demonstrations and, according to Jackson,
tried to sabotage Felicani's committee. Novelist Katherine Anne Porter,
who became involved in the campaign at this time, observed that the Communists "had not originated the protest, I believe, but had joined in and
tried to take over, as the policy was, and is." She claimed that a Communist Party organizer had said: "Saved? Who wants them saved? What earthly
good would they do us alive?"

Herbert Ehrmann, an attorney who joined the legal defense team near
the end, believed that "later appeals might have succeeded if the propaganda campaign had not united the authorities against the two men." Felix
Frankfurter advised civil liberties organizations to back away from public
campaigning because their "entanglement" with radicals "would hurt the
cause of those men. I speak from a great deal of attention to the situation
and a detailed familiarity, I believe, with the governing forces of the community."

In response to the public pressure, the governor of Massachusetts
appointed a special advisory committee to review the conduct of the
case. Gardner Jackson believed that the petitions, Felix Frankfurter's article about the case in the *Atlantic Monthly*, editorials in newspapers around
the country and letters from European intellectuals had forced the governor to appoint the committee.

Jackson persuaded the defense committee to cancel all public demonstrations while the group deliberated. Composed of Boston Brahmins
chaired by A. Lawrence Lowell, the president of Harvard, the advisory committee found nothing wrong with the conduct of the prosecutors or the
judge. The Harvard alumni who were campaigning for Sacco and Vanzetti
felt especially betrayed by the Lowell committee's findings. Jackson wondered later if he had done the right thing in discouraging demonstrations
during this crucial period.

Once the Lowell committee had made its decision, the campaign reached a new level of intensity. The defense committee placed full-page advertisements in *The New York Times*, the Boston newspapers and other periodicals. Felix Frankfurter made a special trip to New York to browbeat Walter Lippmann, then the editor of the *New York World*. Lippmann had published an editorial supporting the Lowell committee; but after a long conversation with Frankfurter, he published another editorial reversing his position.

Oddly, the *Boston Herald*, whose Pulitzer Prize-winning editorial had made opposing the executions almost respectable, also pronounced itself convinced by the Lowell committee's report. But 17,000 letters asking for clemency arrived in the governor's office by May 1927, and large demonstrations in support of the men took place in Union Square in New York, where 10,000 union members rallied in July. Commissioned to write a series of articles for *The New York Times*, H.G. Wells submitted "Outrages in Defence of Order: The Proposed Murder of Two American Radicals" to the paper. The *Times* paid him but did not publish it.

AGONY AND ANTICLIMAX

In August 1927 the drama proceeded inexorably to its tragic conclusion. It was "Sacco-Vanzetti month not only in Boston but all over America and in much of the world. Without television for instant publicity and with radio a luxury rather than a household item, two obscure Italians had become the object of the greatest concern ever accorded two victims before that time and probably since," Feuerlicht observes. Five hundred American intellectuals, including Jane Addams and John Dewey, signed a letter to the Massachusetts governor, pleading for a stay of execution.

"August was a month of appeals, picketing, strikes, demonstrations and bombings . . . [that] only served to reinforce public resentment of the two men," writes Feuerlicht. Hundreds of thousands of American workers went on strike to pressure for commutation. Writers including Dorothy Parker, Edna St. Vincent Millay and Katherine Anne Porter traveled to Boston to demonstrate, along with thousands of others. Some were arrested as they silently paraded in front of the State House and were beaten at the police station.

In London, Moscow, Berlin, Madrid, São Paulo and other cities, hundreds of thousands of workers went on strike. Demonstrations were held in Norway, Sweden, Denmark, Switzerland, Holland, Japan, China, South Africa, Mexico and other countries. Alfred Dreyfus signed a clemency petition and wrote to the condemned men.

Felicani and Jackson went to the governor to plead for clemency. They told him that the reputation of Massachusetts and the United States would suffer "in the eyes of thoughtful people around the world" if Sacco and Vanzetti were executed. "We just didn't get to first base with him," Jackson recalled.

The governor refused to commute the sentence and announced that the men would be executed on August 10, 1927. That evening, as lawyers tried desperately to find a federal judge who would sign a stay, the governor postponed the execution until midnight, August 22.

In the days before the execution, Felicani the anarchist fell into anguished rage. Forty years later he wrote:

> I felt that no action was too violent to protest this crime. . . . It was necessary to keep posted our closest friends in this country and throughout the world. We did not know what else to do. The only hope left was to arouse people to acts of desperation and protest. . . . We asked for action. Action was our only hope for snatching our friends from the hands of the hangman. All legal hope was exhausted. In the large industrial centers of America workers laid down their tools, proclaiming a general strike. Individuals resorted to acts of desperation and terror.

The defense committee office throbbed with frenetic activity. In one day, the staff spent $860 on telegrams.

> We had messengers from Western Union and Postal Telegraph all the time. We had calls from South Africa, Russia, South America, England, Germany, France, Spain. Labor organizations, liberal groups, political parties, religious associations sent wires. Also the most prominent people in public life in every country of the world sent messages. . . . Anatole France . . ., Romain Rolland, Bertrand Russell, Harold Laski, H.G. Wells, Arnold Bennett, Fritz Kreisler . . ., Albert Einstein, Madame Curie . . . also sent words of sympathy and protest. . . . They were all messages written with the burning feelings which consumed everyone. . . . The remembrance of that tremendous wave of human passion will live forever.

The night before the executions, a huge rally took place in Boston. Sacco's wife, Rosa, and Vanzetti's sister, Luigia (who had come from Italy to be with her brother), stood before the crowd. Fifty years later, Katherine Anne Porter remembered:

> The two timid women faced the raging crowd, mostly Italians, who rose at them in savage sympathy, shouting, tears pouring down their faces, shaking their fists and calling childish phrases, their promises of revenge for their wrongs. . . . Rosa Sacco spread her hands over her face, but Luigia Vanzetti stared stonily down into

their distorted faces with a pure horror of her own. They screamed
their violence at her in her own language, trying to hearten her,
but she was not consoled. She was led away like a corpse walking. The crowd roared and cursed and wept and threatened. It
was the most awesome, and the most bitter scene I had ever witnessed.

At this demonstration, Gardner Jackson realized that the crowd was so
stirred up by the speakers' rhetoric that they might try to invade the State
House or the prison where Sacco and Vanzetti awaited death. "There actually began to be formations in the mob of groups that were wanting some
sort of immediate direct action. The cops on horseback, seeing this, began
to break the thing right up."

AFTERMATHS

Sacco and Vanzetti were executed just after midnight, in the first few
minutes of August 23, 1927. One of the most important objects associated with the case is a black armband, with the words "Justice Crucified.
August 22, 1927" in red letters, which the demonstrators wore that day and
the next.

Jackson and Felicani walked the streets until dawn. "Felicani said he
thought we must figure on spending the rest of our lives trying to prove
the innocence of Sacco and Vanzetti, and to develop evidence as to the
actual perpetrators of the crime," Jackson recalled. They decided to
establish a Sacco-Vanzetti Memorial Committee to pursue the case.

All over the world, Sinclair wrote:

> there were mass meetings and protests that night. In London a
> mob marched upon Buckingham Palace and had to be ridden down
> by mounted men. . . . In Berlin there were a score of meetings,
> ending with parades. In Geneva the demonstrants raided the Amer-
> ican Embassy, and when clubbed away broke the windows of the
> League of Nations palace. Even in far-off Tokio [sic] the American
> ambassador had to receive a deputation of labor leaders, and explain
> that he had no control over executions in Massachusetts. In
> Paris there had been a general strike, and on the night of the exe-
> cution there were street demonstrations, with mobs shouting curses
> at Americans whenever they met them. . . . On the evening of the
> 23rd in Paris huge masses of workers were driven about the streets
> by the police. They would scatter, and then reassemble wherever
> Americans were to be met. . . .

A few days later in Boston, some 200,000 watched the funeral procession as it snaked through downtown streets. Mounted police tried to keep

the procession from entering the financial district by riding down the participants and blocking their way. Alice Stone Blackwell, one of the patrician activists who had worked to save the men, described the scene:

> . . . in a driving storm of wind and rain, 50,000 persons started to follow the hearse, containing the bodies of the two Italians, the eight miles to the Forest Hills crematory. They called it 'The March of Sorrow.' The Boston police used every effort to break up the peaceful procession. Repeatedly they closed the street by placing trucks across it; but the marchers made a detour and went on. Traffic was diverted into the procession. Again and again the mounted police rode the mourners down and clubbed them. By every device of violence and brutality, they reduced the 50,000 who had started to a few hundred; and when these reached the cemetery, they found the gates guarded by police who refused them entrance. They stood bareheaded and silent, in the pouring rain, during the services in the crematory chapel.

After the cremation, rival groups fought over the men's ashes. The Communists wanted to take them to New York for a giant rally at Union Square. This was done. Then the ashes, which had acquired the status of sacred relics, were divided into four lots: two to be sent to the men's families in Italy, one to Sacco's family in Massachusetts, one to Felicani in Boston.

Two urns were sent by ship to Italy. The British government refused to let them off the boat when it docked at Southampton. U.S. agents kept the ashes under surveillance until they arrived in Italy. The Italian fascist government had to accept them because the men had been Italian citizens.

Felicani kept his set of ashes until his death in 1967. Then his Sacco-Vanzetti collection, including the ashes, went to the Boston Public Library. For years the urn sat on a shelf in a closet, along with the men's death masks, death certificates, a box of bullets and personal effects. Robert D'Attilio, a local Sacco-Vanzetti scholar, tried to persuade the librarian to scatter the ashes, but the librarian did not want to violate Felicani's final wishes. To this day the ashes remain in a vault in the Boston Public Library, and no one may see them.

Gardner Jackson recounts a meeting he had with a British journalist, a friend of Frankfurter's, soon after the executions.

> He came to see me and asked to talk with me alone. He described his own experiences in his young manhood, which included a case of injustice. He said that he wanted me to benefit by his struggle not to let his failure to get justice in this murder case victimize him the rest of his life. He warned me, with deep feeling, that I

should not commit myself to going on with this case indefinitely. I said that it would be very hard for me not to go on with it for awhile, anyhow, because we were confident we would be able to develop further evidence and proof. He agreed that that was all right, but not to project my life for years ahead into this thing. He kept using that phrase, 'Don't let it victimize you. This is just one experience in your life and you'll become unbalanced if you stay preoccupied with this single case.' In retrospect I think he was right. . . . I think I did take his advice.

Eventually Jackson decided he must get away from Boston and moved to Washington, D.C. He worked there with Drew Pearson, a pioneering investigative journalist. In 1933 he joined the Roosevelt government at the Agricultural Adjustment Administration. The Secretary of Agriculture hired and fired him twice for his independent stands. He was especially concerned about the working conditions of migrant farmworkers. With Roger Baldwin and other veterans of the Sacco-Vanzetti case, he helped secure Tom Mooney's release from prison. During the 1930s and '40s he worked for the CIO (Congress of Industrial Organizations), seeking to expel Communists from the labor movement.

According to Arthur Schlesinger, Jr., "His courage as labor reporter for *PM* in exposing Communism in the unions at the height of the wartime alliance with Soviet Russia led a band of National Maritime Union thugs to set on him late one night in 1944, beating him unmercifully and blinding him in one eye." Later Jackson worked as a freelance writer and labor consultant. In the 1950s he championed the cause of the Bolivian tin miners. Until he died at age sixty-eight in 1965, Jackson continued to believe that Sacco and Vanzetti had been innocent and never hesitated to say so.

During every decade of the Twentieth Century, campaign survivors, writers, artists and intellectuals commemorated Sacco's and Vanzetti's martyrdom. In 1929 H.L. Mencken wrote, "Two years dead, the victims continue to walk."

Before an anniversary meeting, a Communist Party leader came to see Jackson, who had helped him find and pay a lawyer after he was arrested for carrying a placard accusing the governor of murdering Sacco and Vanzetti. He told Jackson:

I just want to warn you that while you're holding the anniversary meeting of your memorial committee . . . I am going to have to hold a meeting on Boston Common, and I'm going to have to call you one of the murderers of Sacco and Vanzetti, because the party felt that you did not follow the right tactics throughout the case and they have ordered me to label you as one of the mur-

derers. I tell you that because I want you know that even though
I say it, as a person I don't believe it myself at all.

Jackson tried but failed to dissuade the leader from this course.

A third memorial meeting took place in 1930 at the Old South Meeting
House in Boston. The program drew parallels with the Mooney-Billings
case and included a letter from Mooney on the inside back cover. The
death masks of Sacco and Vanzetti were displayed there for the first time.

That year, the governor of Massachusetts retired from public life. To
mark the end of his term, he and his family ceremonially descended the
steps of the State House. Gardner Jackson approached him and presented
him with a copy of the recently published *Letters of Sacco and Vanzetti*.
The governor "accepted the book, took it in his hands, suddenly realized
what it was and threw it on the pavement," Jackson remembered.

Many writers and artists found inspiration in the case. Creative works
about the two men included *Winterset*, by Maxwell Anderson; *The Bomb*,
by Frank Harris; poems by Edna St. Vincent Millay and Lola Ridge; *We
Accept with Pleasure*, by Bernard de Voto; and *The Passion of Sacco and
Vanzetti*, by Ben Shahn. Eugene Lyons published *The Life and Death of
Sacco and Vanzetti* soon after the executions, and Upton Sinclair's careful
and extensive research for his novel *Boston* made it a reliable source for
later writers. *The Letters of Sacco and Vanzetti* were published in Britain,
France and the Soviet Union, as well as the United States, between 1928
and 1931.

On the occasion of the Harvard University tercentenary in 1936, twenty-
eight alumni, including Heywood Broun, Malcolm Cowley, John Dos Passos, Varian Fry, Powers Hapgood, Granville Hicks and Gardner Jackson,
printed 5,000 copies of a pamphlet, "Walled in This Tomb, Questions Left
Unanswered by the Lowell Committee in the Sacco-Vanzetti Case and Their
Pertinence in Understanding the Conflicts Sweeping the World at This
Hour." They tried to distribute the pamphlets to visiting dignitaries, but
the university confiscated most of them.

A 1947 manifesto, prepared by Gardner Jackson and Arthur Schlesinger,
commemorated the twentieth anniversary of the executions. Among the
sponsors were journalists F.P. Adams, Joseph and Stewart Alsop, W. Hod-
ding Carter and Marquis Childs; labor leaders David Dubinsky and Walter
Ruether, political figures Eleanor Roosevelt, Senator Wayne Morse and Sum-
ner Welles; activists Roger Baldwin and Arthur Garfield Hays; and academics Robert Hutchins, Clyde Kluckhohn and Gordon Allport. The pamphlet mildly called for "restudy" of the case.

Over the years, numerous books and memoirs reviewed the evidence
and tried to establish the men's innocence or guilt. Participants including
Herbert Ehrmann and Michael Musmanno published studies presenting

evidence of malfeasance by the prosecution, the judge's prejudice and the guilt of a professional criminal gang. These received respectful attention but did not lead to a reopening of the case.

In 1967, Michael Musmanno, then a justice on the Pennsylvania Supreme Court, was still indignant that the governor of Massachusetts had made "the incredibly inhuman declaration that, had it not been for the world-wide pleas for clemency, there might have been another solution to the Sacco-Vanzetti case. This was a miserable confession that there was at least doubt as to the guilt of the two, but that they had to die because otherwise the world might believe that the U.S. had succumbed to foreign intimidations."

On the fiftieth anniversary of the executions in 1977, the governor of Massachusetts, Michael Dukakis, issued a proclamation that Nicola Sacco's grandson delivered to his grandfather's surviving sister in Italy. After many "whereases," Dukakis declared that "any stigma and disgrace should be forever removed from the names of Nicola Sacco and Bartolomeo Vanzetti, from the names of their families and descendants, and so, from the name of the Commonwealth of Massachusetts." Dukakis avoided pronouncing the men innocent and instead emphasized the unfairness of the trial. Nevertheless, he was much criticized for his action in the legislature and the press.

In August 1997, newspapers in Boston and elsewhere remembered the case, but the principal figures were long dead. Nowadays, many people have never heard of Sacco and Vanzetti and know nothing of the passions they aroused two generations ago.

LESSONS TO BE LEARNED

Why remember Sacco and Vanzetti? Were the governor and others correct in saying that the international uproar only made things worse for the men? What can campaigners learn from this case?

In his 1977 proclamation, Michael Dukakis observed that

> all human institutions are imperfect, that the possibility of injustice is ever-present. . . . The trial and execution of Sacco and Vanzetti should serve to remind all civilized people of the constant need to guard against our susceptibility to prejudice, our intolerance of unorthodox ideas, and our failure to defend the rights of persons who are looked upon as strangers in our midst. . . . Simple decency and compassion . . . require that the fate of Nicola Sacco and Bartolomeo Vanzetti be pondered by all who cherish tolerance, justice and human understanding.

These are eloquent and appropriate words, fifty years after the fact. But they do not constitute useful advice for activists who want to learn from history. They leave too many questions unanswered. Why did a highly visible public campaign succeed in saving Alfred Dreyfus but fail to save Sacco and Vanzetti? How did a quiet campaign and sympathetic press coverage succeed in saving Mendel Beilis? Why did it take more than twenty years to get Tom Mooney out of prison, despite secret pressure by a U.S. president and intense grassroots campaigning? Can we learn anything from these old campaigns that applies to present-day conditions? Or do we live in a completely different world?

About the Sacco-Vanzetti case, Gardner Jackson maintained:

> If there had not been the development of the propaganda on their behalf, the setting up of the defense committee, and all the agitation and demonstrations that ensued, these two Italians might very well have been convicted and sentenced and executed without anybody knowing anything about it. Their only chance of getting a square shake in the courts was if we did focus as much public attention as possible on the proceedings. . . . When you have a mass meeting, it's the mass, it's the numbers, that's the indication of a large body of human beings who feel this way, that has its effect.

In recent cases, such as Reuben "Hurricane" Carter's, Leonard Peltier's and Mumia Abu-Jamal's, campaigning has had varying results. Campaigns may pressure the authorities to reinvestigate cases, retry defendants, consider pardon, parole or release, or keep the subject alive for a time. And they may fail after months, years or decades of dedicated grassroots efforts.

The social, political and economic contexts in which such cases occur seem very important, and these factors lie beyond the control of campaigners. In the early 1920s, an economic depression, unemployment, union busting, antilabor court decisions, a restrictive immigration law, prejudice against foreigners, the rise of the Ku Klux Klan and other factors kept many people from expressing their opinions or becoming involved in efforts to save Sacco and Vanzetti.

A situation like that of Dreyfus, in which an entire society mobilized for and against a single person, is rare. In many instances, campaigners have great difficulty attracting sustained public attention to their cause. They lack human and financial resources; the media ignore, bury or misreport the case; powerful and influential people use every weapon at their disposal to defeat them. In the Sacco-Vanzetti case, the Boston elite, personified by the advisory committee, closed ranks with the judiciary and the highest authorities of the state to ensure that the two men would die. Success is unlikely when public opinion and the immense institutional power of the legal and political system are amassed on the other side.

But surely those who claim that campaigning against injustice guarantees injustice are mistaken, since silent acquiescence would lead to the same outcome. To say that things would have turned out better if only the radicals had not made such a fuss is merely a way for powerful people to evade their responsibility. Those who perpetrate injustice, not those who protest against it, are responsible for the wrongdoing. Nevertheless, there are more and less effective ways to protest.

Louis Joughin partly blames the campaigners themselves for failing to save Sacco and Vanzetti. He criticizes them for not providing "a full historical account of the evil done by prejudice and ignorance in the past," for using overly sectarian language, for not translating their "virtuous principles into language which could be understood by the man in the street," for not controlling European radicals, for failing "to unite upon and insistently demand useful positive action." Perhaps all these failures could be most easily perceived with hindsight. He also points out that academics, clergy and the press either remained silent at critical moments or were sharply divided in their opinions and actions.

Jackson admits:

> There was never any complete cohesion between all those committees who were working on the case. They all had their own meetings, fundraising devices, printed material, demonstrations, and so forth. Felicani and his group were the originators of the whole cause and they were recognized as such. . . . The proliferating of the committees in the latter stages of the case was largely as a result of the Communists. They were riding the case hard for their own purposes.

We will see more examples of Communist attempts to control and use campaigns in following chapters.

Joughin fatalistically concludes:

> Could Sacco and Vanzetti have been saved? It does not seem so. Examine the opinions held by the people of this country in the 1920s upon the chief political, economic and social problems of the day. . . . The legacy of Sacco and Vanzetti to society lies in the emphasis which their fate gave to the continuing warfare between the forces of democratic and undemocratic action.

CONSEQUENCES

The campaigners tried to find some redeeming value in the ordeal they had shared. Soon after the executions, campaigner Mary Donovan declared:

> You, Sacco and Vanzetti, are the victims of the greatest plutocracy the world has known since ancient Rome. Your long years of torture and your last hours of supreme agony are the living banner under which we and our descendants for generations to come will march to accomplish that better world based on the brotherhood for which you died. In your martyrdom we will fight on and conquer. Remember Justice Crucified. August 22. Remember.

Similarly, a Communist pamphlet, "Sacco and Vanzetti Labor's Martyrs," trumpeted that the world working class would "march forward triumphantly towards that great victory which is the victory of Sacco and Vanzetti and their final vindication."

At a time of crushing despair, such words helped people go on, though now they may seem tragically naive. There is no doubt, however, that the experience of campaigning for Sacco and Vanzetti impelled thousands or even millions of people to involve themselves in later efforts for human rights and social justice. Some, like Felix Frankfurter and Gardner Jackson, ended up in powerful positions where they had the potential to make substantive changes in social, political or economic conditions. Important institutional changes did take place because of this case. For example, the Massachusetts legislature passed a law in 1939 changing the judicial appeals process, so that a prejudiced judge would never again have the power to squelch every motion for appeal of a case he had already heard.

As a result of their Sacco-Vanzetti experience, Upton Sinclair, John Dos Passos, Edna St. Vincent Millay and others made significant contributions to our cultural heritage. It is difficult to measure the effects of their works, which have enriched so many lives. This cultural legacy may be the principal means by which future generations will learn of Sacco's and Vanzetti's long ordeal, the struggle to save their lives and the tragedy they insisted on calling their triumph.

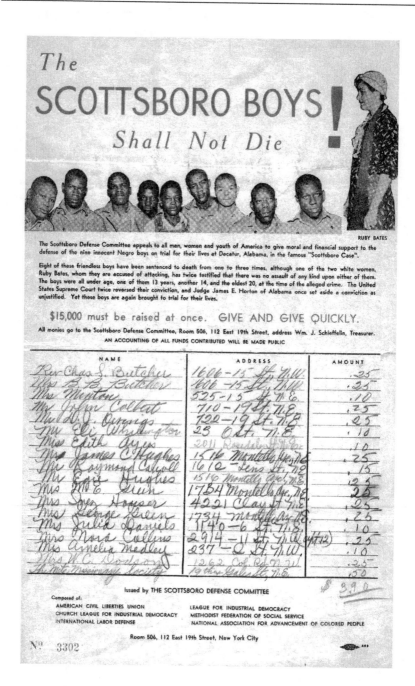

A Scottsboro Defense Committee petition, signed by African-American church members in Kent, Ohio, 1936.

Chapter 7

THE SCOTTSBORO BOYS:
"A TANGLED, UGLY CASE"

In March 1931, as the American artist Ben Shahn was working on "The Passion of Sacco and Vanzetti," nine black boys were pulled from a freight train in rural Alabama and arrested. Someone had seen them fighting with white boys on the train and called police. Also on the train the police discovered two white mill girls and part-time prostitutes, Victoria Price and Ruby Bates. Under pressure from police and fearful of arrest, the young women claimed the black boys had gang-raped them.

By the time the boys reached Scottsboro, Alabama, a mob was waiting at the jail to lynch them. Four days later, a grand jury indicted Olen Montgomery, Clarence Norris, Haywood Patterson, Ozzie Powell, Willie Roberson, Charlie Weems, Eugene Williams, Andy Wright and his brother Roy Wright for the rape of Price and Bates. The boys ranged in age from twelve to nineteen; one was almost blind, and another had such a severe case of syphilis that he could hardly walk. In less than a week, eight had been convicted and sentenced to death. Roy Wright, only thirteen, was sentenced to life imprisonment.

The editors of the Communist Party newspaper *Southern Worker* heard the news of the boys' arrest on the radio the day it happened. They immediately informed the International Labor Defense (ILD), the Communist Party's legal arm, in New York. An ILD representative attended the pretrial hearing and called the ILD to say "they had another Sacco-Vanzetti on their hands."

A regional group, the Interdenominational Ministers Alliance of Chattanooga, Tennessee, paid a local lawyer to defend the boys. He was too drunk to help them in court. In the Jefferson City jail, the boys received a visit from two ILD lawyers. "These were the first people to call on us, to show any feelings for our lives, and we were glad. We hadn't even heard from our own families; they weren't allowed to see us. But these lawyers got in," Haywood Patterson recalled almost twenty years later.

Clarence Norris wrote, "Mr. Brodsky and Mr. Taub made us feel a lot better when they said hundreds of people were working to get us free." Joseph Brodsky, ILD's chief attorney, soon became the boys' lawyer.

The Associated Negro Press, a black news service, sent stories about the trials to black newspapers around the country, and as a result, hundreds of people wrote to Alabama officials to protest. This spontaneous public reaction seems to have surprised the Communists, but they quickly capitalized on it. African-Americans were also writing to the National Association for the Advancement of Colored People (NAACP), the largest and most prestigious black organization in the U.S., asking it to take up the case. Individuals, community groups and churches across the country sent the NAACP donations ranging from five cents to a few dollars. A note from a beauty-shop owner in Nashville read, "Dear Sir, Please enclosed you will find ($1.50) one dollar and fifty cents for the cause of those eight colored boys of Alabama."

Clarence Darrow, the most famous defense attorney of the time, telephoned the NAACP and said that the ILD had invited him to join its legal team for the Scottsboro Boys' appeals. The NAACP's executive secretary, Walter White, warned Darrow to stay away from the Communists; cooperation with the ILD was impossible, he said.

The NAACP had tried to work with the ILD the year before on a case in Atlanta, Georgia. A black friend in Atlanta had written to White, "I suppose their Communist friends will follow their old tactics in taking more interest in the propaganda value of the cases than in really trying to get the people properly tried and defended."

The NAACP kept aloof from the Scottsboro case as long as it could. In April 1931, White wrote to a black newspaper editor:

> We have not rushed into print in this case for various reasons. One of them is that the feeling against the boys was already so bitter that the Association's entrance into the case would unquestionably have inflamed the mobbists [sic] even more against the boys. A second reason has been the intemperate statements made by the International Labor Defense, a Communist organization, have helped, as one man has expressed it, to insure the convictions of the helpless boys.

Meanwhile, the ILD declared that "only the actions of hundreds of thousands in a mass movement of protest" could gain the boys' freedom. As Brodsky started work on the case, protest letters, mass meetings, petitions and marches on behalf of the Scottsboro Boys began to make headlines in the U.S. and Europe. The ILD, Norris later recalled:

> publicized the case through their newspaper, *The Daily Worker*.
> They held rallies, marched and raised money on our behalf. . . .
> They had Haywood Patterson's mother speaking to crowds in Harlem.

Letters, telegrams and petitions poured into President Herbert Hoover and the governor of Alabama demanding our freedom.

COMMUNISTS VS. NAACP

According to James Goodman, the Communist Party had several reasons for working on the case, "By publicizing the plight of the boys and defending them in court, the party saw the chance to educate, add to its ranks and encourage the mass protest necessary not only to free the boys but also to bring about revolution."

The party had started the ILD in 1925, to counter the alarming growth of the Ku Klux Klan throughout the United States. In its early years, the ILD conducted campaigns to save Nicola Sacco and Bartolomeo Vanzetti and to release Tom Mooney and Warren Billings. The ILD declared itself independent of the party, but this was merely a useful fiction to attract non-Communists, such as Eugene V. Debs, to the national committee. Most of the ILD leaders were Communists, and the ILD staff received its orders from the party's Central Committee.

Under pressure from its members to help the Scottsboro Boys, the NAACP finally decided to step in. Walter White visited the "Boys" in May 1931. Norris remembered: "He never came anywhere near us until we were in the death house. By this time the case was international news. A lot of people wanted to know why the NAACP was not involved. . . . He told us we were doomed if we let the ILD lawyers defend us. He said the prejudice against communism and blacks combined guaranteed us going to the electric chair." White persuaded some of the "Boys" to fire Brodsky and sign a statement "asking the Communists to 'lay off,'" Dan Carter wrote. Norris "never did understand why they couldn't work together since they all said they wanted to see us free."

The ILD did not withdraw from the case. It arranged for the "Boys'" relatives to visit them in prison and sent money and cigarettes to them. Haywood Patterson recalled:

> Mail and money was coming to me from Nancy Cunard, of the ship lines. She sent $25 a month. Kay Boyle, an American writer living in France, she sent letters and money and pictures of her family. From people all over money was coming in, so we fellows didn't have to depend on the witched-up stews the prison served us. . . . We heard big shots like Albert Einstein and Thomas Mann came out for us in Europe. We didn't know who these people were but figured from the way Alabama papers quavered about it that they had say-so.

Some of the "Boys" learned how to read and write in prison, so they could follow the case in the newspapers and answer the many letters that came from around the world. Prison conditions were brutal and squalid, and the "Boys" spent many of their prison years in the death house.

In retaliation for the NAACP's intervention, Carter wrote, the ILD released a "stream of vituperation," and a nasty, sometimes public, fight between the two organizations lasted for most of the next four years. When the NAACP's patronizing remarks about the "Boys'" parents appeared in the black press, the ILD sent the news clippings to the "Boys." "The NAACP put out in the papers that we were too dumb and ignorant to realize we were being used by the Communists. Not too long afterwards we all signed with the ILD," Clarence Norris said. The "Boys" went back and forth between the ILD and the NAACP at least half a dozen times between 1931 and 1935.

At the NAACP's annual meeting in summer 1931, ILD supporters tried to force their way in with Haywood Patterson's mother, but the NAACP would not admit her. This incident, reported in the black press, made the NAACP look bad, since the organization was raising funds for the Scottsboro defense at the meeting. ILD supporters tried to disrupt the meeting by circulating a fourteen-page letter accusing the organization of being in league with lynchers to murder the "Boys." Yet the biggest single contributor to the ILD's Scottsboro defense fund at the time was the NAACP.

In January 1932, the NAACP withdrew from the legal case, though it continued to pass donations from its members to the ILD.

A TWO-EDGED SWORD

Some blacks were more tolerant of the Communist Party than the NAACP was. In 1931, 1,300 blacks joined the party. Many drifted away later, and black membership in the party remained small, probably no more than one or two thousand in all. But "Negroes appreciated the Communists' efforts on their behalf. They supported common causes, joined willingly in united fronts, and fought side by side in crusades," Carter wrote. At a time when racial segregation and prejudice pervaded American society, white Communists were often the only white people who would willingly associate and work with blacks. They insisted on integrating their southern chapters and strove to eliminate racist attitudes from their ranks. They also focused attention on racial discrimination, segregation and violations of blacks' human rights, such as voting, freedom of association and freedom of speech—issues that most white-dominated organizations ignored or did not identify as systemic.

The Scottsboro Boys' mothers were particularly appreciative of the Comunists' efforts. Ada Wright, who toured Europe for the ILD for six months in 1932, said: "It looks like the reds are the only ones that want to help us. . . . if it had not been for the reds, and the mass protests of the workers, our boys would have died." Clarence Norris believed that "the spotlight the 'reds' put on Alabama saved all our lives."

At the same time, however, the Communists' tactics alienated government officials, middle-class blacks and moderate white southerners who otherwise might have helped the "Boys." Published white opinion in the South overwhelmingly supported the convictions and death sentences. White politicians read the papers and tailored their statements and actions accordingly.

Protest letters and telegrams arrived by the thousands at the Alabama governor's office, and those coming from ILD groups were said to be threatening, insulting and intemperate. One form letter, used by seventy-five percent of the petitioners in 1932, read as follows:

> We . . . denounce the brutal slave drivers of Alabama, acting through a Ku Klux Klan judge and jury inflamed by race hatred in order to send nine innocent children to the electric chair.
>
> We brand this sentence of the white ruling classes as an attempt at willful, cold-blooded and deliberate murder. We recognize this as an attack against the Negro masses and the working class as a whole.
>
> We demand the immediate and unconditional release of these boys through a new trial—a trial by jury at least half of whom are Negro workers—with the right of an armed defense corps of Negro and white workers to defend the prisoners, jurors and defense attorneys from the bosses' lynching mobs.

Not all the letters were so florid. A German committee of 300 intellectuals begged President Hoover and the governor of Alabama to pardon the "Boys" "in the name of humanity and justice." And hundreds of letters supported the convictions and death sentences.

RISKS OF PROTEST

The overall climate in the South was extremely repressive. Blacks' civil liberties were curtailed, lynchings occurred regularly, and the authorities openly expressed their contempt for the Fourteenth Amendment (which guarantees equal protection of the laws to all U.S. citizens).

In the wake of the Scottsboro trials, the Communist Party sent a small number of organizers into rural areas in the Deep South. Their assignment was to organize a sharecroppers' union. During a meeting to draft a protest to Alabama's governor over the Scottsboro case, white vigilantes broke it up and killed one black man. White mobs then roamed the countryside searching for black "reds." As the Communists organized a conference to discuss Scottsboro, local police raided their office and threw three staffers in jail. Despite threats, 300 blacks and fifty whites did meet.

They held the conference outside, however, because police told them they would have to segregate any meeting they held indoors.

In 1932 a black Communist, Angelo Herndon, was arrested in Atlanta, Georgia, for possessing copies of *The Daily Worker* and was prosecuted under a pre-Civil War law prohibiting the distribution of "insurrectionary" literature. Herndon was sentenced to eighteen to twenty years in prison for this "crime." The ILD campaigned on his behalf, coupling his case with the Scottsboro case. In 1937, the U.S. Supreme Court finally declared the law unconstitutional, and Herndon was freed.

Under such circumstances, it was safer and more effective to organize demonstrations and other events in the North. Scottsboro rallies, marches and meetings took place in many American cities from 1931 to 1937. A mass meeting of 200 Communists in Harlem attracted 3,000 blacks from the neighborhood. Five Scottsboro mothers made public appearances in hundreds of cities throughout the U.S. in 1931. In 1933 they went to the White House with Ruby Bates, who recently had recanted her testimony against the "Boys." Intellectuals, writers and artists, some of whom had campaigned for Sacco and Vanzetti, also participated in the campaign.

THE INTERNATIONAL DIMENSION

From the beginning the Scottsboro campaign was international, perhaps because the Communists were more numerous and better organized outside the United States. Petitions, letters and telegrams from many countries arrived in the governor's office. Thirty-three Members of Parliament signed a petition from Britain. In Germany and other European countries, Communist groups marched on U.S. consulates and embassies during the summer of 1931. Communists played leading roles in the campaign, but they were not the only ones to support the Scottsboro Boys.

A French Socialist newspaper printed a notice of a mass meeting in 1932 that conveys the tone of the European campaign. It starts with a quotation from Tom Mooney, described as "a state [*i.e.,* political] prisoner for sixteen years in California":

> In every epoch of history, certain individuals or groups come to symbolize, by a twist of fate, the struggles of that particular era: In the 1890s, Dreyfus symbolized anti-Semitism in the bosom of the French army; in 1920, Sacco and Vanzetti symbolized the hatred and persecution surrounding foreign-born revolutionaries; in 1916, Mooney and Billings symbolized the struggle between Capital and Labor. Likewise the nine young Negroes of Scottsboro symbolize today the cruel treatment inflicted on blacks by whites, especially in the southern states of the U.S.A.

The announcement continues, "Save the eight innocent young blacks condemned to the electric chair!" and ends with a list of the meeting's sponsors, who included Léon Blum, former Dreyfusard and future premier; the president of the League of the Rights of Man, a human rights organization started during the Dreyfus Affair; Socialist politicians, newspaper editors and trade union officials. This list of names and affiliations takes up half the space of the announcement and is meant to show the campaign's seriousness and respectability.

JUSTICE DENIED

In March 1932 the Alabama Supreme Court upheld the convictions of seven of the eight "Boys"; Eugene Williams' conviction was overturned because he was only thirteen at the time of the trial. Later that year the U.S. Supreme Court reversed the Scottsboro Boys' convictions because by failing to provide adequate legal representation, the state had violated the due process clause of the Fourteenth Amendment. The "Boys" were retried in 1933.

For the new trials, the ILD hired Samuel Liebowitz, a very successful, non-Communist, criminal lawyer, to represent the "Boys." Liebowitz insisted that the Communists keep their propagandizing to a minimum during the retrials, but many southerners held against him the fact that he was Jewish and from New York. Thus anti-Semitic prejudice, especially virulent in the South, became a factor in the retrials. Enraged by the proceedings, Liebowitz gave an interview to a northern newspaper in which he called the jurors "those lantern-jawed creatures—those bigots whose mouths are slits in their faces, whose eyes pop out at you like frogs', whose chins drip tobacco juice, bewhiskered and filthy." His statement was reprinted in southern papers. As a result, his involvement in the case became a liability, but northern blacks hailed him as a hero. In April 1933 he addressed 4,000 in a Harlem church. The next night, 10,000 attended an ILD rally in Union Square on behalf of the "Boys."

The "Boys" were again found guilty in separate trials during 1933 and 1934, despite the weakness of the evidence and Ruby Bates' testimony on their behalf. Because the national press sent reporters to Alabama and followed the trials closely, the American public was much better informed about the case than it had been in 1931. Goodman wrote:

> The hue and cry was deafening. People who had cried out about the trial before cried louder. Many people got involved for the first time. In churches, schools, colleges, on street corners, in parks and other open spaces in cities all over the North there were rallies, meetings, marches and demonstrations. Out of these gatherings scores of new protest organizations were born. . . . Within

twenty-four hours, 25,000 people had sent telegrams to the governor of Alabama.

Again appeals went to the U.S. Supreme Court. In two precedent-setting decisions, the court overturned Norris' and Patterson's convictions because blacks had been excluded from the juries. The ILD insisted that the decisions proved the effectiveness of mass protest and pressure. Nevertheless, even this electrifying event still did not result in the "Boys'" release. More retrials resulted in more convictions, despite the token presence of blacks on the juries. Patterson's sentence was reduced to seventy-five years' imprisonment, but Norris remained on death row. Altogether, eleven Scottsboro trials took place between 1931 and 1937; all but one resulted in convictions.

CRACKS IN THE WROUGHT-IRON FAÇADE

In the mid-1930s several southern newspapers—the *Richmond News Leader*, the *Raleigh News and Observer* and the *Chattanooga News*—began publishing editorials saying the "Boys" were innocent. In Birmingham, Alabama, an integrated committee formed to support them. Members included the president of the local NAACP, a sociology professor, a rabbi from Montgomery and a Presbyterian pastor who chaired the Alabama Interracial Commission. More than 500 blacks and about fifty whites attended a meeting in a church where they spoke. But the initiative went nowhere.

Some of the committee's members suffered as a result of their modest foray into activism. The sociology professor lost his teaching job. The rabbi was forced to resign by his congregation. After receiving threatening telephone calls, he moved to New York. The mayor of Montgomery already had threatened to indict him under the city's new criminal anarchy ordinance, which banned the dissemination of "subversive doctrines" by "word, sign or writing."

It was difficult, even for members of the white elite, to exercise free-speech rights in the South during this period. Mrs. Craik Speed and her daughter Jane were descendants of the founder of Montgomery's First National Bank and Daughters of the American Revolution. They made the mistake of publicly expressing support for the Scottsboro Boys. Jane Speed addressed a united front meeting in Birmingham and was arrested, fined fifty dollars and sentenced to 100 days in jail for disorderly conduct, speaking without a permit, blocking the sidewalk and "addressing a meeting at which there were no physical barriers erected between white and Negro auditors." Released after 53 days in jail, she and her mother moved out of the state.

Meanwhile, vigilante groups in Alabama terrorized black communities and raided homes and meetings, looking for ILD activists. A wave of lynchings took place in Alabama, Georgia, California, Maryland and Missouri, reminding blacks that they could never feel completely safe anywhere.

The NAACP and the ILD continued to argue over strategies and money. An ILD staff member made a speech in which he said that the NAACP "played a reactionary role and practically sided with the legal lynch system of the South." Roy Wilkins, the NAACP's assistant secretary, wrote to Joseph Brodsky: "This is the kind of thing that prevents us from rallying our members wholeheartedly in support of the defense. It is difficult for our members to understand the psychology, to say nothing of the good manners, of an organization which can accept their gifts and then turn around and kick them in the face."

After ILD lawyers tried unsuccessfully to bribe Victoria Price in mid-1934, both Samuel Liebowitz and the NAACP made their dissatisfaction with the Communists public in *The New York Times*. The ILD fired Liebowitz, who set up the American Scottsboro Committee, which lasted for about a year. Liebowitz returned to the case when it went before the U.S. Supreme Court, and the feuding factions suspended hostilities until the *Norris* decision came down in April 1935.

FROM CONFLICT TO COMPROMISE

During the rest of that year, relations among the ILD, NAACP and Liebowitz deteriorated. Finally, thanks to the mediation of Socialist leader Norman Thomas, the ILD and the NAACP agreed to meet with other organizations, including the American Civil Liberties Union, the American Scottsboro Committee and the League for Industrial Democracy, to discuss collaboration. In December 1935 the Scottsboro Defense Committee formed. Its executive committee was composed of representatives from eight political and religious organizations. Decisions would be made by consensus, to prevent the ILD from seizing control. The members selected as chair Rev. Allan Knight Chalmers, the thirty-eight-year-old Congregational pastor of the Broadway Tabernacle Church in New York City.

Chalmers was a conciliator, a quiet worker behind the scenes and a persistent and compassionate man. He saw his first task as helping establish a committee of white Alabamians who would seek to influence the governor and the public, promote the idea that the "Boys" were innocent and work locally for their release. This was a more difficult task than he had anticipated. The moderate southerners he contacted did not want to say the "Boys" were innocent. They were only willing to call for fair trials and clemency. They did not even want the existence of the committee to be publicized. They demanded that Liebowitz be removed from the case in exchange for forming local committees, finding local lawyers to defend the "Boys" and conducting public relations initiatives in Alabama. Their Alabama Scottsboro Fair Trial Committee seems to have done little. In later years, Chalmers graciously gave them much of the credit for his own efforts.

Chalmers did receive substantial help from two newspaper editors, Grover Hall of the *Montgomery Advertiser* and James Chappell of the *Birmingham News*. Time and again over the years, they met with the governor, his aides and the parole board in mostly futile attempts to secure the "Boys'" release or pardon. Their continuing pressure helped create a climate in which secret negotiations between state officials and the defense could take place in 1936-37.

While they bargained, Clarence Norris was retried, reconvicted and resentenced to death. The prosecutor asked the jury for "a death sentence that could be written in golden letters across the Alabama sky to discourage outsiders from meddling in Alabama's affairs."

The attorney general offered Liebowitz a deal he found profoundly distasteful but better than nothing. Four of the "Boys"—Roy Wright, Eugene Williams, Olen Montgomery and Willie Roberson, who had been too young or too physically impaired to be convincingly accused of rape—would be released after charges were dropped. They had spent more than six years of their youth behind bars. Alabama officials insisted that the "Boys" leave the state but not be taken to New York. The other five were to have their sentences reduced, but the authorities reneged on that part of the bargain. In an editorial supporting the deal, Grover Hall wrote that Alabama "had been vilified and denounced in every civilized country of the world. The good name of the state was worth far more than the honor of two 'hookwormy Magdalenes.'" His editorial was reprinted in at least six Alabama newspapers, and the *Birmingham Post* said the evidence was overwhelming that the "Boys" were not guilty.

The New York Times echoed Liebowitz' protest that either all the "Boys" were guilty or none was, but public opinion in Alabama continued to support the convictions. Chalmers, away in Europe at the time, could not understand how Liebowitz could have made such a deal. He redoubled his efforts to secure the release of Patterson, Norris, Weems and Andy Wright. Ozzie Powell could not be helped because he had attacked a deputy sheriff and been sentenced to twenty years for that crime.

Chalmers wrote to a supporter, "I was convinced that the case would never be solved by further agitation, and that quiet and persistent negotiations would be needed if the case ever was to be brought to a favorable solution." He and Hall visited the governor, who agreed that the state's position was untenable but refused to take any action as long as legal appeals were pending. By mid-1938, all appeals had failed, and the governor commuted Norris' sentence to life imprisonment. He promised Chalmers that he would pardon Norris, Patterson, Weems and Wright—and then reneged. Chalmers asked President Roosevelt to have a quiet word with the governor. Roosevelt invited him to a meeting at his retreat in Georgia, but the governor failed to appear. His backers had threatened to end his political career if he pardoned the "Boys." That threat was more important to him than anything the President could say.

THE END OF THE CAMPAIGN

Chalmers exposed the governor's treachery in a pamphlet, "Scottsboro, A Record of a Broken Promise." He then turned his attention to the Alabama Board of Pardon and Parole. The case disappeared from the newspapers; donations dropped precipitously. The public campaign ended, and Chalmers carried on the work of the Scottsboro Defense Committee essentially alone.

With astonishing mildness, Clarence Norris remembered: "As the years rocked around, the letters slowed down to a trickle compared to the earlier years. So much time passed, I guess people forgot about us or went on to other things." Chalmers continued writing to the young men (who were becoming middle-aged as the years in prison stretched to more than a decade). Twice a year he visited them. By 1945, Haywood Patterson was calling himself "three parts dead" and describing "the torture of my daily life" in his letters to Chalmers.

In the mid-1940s, four of the five men were finally paroled, but the conditions of their release amounted to servitude. Norris broke parole and fled Alabama in 1946. Chalmers received an apologetic letter from him and replied that he could understand his flight after what Norris had suffered. Haywood Patterson, the toughest and most resourceful of the men, escaped from prison in 1948. Andy Wright, the last Scottsboro defendant to be released, left prison in June 1950, more than nineteen years after his arrest.

Also in June 1950, I.F. Stone, who would later become famous as an investigative journalist, published a series of articles about the Scottsboro case in a small Pennsylvania newspaper. He had met Haywood Patterson, encouraged him to write about his experiences and helped him find a publisher for his prison memoir, *Scottsboro Boy*. "Fugitive's Book Tells of Nazi-Like Horror Camps in Southland, USA," read the headline of one of Stone's stories. With some justice, Stone compared Patterson to an escaped slave. At the end of the series, Stone suggested the formation of a national committee to secure pardons for Norris, Andy Wright and Patterson. He apparently had no idea that such a committee had already existed for more than a dozen years.

At about this time, Roy Wilkins wrote to Allan Knight Chalmers, "When it came to the delicate, often frustrating, and year-to-year persistence toward the objective, all the others dropped away leaving you to carry on alone."

THE MEANING OF SCOTTSBORO

In December 1950, Patterson was charged with murder after a barroom brawl in Detroit. Convicted of manslaughter, he died of cancer in prison less than a year later. In his book, published not long before his death, he assessed the meaning of his long ordeal. After his escape from prison in 1948, he wrote:

> I saw a few of the people who had helped me in the past. Those people, and others who fought for me, I am grateful to them. To all who helped in the courts, wrote letters, sent money, picketed and marched and died for us boys. They helped me, helped the country, helped my people. I guess my people gained more off the Scottsboro case than any of us boys did. It led to putting Negroes on juries in the South. It made the whole country, in fact the whole world, talk about how the Negro people have to live in the South. Maybe that was the biggest thing of all. Our case opened up a lot of politics in the country. People said more about lynching, the poll tax, and a black man's rights from then on.

In 1955 a terrible crime occurred that reminded many people of the Scottsboro case. A fourteen-year-old black boy from Chicago named Emmett Till had the temerity to whistle at a white woman in a grocery store in rural Mississippi. For this he was abducted, tortured, killed and thrown in the Tallahatchie River. Two white men were charged with his murder. Although Till's great-uncle showed incredible courage in identifying them as the boy's abductors, they were acquitted. In Chicago, Till's mother insisted that a photograph of her son's battered body be published in *Jet*, a popular black magazine. According to Paul Hendrickson, this picture "helped awaken a generation of future young black activists to what would soon, in the next decade, be called the Movement." Three months later, Rosa Parks (an activist in the Scottsboro campaign during the 1930s) ignited the civil rights struggle by refusing to give up her seat in the whites-only section of a city bus in Montgomery, Alabama. She later said that Emmett Till's fate had moved her to action.

In New York City, Clarence Norris lived quietly until the late 1960s, when he decided to find out what his status was in Alabama. The NAACP made inquiries on his behalf to the pardon and parole board, which insisted he return to prison because he had broken his parole by leaving the state in 1946. Norris was in his sixties, steadily employed, with a family, and had no intention of going back to prison for a crime he had not committed. The NAACP contacted the governor of Alabama, George Wallace, and told *The New York Times*, which published a story about Norris. *The Washington Post* published an editorial calling for his pardon, the national media reported the story, and New York politicians expressed their support for him. Even so, the parole board continued to insist that Norris surrender to Alabama authorities.

After several meetings between NAACP lawyers and Alabama officials, "the pressure of adverse public opinion was brought to bear on the governor's office," Norris wrote. The assistant attorney general of Alabama, who was black, recommended a pardon on the grounds that Norris was clearly innocent.

After thirty years as a fugitive, Clarence Norris returned to Alabama to receive a pardon from the hands of Gov. George Wallace in 1976. But this was not the end of the Scottsboro story. In the early 1980s, Victoria Price brought suit against NBC-TV for broadcasting a documentary about the Scottsboro case in which she was portrayed as a liar. She settled for an unspecified amount and died in 1983, insisting to the end, despite overwhelming evidence to the contrary, that she had been raped by the Scottsboro Boys in 1931.

Allan Knight Chalmers, the unsung hero of the story, taught theology at Boston University from 1948 to 1963. He was national treasurer of the NAACP from 1948 to 1957 and president of the NAACP Legal Defense and Education Fund from 1962 to 1972. In the mid-1960s he was still writing occasional letters to one or another Scottsboro Boy. He published five books, including one about the Scottsboro case. His biography of antislavery campaigner William Wilberforce, to which he devoted many years, was never published. Among his papers at Boston University is a reproduction of Thomas Clarkson's slave ship diagram, which had inspired so many early activists.

CAMPAIGNING IN THE MODERN WORLD

The world in which the Scottsboro case unfolded was very different from the one in which earlier campaigns had taken place. Communications were many times more rapid and efficient. During the 1930s, radio became an important medium with a mass audience. "In 1936, a market research firm that studied 53,000 households in sixteen cities found that ninety-one percent of Americans owned radios, compared with fewer than twenty percent nine years earlier," Strasser noted.

Via a radio report, the Communist Party found out about the "Boys'" arrests the day they happened. Party functionaries informed the ILD by telephone, and representatives of the organization arrived on the scene within a few days. The black press reported the trials, and people across the country immediately responded to the verdicts and death sentences with letters and telegrams. It was this spontaneous public response that pushed organizations to get involved in the case. The Communists expeditiously informed their European comrades, who organized a rapid response, both within Europe and to the United States, via telegrams, letters, postcards, petitions and meetings.

In contrast, the NAACP was slow to react and entered the case only under continuing pressure from its members. The NAACP's field secretary at first insisted that "these Scottsboro cases are not political cases." At the same time, Walter White wrote, "We never try any of our cases in the newspapers." As the organization started to clash with the ILD, he saw two options for the NAACP: either drop out of the case and say why publicly, or "get absolute control of the cases." He chose the latter. But the Communists were much more skillful at gutter fighting and did not hesitate to lie, misrepresent, deceive or distort to gain their revolutionary objectives. Nor could the NAACP outdo them in organization and mobilization, not only in the U.S. but internationally.

Nevertheless, the Communist Party operated at a great disadvantage in the United States. In Europe, Communists constituted a formidable political force with a mass following of millions, their own newspapers and elected representatives in multiparty systems. But in the U.S. they were relatively few in numbers, hated and reviled, especially in the South. Although the U.S. Communist Party grew impressively during the 1930s (from 7,500 members in 1930 to 75,000 in 1939), it did not become respectable or popular. After a taste of its military-style discipline and unending meetings, almost as many left the party as joined it.

Few if any American Communists managed to get elected on any level of government. In the 1932 national elections, the Communist presidential candidate received 102,221 votes, while Norman Thomas, the Socialist candidate, received 883,990 votes. Although they exerted considerable influence on intellectuals, students and minority groups, the Communists never managed to establish a mass movement in the United States.

Left-wing and progressive organizations in the U.S. were suspicious of Communists and resented their attempts to control any movement in which they were involved. White's reaction to Communist tactics, in a letter to NAACP officers, typified their sentiments:

> It is patent that the Communists are far more interested in making Communist propaganda out of the Scottsboro cases than they are in saving the lives of the boys. It is equally patent that it is their plan to try to destroy or to discredit every organization or individual which does not submit to Communist dictation. Their official organs have been filled with a number of statements which are nothing but lies in their efforts to harm the NAACP.

It could be argued that the ILD did not want to destroy the NAACP, but rather to use and control it, since the Communists relied on non-Communists to raise sufficient funds for the Scottsboro defense. People who wanted to contribute to the defense but did not want to send money to Communists considered the NAACP a reliable recipient. And according to Walter White, the ILD saw the NAACP as a rival at a time when both organizations were seeking support from the American Fund for Public Service, one of a few foundations that funded progressive groups. This alone would have made for a tense, ambivalent relationship of competition and collaboration.

The Communists could quickly mobilize thousands to sign petitions and send telegrams and letters, but their capacity to keep campaigns going over time was limited. They wielded the greatest influence by wooing non-Communists to collaborate in various causes. According to Howe and Coser, the student movement, which the Communists nurtured in the mid-1930s, became "a training ground for liberals, intellectuals and trade union leaders" for the next thirty years.

Before the Communists decided to cooperate with other groups via the united front in the mid-1930s, their tactics were extremely aggressive, and their rhetoric was more off-putting than persuasive. Alabama officials reacted with outrage to what they perceived as threats, insults and demands in thousands of telegrams that arrived between 1931 and 1937.

It was only when "respectable" (white) public opinion, as expressed in southern newspaper editorials and letters to the editor, raised doubts about the verdicts and sentences that state authorities found it necessary to bargain with the defense. Even then, they insisted on continuing the sacrifice of five lives, instead of the original nine, to the fetish of unsullied white southern womanhood. And it took about six years for Chalmers and his quiet allies to persuade the Alabama Pardon and Parole Board to begin releasing the remaining men.

Thirty years after Clarence Norris' escape to the North, Alabama authorities still resisted admitting that the men were innocent, until unwelcome media attention forced them to give way. By that time the world had changed so much that the high state official recommending a pardon was African-American.

Although the Scottsboro case engaged thousands of people around the world, it was one of many stories in the press and on the radio vying for the public's attention. In the 1930s, people lived in a world pervaded by propagandistic messages and images. The Great Depression made many people desperate, and they craved escape from the daily difficulties caused by worldwide economic catastrophe. In response, advertising sold not only products but also feelings such as sexual fulfillment, happiness, relief from anxiety, adjustment and peace of mind. Political advertising sold revenge, triumph, moral superiority and a sense of security. Election campaigns became marketing extravaganzas, replete with posters, buttons, bumper stickers, radio spots, sound trucks, motorcades, ticker-tape parades, whistle-stop speeches, campaign biographies, movie newsreels, autographed photos, photo opportunities (Calvin Coolidge milking a cow), full-page newspaper ads, torchlight processions, banquets and barbeques.

In contrast, causes like Scottsboro offered guilt, social concern, moral obligation, anxiety, indignation, compassion and danger, all of which were hard to sell to an uncertain, suffering world, moving from one great war to the next. People could focus on causes for only so long before, as Clarence Norris put it, they "went on to other things." In an era of shortening attention spans, campaigners had to find ways to gain the public's interest, commitment, support and courage for more than a few moments.

The ILD perceived that it would be necessary to develop an effective grassroots movement to ensure activists' continuing allegiance and involvement. In the 1937 annual report, its leaders discussed creating local solidarity groups through which ILD followers would have opportunities to work on particular cases in which they were interested. From its relief department in New York, the organization was already providing financial and other assistance to political prisoners and victims' families and sending cards and letters to prisoners in the United States and other countries. Local ILD groups existed; why not turn them into volunteer organizations? There was a proposal to use the radio to advance their work. But the ILD did not have the human or financial resources (or the democratic mentality or framework) to realize these ideas. They came to fruition more than twenty years later with the founding of Amnesty International.

EFFECTS OF THE SCOTTSBORO CAMPAIGN

The Scottsboro case did nothing to resolve vexing questions about the effectiveness of mass campaigning. In the face of the determined, even violent recalcitrance of government officials and citizens ready to defend their racist ideology to the death, even the most persistent, vocal and widespread campaign seemed destined to have little effect, except to stiffen that resistance. As in the Sacco and Vanzetti case, the forces of hatred and prejudice were very strong. The state possessed the power and legitimacy to enforce the reigning ideology through legal repression and violence. Those who wanted to save the Scottsboro Boys or use their case to challenge the dominion of the state were in a terribly weak position. Neither direct action nor force of numbers could overcome the state and its backers.

Allan Knight Chalmers seemed to understand this when he decided to try to influence and persuade, rather than confront, Alabama authorities, using local interlocutors who worked behind the scenes. As Chalmers said, it was a long and painful process, and it was only partly successful. The Scottsboro Boys endured considerable suffering as a result. The State of Alabama ruined their lives.

Scottsboro was a battle for which the time was not yet ripe. The campaign fell into an established pattern of trying to rescue the helpless, rather than mobilizing people who could fight for their own rights. That would happen twenty years later, when Rosa Parks refused to go to the back of the bus. But by bringing issues of racial discrimination to the fore through litigation and agitation, groups like the ILD, the NAACP and the Scottsboro Defense Committee helped prepare the ground for the larger grassroots struggles to come.

"We Have Not Forgotten the Rosenbergs, Killed by Yankee Imperialism Because They Struggled and Died for Peace. We Demand Justice for Morton Sobell, Who Was Abducted in Mexico, Unjustly Convicted with the Rosenbergs and Sentenced to 30 Years in Prison"

Chapter 8

THE ROSENBERGS:
SACRIFICING THE SCAPEGOATS

*And he shall take the two goats, and present them before the Lord at the door
of the tabernacle of the congregation.
And Aaron shall bring the goat upon which the Lord's lot fell, and offer him
for a sin offering.
But the goat, on which the lot fell to be the scapegoat, shall be presented alive
before the Lord, to make an atonement with him, and to let him go for a scapegoat into the wilderness.
. . . Then shall he kill the goat of the sin offering, that is for the people, and
bring his blood within the vail . . . and sprinkle it upon the mercy seat, and
before the mercy seat:
And he shall make an atonement for the holy place, because of the unclean-
ness of the children of Israel, and because of their transgressions in all
their sins. . . .* (Leviticus 16: 7-16)

Physicist Robert Oppenheimer hauntingly quoted the Bhagavad Gita
as he watched the first atom bomb explosion over New Mexico, "I
am become death, destroyer of worlds." After the spectacular end
of the Second World War at Hiroshima and Nagasaki, with Europe in
ruins and the old empires broken, the United States became the world's
most powerful nation, with the world's most devastating weapon under
its sole control.

Convinced that its former ally and emerging rival, the Soviet Union, did
not have the capacity to develop atomic bombs, the U.S. basked for a time
in its nuclear monopoly. Scientists predicted, however, that the Soviet
Union would explode its own atomic bomb within four or five years. Nevertheless, politicians professed shock when the Soviets detonated an atomic
bomb in 1949. Somebody must have stolen the secret, they said. In vain
the scientists insisted that there was no secret.

During the late 1940s, tensions between East and West increased in
Berlin, Eastern Europe, Asia and elsewhere. Winston Churchill gave his
famous "Iron Curtain" speech, and the Cold War was launched. Anti-
Communism became official U.S. policy, inside as well as outside the United
States. Accordingly, President Harry Truman instituted a "federal loyalty

program" in 1947 to oust alleged Communists from government positions. In 1950 the Korean War, which started as a civil war but soon involved Communist China and the United States, exploded. Many believed war between the U.S. and the Soviet Union was imminent. They feared an atomic war, World War III.

"FIVE MINUTES TO MIDNIGHT"

A miasma of paranoia swirled around the United States. Nora Sayre wrote:

> By the beginning of the Fifties many Americans were afraid of one another: the Right feared the Left, the Left feared the Right, and the apolitical feared contact with either side. People of conflicting views felt they were living through a terribly dangerous time. Some on the Left thought fascism could soon be realized in the United States, whereas segments of the Right thought that American Communists would undermine their society, while the Soviet Union would gain control of the globe.

In response to the panic lurking under the calm and prosperous surface of American life, the U.S. Congress passed the Internal Security Act of 1950, also known as the McCarran Act. It provided, among other things, for detention of "dangerous" citizens during an "internal security emergency" or war. By 1954, the FBI had placed the names of 26,174 individuals on its "Security Index," a detention list, which included at least one U.S. senator as a result of his support for the NAACP.

Communists and non-Communist leftists found themselves marginalized, even demonized. They were purged from unions, fired from jobs, placed under surveillance, harassed, threatened, denounced, subpoenaed and indicted for their alleged beliefs. In 1951, eleven Communist Party leaders were sentenced under the Smith Act to five years in prison for *advocating* (not planning) the overthrow of the U.S. government. According to Sayre:

> many on the Left thought they could end up in the internment camps which had been filled with Japanese Americans during the war. The phrase was 'five minutes to midnight'; meaning that fascism was looming, that it might soon be time to leave the country or to live in hiding. Two decades later some discovered through the Freedom of Information Act that they had indeed been on the Security Index: their forebodings had not been irrational after all.

A member of the House of Representatives' Un-American Activities Committee said, "It's a lot better to wrongly accuse one person of being a Communist than to allow so many to get away with such Communist acts as those that have brought us to the brink of World War III."

Anyone who was different risked denunciation. For example, the FBI tracked suspected homosexuals, thought to be susceptible to blackmail and therefore "security risks." In 1953 President Eisenhower signed an executive order legalizing exclusion of homosexuals from government posts. More than 400 employees were discharged from the State Department for their "homosexual proclivities."

African-Americans who criticized U.S. racism while overseas were accused of being Communists. Thus singer and actor Paul Robeson was denied a passport and blacklisted because of his outspokenness while on tour outside the U.S.. In 1951, the federal government accused eighty-three-year-old W.E.B. Du Bois, one of the founders of the NAACP, of being an "unregistered foreign agent" of an unspecified country and put him on trial. The judge dismissed the case for lack of evidence. The NAACP already had expelled Du Bois for his increasing radicalism and his support of Progressive Party candidate Henry Wallace in the 1948 presidential election.

Leftists were denounced not only for recent activities but also for petitions they had signed, meetings they had attended or donations they had made ten to twenty years earlier. The FBI carried out a number of "black bag jobs" (burglaries) of left-wing organizations to photograph their membership lists. The government later used the information gathered in this way to prosecute people for their political activities or to pressure their employers to fire them. The FBI even kept files on contributors and subscribers to left-wing periodicals, such as *The Nation* and *The Progressive*, for decades. Numerous informers provided the FBI with uncorroborated rumors, gossip and slanders about coworkers, neighbors and relatives.

Then there was Senator Joe McCarthy, whose highly publicized crusade against Communists brought him considerable fame and power from 1950 to 1954. McCarthy did not create the anti-Communist juggernaut, but he cleverly used it to advance his political career. His red-baiting tactics influenced many others on all levels of government across the United States. The press seldom challenged or criticized him and his followers.

Organizations that had sought to protect the civil rights of radicals after the First World War remained silent during the 1950s. The American Civil Liberties Union refused to defend Communists in court from 1951 to 1959. Some ACLU officials, including the president, Roger Baldwin, denounced their own colleagues for daring to criticize the FBI. Non-Communist activists, such as Gardner Jackson, worked to expel Communists from the labor movement and the nonprofit sector. New organizations like *Counterattack* and Aware, Inc., sprang up to publish blacklists of suspected Communists or "fellow travelers." Mass communications companies, including CBS, created loyalty oaths, which employees were forced to sign until the mid-1960s.

In this repressive climate, "It was not acceptable to admit to being Communists and attempt to convince the American people that Communists still deserved the protections of the Constitution and the presumption that one is innocent until proven guilty," observed Michael Meeropol, son of Julius and Ethel Rosenberg.

ENTER THE ROSENBERGS

In 1950 the Rosenbergs were an obscure couple in their mid-thirties. They lived not far from where they had grown up, children of poor Jewish immigrants from Eastern Europe, on New York City's Lower East Side. Parents of two sons, ages three and seven, they were not prospering. Having lost his job with the Army Signal Corps because of his alleged membership in the Communist Party, Julius Rosenberg struggled to make a living as an engineer, while his wife, Ethel, struggled to raise two rambunctious children in difficult circumstances. In mid-1950 Julius was trying to close an unsuccessful machine shop he had run in partnership with friends and relatives. His conflicts with one of his partners, his brother-in-law, David Greenglass, were complicated and vexing.

Three weeks after the beginning of the Korean War, on July 17, 1950, Julius Rosenberg was arrested and charged with conspiring to commit espionage during World War II on behalf of the Soviet Union. On August 11, Ethel Rosenberg was arrested for the same offense. A friend of Julius, Morton Sobell, also was charged with conspiring to commit espionage. The principal witness against them was Ethel's brother, David Greenglass, who had worked at the atomic bomb research establishment in Los Alamos, New Mexico, during World War II. The Rosenbergs, Sobell and Greenglass were all found guilty. Julius and Ethel Rosenberg were sentenced to death, Sobell to thirty years and Greenglass to fifteen years in prison.

For fifty years, people have been arguing whether Julius and Ethel Rosenberg were guilty of conspiracy to commit espionage. Numerous books have been published on all sides of the question. In 1993, the American Bar Association's Litigation Section staged a mock trial of the Rosenbergs, and the jury found them not guilty. Since then, former Soviet intelligence agents and interpreters of decoded KGB dispatches have claimed that Julius Rosenberg was a spy but Ethel Rosenberg was not. Depending on their political convictions, scholars and journalists have accepted or rejected this alleged evidence. The dispute may never be satisfactorily resolved. The purpose here is not to enter into the argument over guilt or innocence, but rather to tell the story of the campaign to save the Rosenbergs, determine its significance and analyze its consequences.

WHO WERE THEY?

Both Julius and Ethel Rosenberg had been involved in left-wing political activities since they were teenagers. In an autobiographical statement, Julius recalled participating in the campaign to free the Scottsboro Boys when he was sixteen, in 1933. He referred to Eugene V. Debs, Joe Hill and Sacco and Vanzetti as "innocent men put to death because they were anarchist in times of great labor unrest. The Tom Mooney Scottsboro Boys cases went on for years until final vindication was won for these men."

A modestly talented singer and actor, Ethel Greenglass Rosenberg performed at many events sponsored by the Communist Party or its front groups during the 1930s. She first met Julius at one such event, a benefit concert for the International Seamen's Union, in 1936. Both were steeped in the left-wing culture, ideology and discourse of the era. Later, when they found themselves fighting for their lives against the most powerful enemy in the world, the U.S. government, they interpreted their situation in light of their upbringing, deeply held beliefs and experience. For Julius:

> The lessons of history are very clear: certain powerful entrenched interests needed scapegoats to use as a weapon against those who threatened their positions of power and economic wealth in any way. These movements also started from the grass roots with few supporters and all the power of the newspapers, state, business and so-called respectable organizations were against them. But the people were not dismayed for their cause was just. Where they were able to rally the public and develop a widespread mass campaign they met with success.

When Julius was subjected to government "loyalty" investigations during World War II, he denied being a member of the Communist Party. To the end of their lives, both he and Ethel refused to say they were Communists. This denial helped seal their doom. It also made campaigning on their behalf very difficult, for non-Communists as well as Communists. Considering the ferocity of the American anti-Communist crusade, it would have been hard to save them in any event.

For more than a year after the Rosenbergs' arrest, trial and conviction, the Communist Party ignored their case. Their son, Michael Meeropol, believed the party kept silent for practical reasons:

> The left had been successfully marginalized by the defeat of former Vice-President Henry Wallace and the Progressive party in the 1948 election, the purging from unions of alleged Communist influence, the beginning of the Korean War, and the indictment of the Communist Party under the Smith Act. The Communist and fel-

low-traveling left did not respond to the case. They made a tactical decision to defend the right of the Communist Party to function as a legal political party by attempting to win the Smith Act cases. They also focused on the rights of individuals to refuse to answer questions about their political associations when called by Congressional committees. They chose not to associate themselves with the defense of people accused of espionage.

Cedric Belfrage and James Aronson, who lived through the period as adults, interpreted the Left's silence differently: "Anyone defending Ethel and Julius and Morton [Sobell] was automatically a Moscow agent or tool. . . .The curtain of fear was so dense over America that not one voice was raised."

In his sentencing speech, Judge Irving Kaufman went so far as to blame the Rosenbergs for the Korean War.

> In terms of human life, these defendants have affected the lives, and perhaps the freedom, of whole generations of mankind. . . . I consider your crime worse than murder. . . . I believe your conduct in putting into the hands of the Russians the A-bomb years before our best scientists predicted Russia would perfect the bomb has already caused, in my opinion, the Communist aggression in Korea, with the resultant casualties exceeding 50,000 and who knows but that millions more of innocent people may pay the price of your treason. Indeed, by your betrayal you undoubtedly have altered the course of history to the disadvantage of your country.

Many Americans believed this accusation amply justified a double death sentence, not for "conspiring to commit espionage," of which they had been convicted, but for treason.

Desperate for favorable coverage during the appeal process, the Rosenbergs' lawyer, Emanuel Bloch, begged the Communist Party newspaper, *The Daily Worker*, to write about the case. The editor refused, saying he did not have permission from the Central Committee. Bloch recalled:

> I remember very well those first grim days in March 1951, following the trial and sentencing, when every avenue of information and publicity suddenly closed. . . . a conspiracy of silence settled on the press. Our great newspapers which, during the trial, had seized eagerly upon every propaganda release of the prosecution, closed their pages to all news about the victims. From the government's point of view, and from the point of view of its ally, the press, the Rosenbergs were as good as dead.

The Communist Party did speak out against the death sentence in its West Coast newspaper, but it did not call for any protest or say the Rosenbergs were innocent.

Bloch then went to the editors of *The National Guardian*, a weekly, independent, left-wing newspaper that had started during the 1948 presidential campaign as an organ of the Progressive Party. The *Guardian* decided to take on the case and assigned one of its contributors, William Reuben, to cover it. Using the trial record as his principal source, Reuben concluded the Rosenbergs were victims of a government frame-up. In August 1951 the first of seven articles by Reuben on the case appeared in the *Guardian*. It was called "The Rosenberg Conviction—Is This the Dreyfus Case of Cold War America?"

Reuben was the first—perhaps the only—American journalist to portray the Rosenbergs as innocent. His articles made a great impact, not only on the *Guardian's* 75,000 readers but also on the Rosenbergs themselves, who took heart from Reuben's sympathetic coverage and began describing themselves as "the first victims of American fascism."

Nearly fifty years later Reuben described the reaction to his articles:

> Readers all over the United States wrote in response, enclosing one, two, five and ten dollar bills that amounted to close to $3,000 as contributions 'to the committee.' No such committee then existed. We created it in my Manhattan apartment in October 1951, six months after the end of the trial. We used the contributions to publish the trial record and my *Guardian* articles in pamphlet form.

Reuben and several friends founded the carefully named National Committee to Secure Justice in the Rosenberg Case. Reuben recalled "a lot of discussion" about the name, because the committee wanted to "attract people opposed to the death penalty or putting a woman with two small children to death and people who thought it was a frame-up." Members included Emily Alman and her husband, David Alman, an organizer who had worked with Communist front organizations, including the Civil Rights Congress and the American Peace Crusade; writers Yuri Suhl and Joseph Brainin; Gene Weltfish, an anthropologist at Columbia University; Louis Harrap, a journalist, and B.Z. Goldberg, a Zionist activist. Reuben suggested that the committee invite Helen Sobell, Morton Sobell's wife, who later became "one of the mainstays of the group and its most effective public speaker," Radosh and Milton write.

In late 1951 the committee placed its first public appeal in the *Guardian*. Signers of later appeals included well-known leftist intellectuals such as Waldo Frank, W.E.B. Du Bois, Herbert Aptheker and Nelson Algren. David and Emily Alman did most of the committee's work as paid staff mem-

bers. David Alman later said, "Emily was the brains and I was the organizer."

According to Radosh and Milton, committee members were

> mavericks, not orthodox Communists. . . . the group was only too
> eager to accept support from all shades of the political spectrum:
> civil libertarians, opponents of the death penalty, Jewish organi-
> zations and so on. Potential supporters were not necessarily expected
> to be convinced of the Rosenbergs' innocence as long as they were
> willing to join in the call for a retrial.

David Alman went to the Communist Party to solicit support and was
told that the Rosenbergs were "expendable." With the Smith Act defendants in prison, the party was expecting war to break out between the U.S.
and the Soviet Union and was making preparations to go underground.
Under such dire circumstances, perhaps Communist leaders judged the
Rosenbergs to be unimportant; defending them would only jeopardize
the party.

Nor was Bloch encouraging. He told Emily Alman "that there was really
not much that could be done at this late stage."

The Rosenbergs interpreted the committee's efforts as proof of the validity of their worldview. In January 1952, Julius wrote to Ethel:

> From all sides we hear of new support. The ball is really rolling
> now. More and more people are joining the committee, contributing
> funds, writing letters and increasing thousands of people are being
> made aware of the facts in our case and its nature. . . . there is a
> tremendous wealth of good people who will campaign for right
> and justice when they are aware of the truth. We can feel proud
> that our faith in the American people has borne fruit so soon and
> this is the guarantee of our eventual freedom and complete vin-
> dication.

To say the least, this was an excessively optimistic view of the extent of
public support and the couple's prospects for survival.

For a year the committee struggled to gain public attention and support.
Its first rally had to be canceled because the committee could not find anyone who would rent them a hall in New York City, and a rally held in Far
Rockaway, New York, in April 1952 drew only eighty-five people. On the
other hand, in late 1951 and early 1952, William Reuben and David
Alman had some success traveling across the country, making speeches
and collecting funds. Local committees started forming in several eastern
and midwestern cities, both before and after these tours.

When Reuben returned to New York from his speaking tour, he later
recalled, "I don't know how it happened, but suddenly, I was no longer

part of the committee." In the mid-1980s Reuben told an interviewer he believed that the FBI had infiltrated the committee and worked systematically to blunt its effectiveness. Emily Alman acknowledged that FBI informants might have joined the committee but insisted she was not concerned about this: "We had nothing to hide." Many years later she did research in FBI files on the case and discovered that the government had kept her and her family under surveillance and listed them on the "Security Index" for detention in case of a national emergency.

The Almans stressed that their organizing strategy was "not to organize the opposition." That is, they tailored their speeches and publications to groups they judged persuadable, not to those who seemed prejudiced against the Rosenbergs, and they used unconventional approaches. For example, they would cite the pope to Jews, rabbis to Catholics, Albert Einstein to factory workers. David Alman also looked for conservative or apolitical supporters and managed to find a few.

The national committee compiled a mailing list of about 50,000 names— 20,000 in the New York City area and the rest in other parts of the United States. Emily Alman, the committee's treasurer, recalled raising about $300,000 in less than two years.

The committee recognized the necessity to reach a broader American public by using up-to-date media techniques. Some of the members were communications professionals who understood how businesses and political parties employed public relations and advertising to accomplish their goals.

Public-service advertising was a highly developed and sophisticated means of information dissemination in the 1950s. For example, with the help of public relations expert Edward Bernays, the Mack Truck Company campaigned vigorously for federal funding of interstate highways in 1949-50. Bernays organized press conferences, targeted sectors of industry and the public for direct mailings, arranged speaking tours by Mack executives and employees, and set up front groups and state associations to campaign on the local level. The campaign convinced the U.S. Army Chief of Staff that "trucks were essential for warfare in the dawning atomic age. . . . Congress in 1950 approved $566 million in road building funds," Larry Tye wrote.

With such campaigns featured in mass-circulation periodicals, on radio and television, the Rosenberg committee sought to imitate their methods by gaining coverage and advertising space in the media. Although the *Guardian* published their press releases, advertisements and appeals, many newspapers and radio and television stations refused to accept them. Occasionally during his travels on behalf of the committee, David Alman said, a local newspaper or radio station would interview him. But the mainstream publications that covered the Rosenberg case as it progressed through the appeals courts printed only the government's version of events, along with fiercely negative depictions of the couple in columns, cartoons and editorials.

"J. Edgar Hoover and [prosecutor] Irving Saypol provided the press with a vastly simplified, neatly packaged media frame. . . . Thrown into the bargain was cold-war Americanism and the vibrant secular religion of anti-Communism," John Neville wrote. Although the Rosenbergs had been convicted of conspiracy to commit espionage, the press usually said they had been convicted of treason. Reporters and commentators failed to mention that the Soviet Union had been a U.S. ally when the Rosenbergs allegedly passed secret information to Soviet agents. The media also portrayed the Rosenbergs as unnatural parents, echoing Judge Kaufman, who had condemned them for sacrificing their own children to an alien ideology. The committee struggled against overwhelming odds to replace these harsh images with more benign ones.

GRASSROOTS EFFORTS

A report in the committee archives on the "Midwest Conference on the Rosenberg Case," held in Chicago in August 1952, gives considerable information on the progress and nature of the campaign in the United States. About 300 people had attended a public meeting the night before and contributed almost $700. Some thirty-five people attended the conference, twenty-one from Chicago, the rest from other cities. Seven were black. Unions, front groups, community organizations and religious groups were represented. Delegates planned campaign strategy, suggesting the organization of events, publication of pamphlets and outreach to unions, Jewish organizations, the black community and other groups. The national committee reported that it had published some 400,000 pieces of literature, including pamphlets, fact sheets, letters, the trial record and reprints. In ten months the committee had raised about $50,000 at public meetings, private meetings, through literature sales and in the mail. Expenditures totaled about $59,000.

Delegates discussed difficulties in gaining union support, involving blacks and handling the issue of anti-Semitism. "Because of the general atmosphere," the report noted, "many people were afraid to join [Rosenberg] committees." They debated pressing for a new trial versus campaigning for clemency. A representative from Los Angeles described how the local committee there had come into existence. After great difficulties, the committee finally had begun functioning, and "from there on it was just plug away. Call, contact, visit, mail." Twenty-five to thirty-five people in Los Angeles had distributed thousands of pamphlets and other publications, collected donations, organized meetings and set up a small office.

A report issued in December 1952 by the Boston Committee to Secure Clemency in the Rosenberg Case tells similar stories of grassroots efforts:

> Malden's volunteers have completed their interviews, which included a successful appeal to a local Rabbi. As a result, the Rabbi will speak on the case from his pulpit and will act in concert with other religious leaders to help in obtaining clemency. The Malden people have also accomplished door-to-door distribution of our leaflets and will continue canvassing with the postcard.

Other groups in the Boston area were organizing mass meetings, lobbying local and state officials, placing advertisements in local newspapers, distributing leaflets to shipyard workers and asking pastors to sermonize about the case. "One member from Newton has even had occasion to talk about the Rosenberg case aboard the commuters' train to Boston," the report noted.

Despite these initiatives and the Rosenbergs' appreciation of the committee's efforts, national committee members never had the opportunity to consult with the couple about campaign strategy. Bloch would not allow them to visit the Rosenbergs in prison or communicate directly with the couple. Michael Meeropol explained: "The committee and Emanuel Bloch did not work well together. There were tremendous conflicts over strategy as well as outright distrust between them. . . . despite our parents' willingness to be very actively involved in their own defense, Emanuel Bloch did not credit their participation."

Julius tried to send instructions to the committee via Bloch. "It should be the duty of the Committee to organize and direct this movement into one containing political significance, for that is the only way to secure justice for us," he wrote in November 1952. He also asked Bloch to send him committee publications immediately and to "acquaint the committee with our plans to pursue with dispatch and vigor our next legal moves." He concluded with a request to Bloch to "please help explain our position. Note I am writing for both Ethel and myself and I want the committee to know they have our wholehearted support and I am positive we will be able to work in closer harmony."

Little more than a month before their execution, Julius wrote to the committee via Bloch: "The job that has to be done is clear. All that is required is to go to the people at the grass roots level and inform them of the issues involved—Ring door bells—Put literature in their hands—Hold mass meetings—Demonstrations in the streets, at factories, in public halls and even at the United Nations." Local branches and the national committee already had been doing this kind of work for a year.

THE CAMPAIGN TAKES OFF

When the Rosenbergs' appeal failed in the U.S. Supreme Court in late 1952, the story returned to the front page of major newspapers. Radosh and Milton write:

> Almost overnight, it seemed, the Committee was flooded with eager volunteers and the donations began pouring in. A rally in the New York theatre district sponsored by Paul Robeson, Ruby Dee and Rockwell Kent raised thousands of dollars. By Christmas, the New York City branch . . . was able to charter an eight-car train to carry demonstrators to Ossining, New York, for a show of moral support for Julius and Ethel.

About a thousand people demonstrated outside Sing Sing, where the Rosenbergs were incarcerated, on December 21, 1952.

At about the same time, the Communist Party decided to sponsor an international campaign on behalf of the Rosenbergs. Defense committees sprang up in London and Paris, and by the end of 1952, Austria, Belgium, Denmark, Italy, Sweden, Switzerland, Germany, Ireland, Israel and Eastern European countries had similar committees.

Depending on their ideological predisposition, historians of the case have advanced different explanations for the Communist Party's decision to get involved:

- The party believed the Rosenbergs would not embarrass it by confessing. They had shown they were "good soldiers."
- The Soviet Union hoped to deflect international attention from a show trial of Jewish former Communist leaders then taking place in Prague.
- Many people in countries where the party still had a mass following, such as France and Italy, were appalled by the death sentences and eager to campaign on the Rosenbergs' behalf.
- The party was making an opportunistic attempt to win the support of "a progressive, popular movement [that it could] address, control and win over to Communism," writes Ilene Philipson.

Whatever the reasons, the international campaign to save the Rosenbergs took flight at the end of 1952. Both non-Communist and Communist groups participated. As Emily Alman observed, the international campaign seemed to spread by "spontaneous combustion." According to Radosh and Milton, the case became

> a bigger issue in Europe than it was ever to be in the U.S. In France, in particular, it was practically impossible to pick up a newspaper or a magazine without finding an article sympathetic to the Rosen-

bergs. . . . France was blanketed with posters depicting a malevolently grinning Eisenhower with tiny electric chairs instead of teeth.

Especially for the French, parallels with the Dreyfus Affair were unmistakable. And Europeans of all political persuasions were shocked by the death sentences, which they regarded as barbaric. Clemency, rather than a new trial, became the overriding theme of the international campaign. Letters pleading for clemency from all over the world began pouring into Emanuel Bloch's office and the White House.

DEATH HOUSE LETTERS

For Julius and Ethel Rosenberg, letters were not only a private means of communication, they were also propaganda tools. During almost three years of incarceration, they wrote nearly 600 letters to each other, to family members, to Emanuel Bloch and to friends and strangers. The Rosenberg committee published advertisements in the *Guardian* and other periodicals under the headline, "A Mother Writes from the Death House," quoting from Ethel's letters and soliciting funds. The committee also published excerpts from Julius' and Ethel's correspondence in fact sheets and leaflets. With Julius' encouragement, Ethel worked hard on the letters, looking up words in dictionaries, reworking passages and asking Bloch to change wording before publication. "Ethel's impassioned literary style clearly was seen as a means of garnering support for the Rosenberg case," Philipson writes.

Bloch responded positively to the committee's suggestion that he publish a book of the couple's letters to raise funds for the defense and convince the public of their innocence. He set up a small publishing firm that published *Death House Letters* in June 1953. The letters were carefully selected and edited to portray the Rosenbergs as dedicated and idealistic progressives, devoted parents and innocent victims. Some readers have complained that the book reduces the couple to "relentless ideologues for whom all topics serve a political agenda." But others have recognized that "regardless of their rhetorical excesses, the Rosenbergs' published letters had a tremendous impact, both in America and abroad," Radosh and Milton write.

The committee also used photographs and letters of the Rosenbergs' sons, Michael and Robert, to generate sympathy for the family. Ten-year-old Michael was featured in the newspapers when he personally delivered a letter to the White House asking President Eisenhower to "please let my mommy and daddy go."

ATTACKERS AND DEFENDERS

The U.S. government had its own propaganda goals for the Rosenbergs. Under the Freedom of Information Act, the historian Blanche Wiesen Cook obtained a CIA memorandum dated January 22, 1953, suggesting that the Rosenbergs' death sentences could be commuted if they would

> appeal to Jews in all countries to get out of the Communist movement and seek to destroy it. . . . The couple is ideally situated to serve as leading instruments of a psychological warfare campaign designed to split world Communism on the Jewish issue, to create disaffected groups within the membership of the Parties, to utilize these groups for further infiltration and for intelligence work.

This plan seems as unreal as the Rosenbergs' dreams of "eventual freedom and complete vindication."

Jews played central roles in the campaigns for and against the Rosenbergs. The judge, prosecutors, defense attorney and most of the defendants, suspects and witnesses in the case were Jews, but not one juror was Jewish. Several of the columnists who crusaded against the couple—Walter Winchell, Eugene Lyons and others—were Jewish. Winchell falsely accused the Rosenbergs of insulting the prison rabbi, and Lyons denied they had written the *Death House Letters*. The American Jewish Committee called loudly for the Rosenbergs' executions. Jewish newspapers generally remained silent about the case. The most prestigious newspaper in the United States, *The New York Times*, owned and published by Jews, did not question some of the prosecution's more dubious tactics or follow up a *Guardian* reporter's discovery of a crucial piece of missing evidence. The paper refused to accept committee ads offering the trial record for sale. The Times' radio station, WQXR, also refused to air committee advertisements.

The judge and prosecutors were rewarded for their participation in the case with high offices. According to Belfrage and Aronson, defense attorney Emanuel Bloch suffered a very different fate:

> In January 1954, the Bar Association of the City of New York petitioned the Appellate Division of the New York State Court to take action against Manny for his characterization of the trial, at the victims' funeral, as 'an act of cold, deliberate murder.' On January 30, Manny was found dead in his Manhattan apartment, victim of an apparent heart attack. Rather, it could be said, his heart had given out in exhaustion and despair.

Despite the defeat of Nazism, anti-Semitism had not withered away in the United States or elsewhere, and Jews were painfully aware of its power in their daily lives. They responded to the Rosenberg case much as many

Jews in late Nineteenth-Century France had reacted to the Dreyfus Affair: in silence, with averted eyes. Garber and Walkowitz write:

> The Jewish community as a whole distanced itself from the Rosenberg case, fearing that the alleged connection between Jews and Communism could unleash a powerful anti-Semitic backlash. Even Jewish groups on the Left, including groups affiliated with the Communist Party, remained unusually silent.

On the other hand, most of the members of the National Committee to Secure Justice in the Rosenberg Case were Jews, and many who signed petitions supporting the Rosenbergs were evidently Jewish.

One Jewish organization that did not shrink from defending them was the Emma Lazarus Federation of Jewish Women's Clubs. ELF was a national organization with seventy local chapters. Ann Meeropol, who later adopted Michael and Robert Rosenberg, was an active member of ELF.

One of ELF's leaders, Clara Lemlich Shavelson, was prominent in the Rosenbergs' defense. A longtime labor activist who had organized women garment workers in 1910, she "became a delegate to union conventions, an activist with the Women's Trade Union League, an outspoken Socialist and suffragist, and a tireless organizer of women workers," Garber and Walkowitz write. In 1934 she was the only woman to run for the New York state Senate. During the McCarthy years, the federal government took away her passport because of her early membership in the Communist Party. To Shavelson and ELF, Ethel Rosenberg was "the symbol of an activist, committed Jewish woman working on behalf of the wider interests of mothers and children all over the world as well as for her own family."

Others who spoke up for the Rosenbergs included Harold Urey, one of the developers of the atomic bomb, who showed great courage by questioning the validity of the government's scientific evidence against the couple in a letter to the editor of *The New York Times*. Nobel Prize winner Albert Einstein joined Urey in publicly calling for clemency in early 1953.

THE FINAL MONTHS

In January 1953, about 2,500 people went to Washington to keep a twenty-four-hour vigil in front of the White House, visit the Justice and State Departments and lobby Congress members for clemency. Large rallies were held that month in New York, Chicago, Los Angeles and other cities. Walter and Miriam Schneir write:

> Not all of those who participated in these and related activities necessarily were convinced of the innocence of the Rosenbergs. A typical handbill publicizing a clemency meeting at the time read,

in part: 'Millions all over the world are appealing to the President to commute their death sentence! Some believe the Rosenbergs are guilty. Some believe they are innocent. Some do not know. But all agree that the death sentence should be commuted by the President.'

A "Partial List of Persons Who Favored Clemency for the Rosenbergs" in the committee's files includes Christian clergy, rabbis, physicians, journalists, scientists and artists. Letters and petitions went to Presidents Truman and Eisenhower from Mary Church Terrell, one of the foremost African-American activists of the time; the Union Federation of Indonesia; Bartolomeo Vanzetti's sister; relatives of Alfred Dreyfus; and thousands of others from Iceland, France, Israel, Switzerland, Italy, Ireland, Japan, Britain, Australia, Argentina and elsewhere. Even the chief justice of the Utah Supreme Court wrote to the President requesting clemency, because "the conviction rests on too shaky a foundation."

President Eisenhower denied clemency just three weeks after taking office in January 1953. His statement echoed Judge Kaufman's sentencing speech:

> The nature of the crime for which they have been found guilty and sentenced far exceeds that of the taking of the life of another citizen: it involves the deliberate betrayal of the entire nation and could very well result in the death of many, many thousands of innocent citizens. By their act these two individuals have in fact betrayed the cause of freedom for which free men are fighting and dying at this very hour.

As the scheduled execution date, June 18, 1953 (the Rosenbergs' fourteenth wedding anniversary), approached, the stream of letters became a flood. According to *The Washington Post*, during the first six months of 1953 the White House received some 200,000 letters and telegrams about the case, most requesting clemency. The pace of legal actions quickened, and the committee scheduled benefits and other events to finance them. A British Labour Member of Parliament was scheduled to speak at a clemency dinner in New York in March 1953, but the U.S. government refused to give him a visa under the McCarran Act.

U.S. consulates and embassies in Europe "were so deluged with letters and delegations on behalf of the Rosenbergs that officials had little time for routine duties," wrote Jonathan Root. Privately, U.S. Ambassador to France Douglas Dillon urged President Eisenhower to commute the death sentences because of their adverse effect on international public opinion.

In early June, prominent French clergy, politicians (including four former premiers and the President of France) and 8,000 others telegraphed the U.S. Embassy in Paris, pleading for clemency. The Vatican broadcast the pope's appeal for clemency in four languages and sent it via the papal nuncio to President Eisenhower, but somehow it did not reach him. Thousands of clergy from the U.S. and other countries also sent appeals to the White House.

Only one mainstream newspaper in the U.S., the *Laredo* [Texas] *Times*, editorialized against the government's last-ditch attempts to force the Rosenbergs to "confess or die."

LAST-DITCH EFFORTS

A member of the Los Angeles Rosenberg committee discovered in early June that Emanuel Bloch had made a technical error during the trial. When he suggested that Bloch had been wrong, the committee summarily expelled him. So he wrote a pamphlet, had it printed at his own expense and sent it to the *Guardian* for publication as an advertisement. The *Guardian* rejected it. But the pamphlet made its way to an attorney, Fyke Farmer, who hurriedly did some research and confirmed that the Rosenbergs had been prosecuted and sentenced under the wrong law. Farmer tried to convince the committee to help him but found, "A funny thing about these people is that they do not seem to want any outside comment or help."

Without any cooperation from Bloch or the committee, Farmer took a last-minute habeas corpus appeal to U.S. Supreme Court Justice Douglas, who signed a stay of execution. But the next day, in an unprecedented action, the full Supreme Court overturned the stay, and preparations for the execution proceeded.

William Reuben believed that the government pressured the Supreme Court to overrule Douglas and rushed to execute the Rosenbergs to forestall the huge international movement that was calling increasingly loudly for clemency.

The world watched in morbid fascination as Michael and Robert Rosenberg made their final visit to their parents in the death house. Neville writes:

> For two years, the Rosenberg children had been nearly invisible to the public. Now their every move became woven into the agenda-setting ritual of the last-minute death watch. It was an agonizing moment. But on another level, it was almost unreal. For the first time since their arrests, the Rosenbergs were shown by the news media as a complete family. Before then they had been the disembodied parts of a story too politically sensitive for the news media to present fully. Now with the end near, the characters were hastily assembled center-stage for the last tormented scenes of one of the most excruciating international news-media productions of modern times.

The rescheduled execution date, June 19, 1953, was the eve of the Jewish Sabbath. Rather than delay the executions for one more day, federal officials moved the time from 11 p.m. to 8 p.m., to carry out the death sentences before nightfall. Police barricaded all the roads to Sing Sing to prevent a "Communist demonstration."

In fifty cities throughout the world, large, sometimes violent, demonstrations took place before and after the executions. The Schneirs write:

> In Paris that day, thousands had been participating in daylong rallies to 'save the Rosenbergs.' One youth was shot and over 400 persons arrested as demonstrators clashed with massive police formations blocking approaches to the locked American Embassy. ...Across the Channel, English supporters of the Rosenbergs made vain last-minute attempts to persuade Prime Minister Winston Churchill to intervene with President Eisenhower on behalf of the doomed pair. Thousands of clemency demonstrators roamed through London's West End.

In New York's Union Square, a traditional venue of left-wing and labor demonstrations, 5,000 people gathered. "When news reached them that the Rosenbergs were dead, a wail of grief went through the crowd. For minutes there was no speaker, no program, simply grief," Joseph Sharlitt writes. One account claims the police disconnected the loudspeakers in the square to silence any protest.

William Reuben was not aware of any loudspeakers being turned off. He stood in Union Square, watching the sun setting beyond the concrete canyons of Manhattan. As it slowly went down, "You could feel the life of the movement draining away." All around him, people were wailing. For Reuben, it was the "saddest moment as an American I've ever felt." He spent a sleepless night struggling with a sense of guilt and shame despite his efforts to save the Rosenbergs. The next morning he felt that a "calamity" had taken place, but nobody seemed aware of it.

In Brooklyn, Neville writes, a "long line of graveside speakers," including W.E.B. Du Bois, carried out the traditional final ritual of the *cause célèbre*. People from around the world sent messages of sympathy to the committee and the Rosenberg family. Emanuel Bloch began raising $50,000 to provide for the care of Michael and Robert. As adults, they would establish the Rosenberg Fund for Children, which they described as a foundation that "provides for the educational and emotional needs of children in this country whose parents have been targeted because of their progressive activity."

THE MEANING OF THE ROSENBERG CASE

The Rosenbergs' condemnation occurred in the midst of a national witch-hunt, which Belfrage and Aronson call the purging of the "Red cancer in the American body politic." The anti-Communist campaign peaked just before, during and after the Korean War, when fears were heightened and civil liberties curtailed. The case may be seen as a sacrificial ritual—American society's propitiation of "death, destroyer of worlds," after the searing experience of Hiroshima and Nagasaki, at a time when the United States was contemplating using the atomic bomb again, in Korea or China. To maintain its sense of righteousness and moral superiority, America needed to cast responsibility for mass slaughter elsewhere.

And so the forces of law and order plucked the Rosenbergs, members of a demonized minority, from obscurity to serve as scapegoats. Although the FBI identified ten members of the alleged espionage ring, six went free in exchange for their testimony. None of the other "atomic spies" of the era was sentenced to death. Only the Rosenbergs were forced to assume the fatal burden of unacknowledged fear and guilt.

In the process, the ritual drama of the *cause célèbre*, which had been developing over more than a century in Europe and the United States, became a morbid, fruitless spectacle. The pleas of thousands for mercy could not overcome the fierce determination of the world's most powerful government, whose judges and prosecutors assumed the role of pitiless high priests carrying out a human sacrifice.

The anti-Communist hysteria of the time, which the government skillfully stirred and manipulated, was deadly for the Rosenbergs. Reduced to mere effigies, they tried to make sense of what was happening to them by casting themselves as the central figures in a left-wing morality play. At the end of her life, as she struggled to maintain her dignity and sanity, Ethel Rosenberg compared herself to Joan of Arc. This scenario might have been acceptable to the Rosenberg's small political community, but to the larger society it seemed incomprehensible, twisted, even evil. It was all too easy for critics like Leslie Fiedler to ridicule Ethel's overblown sense of her own heroism, as long as they forgot that she firmly believed in her own innocence.

Despite his contempt for what he considered the Rosenbergs' pretentiousness, dishonesty and deviousness, Fiedler believed that executing them was wrong on pragmatic grounds. "Before the eyes of the world we lost an opportunity concretely to assert what all our abstract declarations can never prove: that for us at least the suffering person is realer than the political moment that produces him or the political philosophy for which he stands," he wrote in his well-known essay, "Afterthoughts on the Rosenbergs."

Fiedler the anti-Communist liberal was especially angry at the Rosenbergs because he believed they had degraded and betrayed a heroic tradition of which they falsely claimed to be part. He wrote: "We were called upon to judge in their places Sacco and Vanzetti or Dreyfus. And how did they get in? Through the evocation of these almost traditional victims, a kind of moral blackmail was practiced on us. . . ."

In countries where Communists were not seen as demonic figures and the death penalty for political crimes was considered an atavism, many people had difficulty grasping the logic of scapegoating. Nor could they approve of the U.S. government's use of totalitarian methods—secret surveillance, harassment and threats, blacklisting, "black bag jobs," wiretaps, purges, show trials, abridgement of civil liberties, use of informers, forced confessions, death sentences for political crimes—that became known during and after the Rosenberg trial. The international protests may have expressed people's disappointment with the United States, their erstwhile liberator, as much as their desire to rescue two obscure leftists who might or might not have passed secrets that were no secret to a wartime ally.

Many of those who watched the overwrought drama of the anti-Communist crusade from outside the United States expressed horror, disapproval or incomprehension. They found implausible the U.S. government's attempt to blame the Rosenbergs for the Korean War. To accept this extravagant claim, one had to share the belief in the demonic nature of the "Communist conspiracy" that gripped the United States at the time.

The Rosenbergs' defenders, both inside and outside the U.S., had a different vision of justice from those who exulted in their executions. Whether or not supporters believed the Rosenbergs were guilty, they did not subscribe to the notion that someone had to be sacrificed to uphold the moral and political order. They could not persuade the American public, however. A well-organized, prolonged propaganda barrage by the U.S. government and its allies drowned out their calls for clemency.

As in the Haymarket and Sacco-Vanzetti cases, the defendants' unacceptable political opinions made a fair trial and evenhanded press coverage impossible from beginning to end. After World War II, the government and the press had a "close relationship. . . . the political mechanics of agenda setting, i.e., gatekeeping, had long ago excluded from mainstream publications exposés and press releases from radical sources and newspapers. . . . the news media simply averted their heads," Neville writes. Over the following twenty years, the Vietnam War and the Watergate scandal would make the U.S. press somewhat more skeptical and critical of government news sources. But during the anti-Communist crusade of the late 1940s and early 1950s, the government-media partnership worked with chilling effectiveness. Few in the U.S. dared (or even thought) to question its version of reality. Locked out of the media, without broadly based public backing, the Rosenberg committee and its supporters could not successfully challenge it.

Emily Alman had a more optimistic interpretation of the case's significance. She believed that the Rosenbergs "kept the doors [of the anti-Communist detention camps] shut" by refusing to confess and that the campaign "turned back fascism" in the United States.

THE AFTERMATH

Emanuel Bloch published *Death House Letters* only days before the Rosenbergs were executed. They apparently never saw a copy of the book. After their deaths, thousands of people all over the world read the letters, which were reprinted in many editions and languages over the years. Translations were published in French, German, Swedish, Czech, Hebrew, Spanish, Yiddish (in Warsaw and Buenos Aires) and Japanese. The French translation went through at least thirty-four editions.

As a piece of propaganda, the book had long-lasting and powerful effects. It provided a rare alternative version of a period of American history dominated by triumphalist accounts and interpretations. Its positive portrayal of the Rosenberg family strengthened opposition to the death penalty on moral grounds. And as she would have wished, Ethel Rosenberg became a martyr in the Soviet bloc and for the European Left.

It is difficult to measure the effects of the case on the next generation, the New Left activists who came of age in the 1960s, but it seems likely that it did influence them.

Jonah Raskin, a "red-diaper baby" (child of Communists) and a 1960s radical, recorded the Rosenbergs' enduring but usually unacknowledged influence in his 1974 autobiography. As a child whose family was under FBI surveillance, he identified with the Rosenberg sons. But when he reached his twenties, he later wrote, "No one in the new left talked about the Rosenbergs. . . . John Brown was our hero, an American guerrilla warrior from bloody Kansas, a madman in the eyes of America, who had taken up arms to free slaves."

After Raskin's wife became involved in the terrorist "Weatherman" movement in the late 1960s, he went underground to avoid interrogation by the FBI. During this frightening time, he had strange dreams, including one in which Ethel Rosenberg and the Weatherwoman Bernardine Dohrn "had their arms around one another. They looked like mother and daughter."

Raskin ends his autobiography (written at age thirty) with an evocation of the Rosenbergs by recounting his friendship with Michael and Robert Meeropol in the 1970s. He compares them to the sons and the daughters of many other thirties radicals who were investigated, exiled, fired and jailed. Like Michael and Robby, the children were frightened by McCarthyism and the FBI and conformed, but in the thaw of the sixties they surfaced and rebelled. They joined the movement, the crowd in the streets, looked like freaks and hippies, lived in communes, dropped out. They connected the old left with the new left, they linked the thirties with the sixties.

Even for those uninvolved in politics, the Rosenbergs became part of the grim folklore of the Cold War, casting a long shadow over a decade that later politicians tried to portray as "the good old days."

Critical writers and artists on both sides of the Iron Curtain found inspiration in the case for many years. During the appeals process, community theatre groups performed hastily written plays based on the Rosenbergs' published letters to raise funds for the defense. Picasso drew idealized portraits of the couple that illustrated campaign leaflets around the world. Jean-Paul Sartre and other eminent intellectuals published articles denouncing the U.S. government's conduct of the case.

Almost twenty years later, E.L. Doctorow published a well-received novel, *The Book of Daniel*, based loosely on the story of the Rosenberg children. Another novel about the Rosenbergs, Robert Coover's *The Public Burning*, appeared in 1977. Coover had great difficulty in finding a publisher because he used still-living public figures, including Richard Nixon, as characters without changing their names. According to author William Gass, who wrote the novel's Introduction, the publisher became so alarmed by the possibility of legal action that when the book reached *The New York Times'* bestseller list, "The novel's name was removed from the publisher's catalogue, no advertising was permitted, and copies were quietly withdrawn from the stores."

Michael and Robert Meeropol, the sons of Julius and Ethel Rosenberg, were instrumental in keeping the case before the public for decades. They led efforts to reopen the case in the 1970s and '80s. In 1975 they published a memoir, *We Are Your Sons*, and later Michael undertook the labor of compiling a complete edition of his parents' letters. It was published in 1994. Scholars and long-lived survivors, such as William Reuben and Morton Sobell, remained emotionally involved in the case, debating it passionately at conferences and in books and articles. The National Committee to Reopen the Rosenberg Case continued to operate in 2001. Thus the campaign on behalf of the Rosenbergs entered its sixth decade.

Mostly overlooked during the clemency campaign, Morton Sobell, the Rosenbergs' co-defendant, maintained his innocence during more than eighteen years in prison. After the executions, the Committee to Secure

Justice in the Rosenberg Case changed its name to the Rosenberg-Sobell Committee, and Morton's wife, Helen, was its most active and effective member. She worked ceaselessly to obtain decent prison conditions and early release for her husband. The records of the Rosenberg-Sobell Committee contain hundreds of letters she wrote to supporters in the U.S. and abroad, prison officials, other government officials, Congress members—anyone she thought might help. The unsung hero in this long and tragic saga is Helen Sobell, who devoted almost twenty years of her life to getting her husband out of prison.

Despite the concentrated and persistent efforts of Helen Sobell, the Committee to Secure Justice in the Rosenberg Case and millions of others, the international campaign to save the Rosenbergs failed. All those Herculean efforts delayed the Rosenbergs' executions for only a few months. Furthermore, this unsuccessful campaign seemed to exhaust the possibilities of the *cause célèbre* in the modern world. If all that work, money and time could not save two people condemned to death for political offenses in America, what could save thousands of others, accused of crimes against the state, whose names nobody knew and who languished, forgotten, in prisons, jails and concentration camps around the world?

Founder Peter Benenson lights the Amnesty International candle during the organization's 20th anniversary commemoration, London, 1981.

Chapter 9

AMNESTY INTERNATIONAL: MYTH AND REALITY

The Cold War intensified throughout the world during the 1950s. The United States, Western European countries and the Soviet Union competed for international dominance in trade, weapons and politics. In their former colonies and spheres of influence, the industrialized nations of Europe sought to maintain and perpetuate their control through indirect means. The United States sought to dominate other nations through treaties, defense agreements, trade pacts, covert actions, propaganda offensives and armed intervention. The Soviet Union established its control over neighboring states through force of arms and installation of friendly regimes, while waging worldwide ideological warfare. The new Communist regime in China, the world's largest nation, intervened in the Korean War and became isolated as an "outlaw state" for the next two decades.

After their victory in World War II, the world's major powers conducted trials of war criminals for crimes against humanity, established the United Nations and signed a series of international declarations and agreements guaranteeing human rights. In 1948 the Universal Declaration of Human Rights was promulgated. Yet at the beginning of the Twenty-First Century, the International Covenant on Civil and Political Rights or other human rights conventions and protocols remained unsigned or unratified by nations including Brazil, China, Indonesia, Japan, Malaysia, Pakistan, Saudi Arabia and the United States.

Even the signers of these agreements continued to commit systematic human rights abuses against their own people. These violations included abridging freedom of religion, assembly, expression and association; imprisoning political opponents without warrant or trial; conducting unfair trials; using torture to force confessions; executing political prisoners; exiling and "banning" political opponents and many others.

One of the British originators of Amnesty International observed:

> There was a gradual realization that there were a lot of governments with a lot of political prisoners after the war. . . . Then

there was the slow build-up of new states in Eastern Europe. The character of the regimes in Eastern Europe was gradually shaped, and so was our awareness of how near we were to them. And the third world dictatorships came along. . . . Many proved to be single-party states with political prisoners. . . . It sort of shocked people to think that all these nice little new countries were going to be just as bad as the old ones.

It was in response to these confounding realities that Amnesty International came into existence.

THE CREATION MYTH

Amnesty's "creation myth" goes like this: One day in late 1960, a British lawyer named Peter Benenson was reading the *Daily Telegraph* in the London tube when he saw a brief article about two Portuguese students who had been arrested for making a toast to freedom in a Lisbon bar. As Benenson told the story:

> This news item produced a righteous indignation in me that transcended normal bounds. At Trafalgar Square station I got out of the train and went straight into the Church of St. Martin's in the Fields. There I sat and pondered on the situation. I felt like marching down to the Portuguese Embassy to make an immediate protest, but what would have been the use? Walking up the Strand towards the Temple my mind dwelt on World Refugee Year, the first of those years dedicated to international action. What a success it had been! The DP [displaced person] camps in Europe had been finally emptied. Could not the same thing be done for the inmates of concentration camps, I speculated. What about a World Year against political imprisonment?

In May 1961, the myth goes on, Benenson published an article, "The Forgotten Prisoners," in the London *Observer*. (In some versions, Benenson's inspiration for the campaign happens on the same day as the publication of the article.) Immediately thousands of people responded, and Benenson set up Amnesty International. Soon its members were writing so many letters to heads of state and other officials that political prisoners were being released all over the world. A member designed the organization's logo, a candle encircled by barbed wire. Amnesty International became the world's most successful, largest and most influential human rights organization, winning the Nobel Peace Prize in 1977. Amnesty's members commemorate the circumstances of its founding by ending every annual general meeting with a "toast to freedom."

This story lacks only a happy ending: Forty years after Amnesty's founding, governments throughout the world continue to violate human rights, often on a massive scale. As an Amnesty pioneer commented, "It seemed like an unending battle. . . . for every one you got out, about a hundred went in."

The immediate impetus to form Amnesty did come from Peter Benenson's righteous indignation while reading a newspaper in the London tube on November 19, 1960. But more than twenty years' involvement in civil liberties initiatives led Benenson to that moment of angry inspiration. And he was not alone in his effort. Without the active collaboration and participation of Benenson's "fierce legion of friends," Amnesty International would not have come into being.

The creation myth has a large kernel of truth, but the real story of Amnesty's beginning is much more complicated and drawn out. The difficulties, twists and turns of its founding and early years are reminiscent of its precursors' experiences during the previous two centuries. The goals, tactics and strategies that its originators developed owe much to earlier campaigns and organizations. Whether unconsciously or deliberately, they were responding or reacting to earlier successes and failures by recreating old structures and tactics or inventing new ones.

AMNESTY'S ANCESTORS

Even before Peter Benenson's birth in 1922, some direct precursors of Amnesty International were operating. In 1907, British and American anarchists founded the Anarchist Red Cross (ARC) to send funds and letters to anarchist political prisoners in Russia. They arranged for lawyers to defend the prisoners in court and even sent them false identity papers.

At least one prisoner used the money he received from the ARC to escape from Siberia. "Three weeks after the war broke out I received one-hundred dollars from the ARC. I was overjoyed. In my high spirits I thought I would take a chance. I left the village [in Siberia] and walked for sixty-three hours to a small city, from which I made my way to Irkutsk. . . ." This prisoner, Morris Schulmeister, ended up living in the United States.

The ARC had branches in Detroit, Chicago, Philadelphia and other U.S. cities and an office in London. Its New York center's sixty to seventy members met weekly. Avrich collected a member's reminiscences:

> Only the correspondence committee could write to the prisoners, and each member of the committee had ten or twelve prisoners to write to. We pretended to be brothers, sisters, fathers or mothers, otherwise the Russian government would not deliver the letters and money. . . . Only the members of the committee knew the names of the prisoners. . . . The whole thing got started when we heard that socialists were being helped in Russian prisons but that the anarchists got nothing. . . . We also published a paper once a year . . . half Yiddish and half Russian.

The organization raised funds by sponsoring social events, such as dances. Avrich says the ARC lasted until 1917, when some of its members returned to Russia to participate in the revolution there.

They, too, were persecuted and imprisoned by the new Bolshevik government. Alexander Berkman, Emma Goldman's companion, set up a relief fund in the early 1920s for anarchist prisoners and revolutionaries in Russia and other countries.

In the wake of the American "red scare" of 1920, Roger Baldwin, the founder of the American Civil Liberties Union and a self-proclaimed follower of Emma Goldman, set up the International Committee for Political Prisoners. According to Peggy Lawson, its purpose was "to raise money for the deported aliens and to get in touch with agencies in foreign countries that could help them."

Baldwin recalled, "We set up a network of correspondents in the various countries, and we had contacts with the Communist movement and with the Socialist International in New York, plus a very strong committee." The ICPP was much more overtly left-wing than the ACLU. For more than fifty years Baldwin (who lived to the age of ninety-seven) acted as the bridge between the radical Left and liberal civil libertarians in the U.S. and other countries.

Baldwin compared the ICPP to Amnesty, "but [it had] far more limited means and results. We got some prisoners out—I don't remember how many, but we wrote a lot of letters to officials and put out a regular bulletin and irregular reports."

After Baldwin retired from the ACLU in 1950, he focused his efforts on the International League for the Rights of Man, of which he was chair. (Ludovic Trarieux had founded its precursor, the Ligue des Droits de l'Homme, during the Dreyfus Affair in 1898.) With Baldwin gone, the ACLU became a more grassroots organization. In 1949 it had 9,000 members; but by 1970, there were 250,000 members, forty-nine state affiliates and 400 chapters. In Baldwin's day, only fifteen to twenty chapters had existed.

Baldwin became a close friend of Peter Benenson after World War II and helped him set up Amnesty's U.S. Section in the early 1960s.

In 1955, a small group of anarchists in the United States founded the Libertarian League, which sponsored lectures and benefits, published a newsletter and demonstrated at the Spanish Consulate in New York on behalf of political prisoners in that country. During its ten years of existence, "We saved at least five lives of anarchist workers condemned to death [in Spain]," Sam Dolgoff recalled in an interview with Avrich. The league criticized Fidel Castro for his repressive policies in Cuba. Other ad hoc campaigns also sought the release of political prisoners in the East and West during this period.

Peter Benenson's personal involvement in human rights went back to the 1930s. He traced the origins of the Amnesty idea to the Spanish Civil War, which broke out when he was fifteen. At that time he read and was much affected by Arthur Koestler's *Spanish Testament*, on political imprisonment and execution.

Benenson was part of a privileged family. His grandfather, a fabulously wealthy Russian mine owner and banker, moved to Britain and then to the U.S. just before the revolution. Until 1930, he sent his daughter, Flora, Benenson's mother, a £1,000 monthly allowance. Flora's husband, Colonel Harold Solomon, was an official in the British colonial administration in Palestine after World War I. Solomon ran for Parliament as a Tory in 1929 but lost. He died when Peter was nine, in 1931.

A widow during the Depression, Flora Solomon had to work to support herself and her son. She became an administrator at Marks and Spencer, the British department store chain. During World War II she organized food distribution for the British government and won a decoration, the Order of the British Empire, for her work.

THE MAKING OF AN ACTIVIST

Benenson attended Eton, Britain's most prestigious private school, in the late 1930s. It was there that he became politically active. He and his classmates "adopted" orphan children in Spain during the civil war and sent funds to a relief committee there. He left school when he was sixteen or seventeen to work for a refugee children's group in London, finding countries where German Jewish children could emigrate. He would go to various embassies to wangle or buy visas for the children. One of the Amnesty pioneers, Marlys Deeds, and her brother were among the children Benenson rescued from Germany.

Benenson went to Balliol College, Oxford, then served as an army intelligence officer during the war. After the war he became a lawyer, but he soon found he was more interested in politics than in practicing law. He ran a legal advice bureau for the Labour Party in North Kensington, London, and unsuccessfully ran for Parliament several times in the 1950s. During all those years he was garnering hundreds of contacts in the worlds of politics, law and journalism. These would serve him well when he organized the one-year campaign that became Amnesty International.

In the 1950s the Trades Union Congress (TUC) asked Benenson to observe political trials in Spain. As a result he became interested in political trials in several countries, including Cyprus, South Africa and Hungary. Spain was still suffering under the apparently eternal dictatorship of Francisco Franco. Cyprus was struggling to gain independence from Britain. In South Africa, the apartheid government was targeting the African National Congress for persecution and prosecution. The 1956 revolution in Hungary had briefly given many in the West hope that Eastern Europe could free itself from Soviet domination.

His experiences in Spain and Cyprus taught Benenson some direct methods of international pressure:

> Gradually I learned the techniques by which an observer could make his weight felt: demanding to sit in counsel's seats, trying to inspect all the documents, making grimaces when the prosecutor overreached himself, making obvious notes about the conduct of the tribunal, talking to the accused whenever there was an adjournment, learning enough Spanish law to be able to make a constructive suggestion here and there to the military defenders.

After seeing the conditions of imprisonment and the situation of political prisoners' families, he suggested that the TUC set up a Spanish Prisoners' Defense Committee to send financial aid and food parcels to the families.

Through these activities, Benenson got to know other lawyers and organizations involved in civil liberties work. He later told an interviewer:

> I didn't think you could be interested in human rights in another country, like I was in Spain, unless you were concerned with human rights at home, so I became much involved with human rights in Britain at the time, and was very upset to find, as indeed others were too, that the only organization that was active on that field . . . was the National Council of Civil Liberties, which was then a Communist front organization. And though its aims and objectives were perfectly laudable, its personnel were not. . . . And that's how and why I decided that we ought to try to set up an organization very much like the American Civil Liberties Union.

At the time the ACLU was encouraging the development of the Society of Labour Lawyers in the U.K., and Benenson joined its executive committee. "I made it my determination to try to build . . . a nonparty, all-party body supported by all lawyers enthusiastic for civil liberties," he recalled. In 1956 he founded a new organization, called Justice, which became the British branch of the International Commission of Jurists (ICJ).

A friend, Tom Sargant, became Justice's executive secretary, a post he held for twenty-five years. Sargant had met Benenson through a Labour Party colleague, and the men's wives taught at the same school. In 1956, Benenson called Sargant and said, "Tom, I'm trying to do something about Hungary and South Africa; would you come down and help me?" Benenson was trying to find lawyers from the three major political parties in Britain to observe treason trials in the two countries. Justice grew out of this initiative; its other programs included a court ombudsman, a victim compensation scheme and legal aid. Branches were established in Trinidad, Jamaica, four British colonies in Africa and Hong Kong. The policy of Justice was not to work on individual cases, but Sargant did some of this kind of work "on the quiet." With a few volunteers and a staff of four or fewer, Sargant found such work overwhelming.

Benenson became restless and dissatisfied with the organization. Sargant remembered: "He got . . . totally involved in . . . things like torture, and capital punishment, and things that were not within the purview of Justice. . . . he always had this wider vision of a humanitarian organization involving not just lawyers but all the other professions."

Besides Justice, Benenson said he was "involved in all sorts of committees against torture of prisoners in Iraq and Syria and different parts of the world. . . . All this was part of my daily bread, really."

In 1959 Benenson followed the activities of the International Refugee Year, a one-year United Nations campaign, with great interest. That year he became seriously ill with what was later diagnosed as coeliac, an intestinal disorder. He retired from the bar and went to Italy to convalesce. While he was there, he became a Roman Catholic and pondered his future.

As an organization, Justice seemed to him "excessively cautious." Suspicious of the ICJ, he concluded that "its copious finances must derive . . . from some organ of the American government; it turned out to be the CIA." As his time in Italy came to an end, he decided "it was necessary to form an all-embracing organization to fight for civil liberties, not just in Britain but in all the countries where there was a free Bar. And, perhaps more important, the organization must be open to the general public." A few weeks later he was in the London tube reading about the Portuguese students in the *Daily Telegraph*.

EARLY COLLABORATORS

Benenson took his idea for a political prisoners' campaign to a friend and legal colleague, Louis Blom-Cooper, the chair of the Howard League for Penal Reform, an organization dating back to the 1860s. He had worked with Tom Sargant on the Justice victim compensation scheme during the 1950s.

Like Benenson, Blom-Cooper was Jewish but not religious. His father's family had migrated from Holland to Britain in the 1880s. He told an interviewer he had never experienced anti-Semitic discrimination at school because he was good at sports. As an army officer and later as a lawyer, he traveled to Africa, India and Burma. Benenson would send him on missions for Amnesty to Sri Lanka and Pakistan.

Blom-Cooper suggested that Benenson approach the London *Observer* about publishing an article to launch the Amnesty campaign. Blom-Cooper was the *Observer's* legal correspondent, and he spoke to his editor, David

Astor, about the idea. Astor recalled: "I myself thought the idea was a bit
far-fetched. I didn't see how you could possibly hope to influence foreign governments to let out political prisoners just by making a noise here.
. . . This attempt to agitate, particularly against the Communist regimes,
seemed very unlikely."

But Astor himself had written to the Soviet ambassador about a correspondent of his who had vanished in Korea during the war, and the correspondent's situation in prison had improved as a result. So Astor had
seen the tactic could work. He also admired Blom-Cooper, describing him
as "a person who's very bold—in standing up and speaking out, and making himself heard." The *Observer* had already run articles supporting campaigns, including one to abolish the death penalty in Britain, which
Blom-Cooper had spearheaded.

Benenson developed the Amnesty campaign idea with another colleague,
Eric Baker, a Quaker who headed the Friends Home Service Committee
in London. He was general secretary of the National Peace Council and
one of the founders of the Campaign for Nuclear Disarmament. Like Benenson he had a long history of involvement in humanitarian initiatives. As
a conscientious objector during World War II, he had worked on the "Star-
vation in Europe" campaign, raising funds to send food to the war-torn
continent, "getting people aware and putting pressure on the government."

Baker and Benenson met while working on the issue of Cyprus in the
late '50s. During his stay in Italy in 1960, Benenson corresponded with
Baker, sometimes about political matters but just as often about religious
belief. On his return to Britain, he used Baker as a sounding board. Another
Amnesty pioneer, Peter Archer, remarked, "To some extent Eric was restraining Peter's exuberance."

On January 13, 1961, Benenson wrote to Baker:

> I am working on a scheme to make this year (anniversary of U.S.
> Civil War and emancipation of serfs in Russia) an occasion for
> launching a general appeal for an Amnesty for all political pris-
> oners everywhere. The appeal will be made on 11th November
> to link up with the idea of the Armistice. The *Observer* is offering
> its centre supplement on 12th November for the occasion, and I
> am finding a great deal of goodwill everywhere for the scheme.
> If you know of any people willing to undertake a little work on
> their own in this connection, I would be grateful. I am compiling
> a list of all political prisoners in each country for publication on
> Amnesty Day, and am looking for people who would undertake
> the responsibility of getting as much information about one or
> more countries, thus dividing the labor into compartments.

As he organized his thoughts, Benenson kept in close touch with Baker, whose wife later remarked, "There were very few nights when they were not talking [on the telephone] about something."

Benenson decided to compile a book of cases of political prisoners, *Persecution '61,* to be published as part of the Amnesty campaign. Baker did much of the research, and Benenson later said the book would not have appeared without his help. The two gathered information on about 100 prisoners, but the book contained the cases of just nine, from the First, Second and Third Worlds.

During the first six months of 1961, Benenson and several colleagues met weekly for lunch at the White Swan, a pub near his legal chambers. There they planned the Amnesty campaign, noting their ideas on paper napkins and the backs of envelopes that still repose in Amnesty's archives. This quaint way of doing business harked back to early British campaigners who met regularly in taverns and coffeehouses.

Peter Archer was one of the colleagues with whom Benenson met at the White Swan. The son of a toolmaker, he became interested in politics at school. Later he was a barrister, a Methodist lay preacher, chair of the Fabian Society, a Member of Parliament, U.K. Ambassador to the United Nations, chair of Amnesty's British Section, Solicitor General in Harold Wilson's government and chair of the Society of Labour Lawyers. He met Benenson around 1953 and later joined Justice. His wife, Margaret, organized and managed the first local Amnesty groups. Archer became a parliamentary expert in human rights as a result of his work for Amnesty.

With these friends and colleagues, Benenson was defining the goals and purposes of the "Appeal for Amnesty, 1961." At first, he had thought to call the campaign "Armistice," linking the release of political prisoners to an armistice in the Cold War. When he wrote to Eric Baker in January 1961, he mentioned launching the campaign on November 11, Armistice Day. Later he said: "I do believe that anniversaries are important, the anniversaries of deaths and of events. . . . they have great significance in human life, and I think one can use these occasions to good effect. . . . If you pick the right anniversary, what appeals to people, you can get a lot out of it."

As Benenson discussed and developed the idea with Blom-Cooper, Baker, Archer and others, he changed some of the guiding concepts of the campaign. It would start, he decided, on Trinity Sunday, May 28, 1961. Perhaps his choice of a religious holiday had something to do with his recent conversion to Catholicism. In later years he explained, "The world was then divided into three, and should really be one, in that suffering in one point of the world is equally as important as suffering in another part of the world."

LAUNCHING THE APPEAL FOR AMNESTY

In the spring Benenson went to Italy to write *Persecution '61* and the article, "The Forgotten Prisoners," that would appear in the *Observer* on May 28. David Astor put the article on the front page of the *Observer Weekend Review*. It included photographs of six prisoners: Constantin Noica of Romania, Rev. Ashton Jones of the United States, Agostinho Neto of Angola, Archbishop Beran of Czechoslovakia, Toni Ambatielos of Greece and Cardinal Mindszenty of Hungary. Other prisoners mentioned were from South Africa and Spain.

The article begins with a sidebar:

> On both sides of the Iron Curtain, thousands of men and women are being held in gaol without trial because their political or religious views differ from those of their Governments. Peter Benenson, a London lawyer, conceived the idea of a world campaign, APPEAL FOR AMNESTY, 1961, to urge Governments to release these people or at least give them a fair trial. The campaign opens today, and "The Observer" is glad to offer it a platform.

The article cites Articles Eighteen and Nineteen of the Universal Declaration of Human Rights, on freedom of thought, conscience, religion, opinion and expression. It describes repression in eastern and western countries, defines the "Prisoner of Conscience," describes the campaign's principal aims and activities, gives several examples of prisoners' plights and links their persecution to larger social and political forces. Benenson concludes by drawing a parallel with the antislavery campaigns of the Nineteenth Century: "Experience shows that . . . governments are prepared to follow only where public opinion leads. Pressure of opinion a hundred years ago brought about the emancipation of the slaves. It is now for man to insist upon the same freedom for his mind as he has won for his body."

The article's central paragraph describes how the campaign will work:

> The campaign, which opens to-day, is the result of an initiative by a group of lawyers, writers and publishers in London. . . .We have set up an office in London to collect information about the names, numbers and conditions of what we have decided to call 'Prisoners of Conscience,' and we define them thus: 'Any person who is physically restrained (by imprisonment or otherwise) from expressing (in any form of words or symbols) any opinion which he honestly holds and which does not advocate or condone personal violence.' We also exclude those who have conspired with a foreign government to overthrow their own. Our office will from time to time hold press conferences to focus attention on Prisoners of Conscience selected impartially from different parts of the

world. And it will provide factual information to any group, existing or new, in any part of the world, which decides to join in a special effort in favour of freedom of opinion or religion.

The Appeal for Amnesty had four aims, listed in a box in the middle of the article:

1. To work impartially for the release of those imprisoned for their opinions.
2. To seek for them a fair and public trial.
3. To enlarge the Right of Asylum and help political refugees to find work.
4. To urge effective international machinery to guarantee freedom of opinion.

The box also contains an announcement of a press conference whose speakers include Conservative, Labour and Liberal Members of Parliament and gives the campaign's mailing address (Benenson's chambers in the Temple Bar).

Benenson and his colleagues conceived of the Appeal as a "one-off," one-year campaign. "My idea," he said later, "was to put my foot in the water for one year and see how warm or cold it was, and if the reaction was favorable and it seemed the water was good, to go on in for a long swim."

As the creation myth claims, the public responded to "The Forgotten Prisoners" immediately, in overwhelming numbers. Thousands of people, from parliamentarians to schoolchildren, from London to Uruguay, wrote to the Appeal's offices, sending contributions and offering to do volunteer work. Newspapers around the world reprinted "The Forgotten Prisoners," radio broadcasts mentioned the campaign, pastors sermonized about it.

Celebrities, artists, intellectuals and other prominent cultural and religious figures also endorsed or participated in the campaign. Among those listed in early appeals and reports are composer Benjamin Britten, violinist Yehudi Menuhin, sculptor Henry Moore, the Anglican Bishop of Birmingham and a Catholic archbishop.

Peter Archer later admitted he had been dubious about the idea of the campaign:

> I didn't think we could get over to the public the concept of a political prisoner. . . . I didn't think people would understand it, and I was totally wrong about that. . . . I don't think [Benenson] ever had doubts . . . although I think the reaction to the May '61 article surprised him. . . .

THE PIONEERS

Among the thousands who wrote to Benenson were several people who became intimately involved in the campaign. One of the best known was Sean MacBride, Irish revolutionary, statesman and diplomat. MacBride had met Benenson through Justice. For several years, as secretary general of the International Commission of Jurists, he had traveled to various countries, trying to persuade governments to release political prisoners. Sometime before Amnesty was formed, for example, he went to South Africa and persuaded the foreign affairs minister to release about 2,000 prisoners.

MacBride came from an Irish political family. The British had executed his father as a result of his participation in the Easter Uprising of 1916; during that era his mother spent some time in prison, as did Sean MacBride—the first time when he was only fourteen. During the Irish Civil War in the early 1920s he spent a year in jail, and his cellmate was executed. MacBride's mother "spent her life . . . getting people out of jail." He told an interviewer that she had run a campaign called "Amnesty" well before 1914.

As a diplomat and international lawyer, MacBride also had participated after World War II in drafting the European Declaration of Human Rights, which set up "the first international body for receiving complaints of any individual, even against his own government." As a result of these experiences, he realized "the importance of having a nongovernmental organization that would not be tied to governments and that could investigate the situation and that could report on them and draw public attention to them." He saw the need for "a humanitarian organization that would do for political prisoners what the Red Cross did for prisoners of war."

MacBride became the chair of Amnesty's board, lending his personal prestige to the organization at an early stage.

Another colleague who wrote to the Appeal was Neville Vincent, who had met Benenson when both were involved in Labour Party politics. He was a member of the Howard League for Penal Reform and the Society of Labour Lawyers. One of Benenson's closest associates and advisers during Amnesty's early days, he raised funds, recruited members and went abroad on missions to visit political prisoners.

Vincent said he got involved in Amnesty out of his "hatred of injustice." Marlys Deeds, who worked in the Amnesty office for about five years, said he "had a wonderful way of summing a situation up. He was not a genius, but as brilliant as Peter in a totally different way, with a frantic sense of humor. And he could assess a situation fairly accurately, and this is why he is such a successful businessman." She believed he "felt really guilty about being so rich." Vincent contributed his financial skills to Amnesty as the organization's first treasurer.

Norman Marsh, former secretary general of the ICJ, phoned Benenson at his wife's urging after the publication of "The Forgotten Prisoners." He had seen a draft of the article but had not been enthusiastic about the idea. He became involved in the new organization as a member of the policy committee and one of the "godfathers" who counseled Benenson at difficult moments.

Like MacBride, Marsh had traveled to several countries for ICJ, trying to persuade governments to release political prisoners. During the mid-1950s, he recalled, Benenson would write to him at ICJ, "telling me what I ought to do and what I ought not to do, always pushing me into action."

From his own experience, Marsh could understand why Benenson had decided to start Amnesty:

> It is very likely that one of the factors that persuaded Peter to take up Amnesty was the realization that there was room for a body concerned simply with intervention, protest, relief, as distinguished from a body like the ICJ, which is working much more long-term on the principle of the rule of law, cooperation of lawyers, and incidentally protesting about misuse of legal procedures, but nevertheless cannot be sending telegrams at the last minute to save people from the gallows, or sending out relief to people in prison.

Marsh's wife, Christel, became even more intensely involved in Amnesty than her husband. She was the first coordinator of the "library," which later became Amnesty's research department. Her job was to collect and document cases. She remembered: "I bought two small boxes of cards in which I then started copying. . . . It was all very primitive."

At first Benenson paid a clipping service to collect news reports about political prisoners. These were often only a few lines long. Some of the early case files that Christel Marsh created may be found in the Amnesty archives; they are little more than lists of names by country, with brief descriptions of prisoners' occupations, reasons for imprisonment and the source of the information.

Later Christel Marsh expanded her activities to include corresponding with overseas Amnesty groups. Her husband remarked, "She would come home with piles of letters, drafting letters to people and causes and groups and who knows what else all over the world." She worked at the Amnesty office from 1961 to 1973.

Christel Marsh was born in Germany, the daughter of a teacher and Protestant theologian. In 1939 she was arrested and interned by the Gestapo for political reasons. After fleeing Germany she met and married Norman Marsh in England. The war destroyed her family in Germany. She was one of three German refugee women among Amnesty's founding members.

Keith Siviter also responded to the *Observer* article, but he was not a friend or colleague of Benenson. A Congregational minister, he received "an excited phone call" on Trinity Sunday 1961 about the article from a friend and parishioner. "We were both enormously interested at the very outset, as we had been concerned for several years about prisoners and repression," he recalled. The two visited the Appeal office in June or July and attended the first meeting of their local Amnesty group in November; 250 people came. Siviter described his reaction to the article:

> One had felt there was nothing you could do and there was this repression going on. We were reading the papers, so much of it, all the Russian business, you know. We were hearing of dreadful things happening in Europe—East Germany, Hungary, Rumania—terrible lot of oppression. One felt helpless, and here was this article, something you can do about it! Pick up your pen and write, it's doing something. It's actually something to heal this world.

In 1963 Siviter's friend joined the Amnesty staff and asked him to volunteer. He joined the staff part-time in 1966, while still a pastor. Later he resigned his ministry and went to work for Amnesty full-time. He was the organization's financial officer until 1986.

Peter Archer, an early member of the policy committee, admitted: "I don't think we had any clear idea what to do with the people who replied to the article. . . . the letters from the article were spread over two to three weeks, and then we were all saying, 'What in hell do we do with all this?'"

The answer was the "Threes."

THREES' COMPANY

Apparently Benenson came up with the idea. Headquarters would send prisoners' names and other information to local Amnesty groups, each of which would work on three cases, one from each political bloc. The groups, called "Threes," would do further research, write to officials, send relief to families and prisoners, help released prisoners gain asylum and rebuild their lives in a new country, raise funds to support the work at headquarters and educate the public.

Headquarters sent pages of instructions to the new groups. For example, under the heading "HOW TO SET TO WORK," one such document suggested:

> If possible enlist the support of some group to which you already belong, *e.g.*, church, political party, Rotary Club, trade union, school,

university, etc. Alternatively make up a THREES group with your friends—a dozen or twenty people should be a satisfactory number. What is important is that, even if the work is shared out between you, everyone should accept the impartial and humanitarian purposes of the movement and that the group as a whole should be prepared to sponsor all these prisoners equally.

Groups were told to consult with headquarters before undertaking certain actions, such as writing to prisoners' relatives or obtaining information about their families. "Failing all else, one of the THREE members should set off to the country (or make use of the already-arranged journey of a friend) and start the search. BUT PLEASE DON'T SET OFF ON A JOURNEY WITHOUT FIRST CONSULTING U.S.—some such journeys are not advisable," one directive stated. Perhaps Amnesty staff later rued having advised, "The great thing is to use your own initiative, not to wait for leadership from the Centre."

The instructions conclude, "If at any time you receive a letter from the Centre asking you to desist from some project, please accept the request graciously. There are some actions that look harmless in themselves, which could have repercussions on the wider international movement." These statements show an amusing but touching combination of naiveté, audacity and astuteness. Whoever wrote them (probably Benenson) had associated with the powerful and found it possible to do business with them.

Indeed, his colleagues and friends repeatedly mentioned Benenson's talent for making contacts. Said Tom Sargant, "He had this fantastic capacity for getting in with people in high places. That was Peter's genius. . . . Peter could go and talk to them on equal terms and get them to do what he wanted. . . . And this I attribute in part, not wholly, in that he went to Eton, and Balliol . . . where all the high and mighty went so he could mingle with them on level terms."

Benenson's friends Marsh, MacBride, Archer and Vincent also were accustomed to operating on the higher levels of government, and they may have made certain assumptions about others' capacity to persuade rulers and bureaucrats to free prisoners. When they went on mission alone to Spain, Portugal, Czechoslovakia, Ghana and other countries, they sometimes got their way by going directly to the top and making a personal plea for mercy.

Housewives in Holland or university students in Sheffield had a harder time, however. Marlys Deeds, who worked directly with local groups, observed, "They were discouraged when they heard absolutely nothing. They got no replies from the usual sources that were given to them."

In November 1961, the policy committee met to discuss the future of the Threes. The minutes conclude:

Unfortunately, so far the work of the Threes has not prospered, largely because the task set them has proved in practice almost impossibly difficult to fulfill. There are about twenty groups in Britain, anxious to do something for Amnesty, but reports indicate that most of them feel that they are not really able to make any progress. They need more help from the centre and the work involved means that in fairness this can only be done by paid central office staff.

The Threes, which had begun as part of an inspired, creative and innovative project, Peter Benenson's brainchild, eventually became the mainspring of a bureaucratized and hierarchical organization. This transformation should not be surprising, since apparently none of the pioneers had any previous experience organizing or participating in a grassroots group. They were making it up as they went along, discovering through trial and error just how complicated consolidating a far-flung, rapidly growing, international organization could be.

They sought, however, to make the volunteer part of the organization its engine. Benenson, MacBride and the other pioneers wanted to directly involve ordinary people around the world in the struggle for human rights. Archer commented, "We were working for people, not ideologies or anything else, and it was people who were going to work for them. So it was people working for people."

If there must be a central office, its *raison d'etre* would be to serve the groups and individuals who would write the letters, raise the funds and educate the public. Amnesty always billed itself as a "volunteer-run organization." Accordingly, the pioneers tried to set up a democratic form of governance on the international level, with an elected International Executive Committee (IEC) and International Council Meetings (ICM), where volunteer delegates would make policy.

The reality, however, was more complicated and contradictory. Tension developed between the increasingly professional headquarters and the "amateurs" who comprised the international movement that gave the organization its force and legitimacy.

One policy committee member, Keith Wood, expressed this tension in his resignation letter:

> I have never really believed that direct action by small, and mostly ill-informed, groups scattered around the world could ever be effective. Indeed . . . the scope of their doing actual harm positively alarms me. . . . So I must leave the 'three's' and all other such amateur 'do-gooder' movements to whose who can have faith in them. And good luck to them.

GLORIOUS AMATEURS

In the early days, the Appeal for Amnesty was a kind of cottage industry that operated on a piecework basis. The office consisted of two "very tiny, very dark cellar rooms," recalled Christel Marsh. The men and women who worked there every day vividly described its chaotic but productive ambience. Keith Siviter, who worked first as a volunteer, then as a staff member, reminisced:

> It was very good fun. . . . when you had Peter around, you'd never had . . . a closed door. Whatever was going, it would be an open office, very much so. [There were] Library meetings, when all the staff, volunteer and paid, met on Friday lunchtimes. If there was a problem over a prisoner or a group, that was the place it was discussed. By everybody, including the telephonist. . . . There was no sense of a hierarchy and a structure and authority and all those things. Just a job to be done.

Christel Marsh, the head of the "library," recalled: "In the beginning, I was 'maid for all work.' . . . If you think how absolutely amateurish it was, it's quite staggering. . . . We experimented all the time—trying to improve, making it more professional, quite simply because it was so terribly unprofessional."

Peggy Crane, the Appeal's first "executive officer," observed: "And you had this sort of feeling, after about six months or so, that we had just the beginnings of an organization. And when it had been going on for about a year . . . there was a sort of general feeling that we'd got much more of . . . a proper organization."

Crane did not stay long at the office—she soon found working for Benenson "almost impossible," and she wearied "of just being a dog's body." But Christel Marsh remained for twelve years. "For years it was simply a struggle to keep it going," she said later. "I often had the feeling that if I stepped down there'd be nothing more. The whole card index would stagnate and the whole thing would come to an end!"

Benenson was inspiring and stimulating to be around but not an organizer or a manager by temperament. Sean MacBride complained: "The trouble with Peter was he used to keep things on bits of paper, backs of envelopes and things. . . . Peter was a marvelous ideas man . . . but when it came to the implementation of the ideas, he was . . . inexperienced or unorganized in converting them into concrete projects."

Peggy Crane believed Benenson did not want to create an administrative structure. "You could come or you could disappear, but if you came, you must be there. Time was nothing. . . . For those who were working with him he was like part of a volcano."

Marlys Deeds said Benenson "often had so many ideas, all at the same time, he'd give directions to everybody to get on with it because he felt the inner urgency that it must be done at that very moment. Not tomorrow. . . . all the people were tools for his ambitious scheme." She found the environment extremely stimulating but broke down in 1966 and left the organization.

Neville Vincent had a broader perspective:

> It was a new movement, a bit strange and mad on the face of it. And it was not always easy, if one was being honest, to know if one was doing good, I mean bearing in mind the amount of effort involved, the amount of money, the amount of time. . . . one was imbued with more zeal because very often people came back who'd been let out of prison . . . and said, 'About those postcards of yours, they kept me alive in a time of darkness.'

THE BEEHIVE

During the Appeal's first year, a great number of activities were going on simultaneously. Benenson did not want the organization to be only British. "As soon as it was launched in England I went to Paris to have this meeting of theological leaders . . . and got the thing going in France," he recalled. He and other pioneers organized and participated in international meetings in Luxembourg and Belgium, and Benenson flew to New York to see if a U.S. section could be established. By mid-1962 Amnesty claimed to have groups working or forming in Argentina, Australia, Belgium, Burma, Canada, Ceylon, Congo, Ethiopia, Ghana, Greece, India, Ireland, Israel, Jamaica, Malaya, Mexico, Netherlands, New Zealand, Nigeria, Norway, Sweden, Switzerland, West Germany and the United States. Threes were at work in Australia, Britain, Ireland, Norway, Sweden, Switzerland and the United States.

Marlys Deeds organized an event to take place on December 10, 1961, commemorating the anniversary of the adoption of the Universal Declaration of Human Rights. With the help of a public relations firm, she booked Yehudi Menuhin and Jacqueline du Pré to give a concert at St. Paul's Cathedral. The most dramatic part of the commemoration occurred at St. Martin's in the Fields Church, where Benenson had meditated on the Portuguese students about a year before. Handcuffed, with a cord linking the handcuffs, Calypso singer Cy Grant and actor Julie Christie walked solemnly into the church. The Amnesty candle was used to burn through the cord, freeing the "prisoners." After the ceremony, former prisoners of conscience living in exile in Britain kept vigil over the candle. To this day in Britain, many churches commemorate Human Rights Day on the Sunday closest to December 10 with a special "Amnesty service."

AMNESTY ON THE GROUND

The image of the candle became associated with Amnesty. A local group member, Diana Redhouse, designed the original candle-in-barbed-wire logo in June 1961. Redhouse was Jewish and had experienced anti-Semitism at school in London and later on the job. Like some of the other Jews involved in Amnesty, she was not religious; but unlike Benenson and Vincent, she did not convert to Christianity.

Strongly affected by the *Observer* article, she wrote to Benenson, who asked her to start a local Amnesty group. She later recalled: "I felt it was something I had to do. That who's going to do it if I don't?" With Margaret Archer's help, she and some others founded what she believed to be the very first Amnesty group, in Hampstead, Northwest London; she was its secretary for sixteen years.

She remembered: "I thought it was a bit haphazard, the whole thing. . . . It took a long time and we got a prisoner," a Ghanaian. The group raised five pounds at a "bring and buy" sale and sent it to the prisoner's wife. Later they wrote to the government asking for his release.

Another important early group was in Eltham, a London suburb. Dorothy Warner, its first secretary, was born in Germany to a Protestant mother and a Jewish father in 1920. Although she was baptized and educated at a convent school, she became a victim of the Nazis with the rest of her family. The Gestapo arrested her and her father, a judge, in 1944 and sent them to forced-labor camps. Both escaped after a bombing. After the war her father returned to being a judge in West Germany. Dorothy's future husband, Henry Warner, also German and half-Jewish, had escaped to Britain before the war. He was posted as a British army officer to serve as Dorothy's father's clerk. She and her husband later moved to Britain.

"In 1962 we heard our minister at the United Reform Church . . . telling us about the plight of some Portuguese students who had been overheard expressing some dissatisfaction with their government," she recalled. Soon after, she formed the Eltham Amnesty group. Asked why Amnesty appealed to her, she replied: "If you had lost your liberty you can't do anything else but. . . . I mean, if you are interested in people, as I am, you couldn't possibly close your heart and eyes and ears to that, could you? You had to respond in some way. So this is what I did." Warner was the only member of her church who had been a prisoner.

In the beginning, Warner and other group members would go to the Appeal office in Mitre Court and select prisoners from Christel Marsh's card files. At one time, the Eltham group was working on twenty-one prisoners' cases.

Warner wrote a letter to a prosecutor in East Berlin about a couple jailed there for fleeing to the West. The prosecutor replied, saying they were criminals who had abandoned their baby, who had died. She wrote back to apologize for her mistake but added questions about other prisoners. "We had quite a correspondence, this chief prosecutor and myself."

Warner left the Eltham group in 1966 but returned around 1978. Things had changed.

> [In the 1960s] the whole group work was so different because we, of course, had to find our own feet. We had to have our own contacts. Right from the beginning, we used our own initiative. . . . We found channels to get going. But now [1978], when I suggested that we should get more prisoners, there wasn't the rule anymore that they must be strictly one from the West, one from the East and one from . . . the Third World."

In the early days, not all groups were as resourceful as Warner's. Responding to their pleas and complaints, headquarters expanded the range of activities that groups could carry on locally. Newsletters and circulars from the central office suggested that groups undertake human rights education and public outreach, fundraising, recruiting new members, lobbying for adoption of human rights agreements and helping refugees and asylum seekers.

VISIONS VS. PRACTICALITIES

Beneath Benenson's idea of an international, grassroots organization lay a visionary impulse. In an unsigned paper dated June 5, 1961, he reveals his true intentions in launching the Appeal for Amnesty.

> The underlying purpose of this campaign . . . is to find a common base upon which the idealists of the world can co-operate. It is designed in particular to absorb the latent enthusiasm of great numbers of such idealists who have, since the eclipse of Socialism, become increasingly frustrated; similarly, it is geared to appeal to the young searching for an ideal, and to women past the prime of their life who have been, unfortunately, unable to expend in full their maternal impulses. . . . it matters more to harness the enthusiasm of the helpers than to bring people out of prison. . . . Those whom the Amnesty Appeal primarily aims to free are the men and women imprisoned by cynicism and doubt.

On a more practical level, his report on the Appeal's first six months recognized that its goals were very ambitious indeed.

> Experience shows that the cost of maintaining a network of local groups even in one country is that of having a paid central organisation, devoted exclusively to this work, in each country. It has

not been possible to raise sufficient funds for this purpose even in Britain. It is, I believe, impossible to envisage raising enough to promote a world-wide network of groups at any rate for some years to come. That being so, I think it more realistic to recognise that in the present state of the world there is no practical voluntary machinery for securing the release of 'prisoners of conscience.' If this deduction is correct, then it is necessary to decide whether it is right that the appeal, conducted on the emotional level, should continue.

He recommended that the policy committee decide in December 1961 to continue the campaign until June 30, 1962. But, he added, "if at that date, it has not been possible to collect £5,000 from 10th December 1961, then a decision should be taken to close down the operation on 31st July, 1962." They found the money. Their first yearly financial statement showed total income of more than £7,500.

Nonetheless, the organization was often "hard up." This was because Benenson could not convince government officials that Amnesty was a charitable, humanitarian, apolitical organization. A 600-year-old law kept the "Prisoners of Conscience Fund," a popular destination for contributions, separate from the Appeal's operating budget. As a result, Neville Vincent had difficulty finding sufficient funds to run the office. Staffers were sometimes reduced to conducting raffles to raise their operating expenses. Amnesty went to court several times over the years to change its status and release the money tied up in the POC Fund.

THE MANDATE

In the early days the organization's mandate was very simple, focusing only on Articles Eighteen and Nineteen of the Universal Declaration of Human Rights and the release of prisoners of conscience (POCs). Apparently no rule existed to keep members from working on cases in their own countries—that came in the mid-1970s. But in practice, from the beginning, most Threes groups were working on cases of unknown people in faraway countries.

This system had certain advantages. The *causes célèbres* of the past had centered on notorious members of despised social and political groups. Public campaigns failed to overcome the intense animus and prejudice against the Haymarket anarchists or the Rosenbergs. Or it took many years of campaigning to change public opinion, as in the Dreyfus Affair and the Scottsboro case. Amnesty members were much quieter, eschewing polemics, writing polite personal letters about unknown people to government officials thousands of miles away. The pressure they exerted was subtle and cumulative. They wrote as individuals on behalf of individuals, and they exercised their human rights by standing up for the human rights of others. Therein lay the brilliance of Benenson's idea.

When Benenson proposed broadening the mandate to include torture cases, "there was great outcry . . . we're dissipating our energies, we ought . . . only to keep to our work for prisoners of conscience. Then we moved into capital punishment. Exactly the same thing," Siviter remembered. This outcry would be repeated many times over the years as the mandate continued to expand.

A NEUTRALIST INITIATIVE

Another challenge of Amnesty work was cooperating (or not) with Communists. The pioneers had agreed the organization would work only on cases of prisoners who had not advocated violence or overthrow of the government or carried out violent acts. This limitation excluded committed revolutionists of all sorts. They also decided not to work on espionage or treason cases (perhaps in reaction to the Rosenberg case and others, East and West, during the 1950s). But in many countries, Communist or Communist-front organizations were seeking the release of non-Communists or of people merely accused of expressing "Communist" opinions. Amnesty groups tried to steer a middle course.

The Eltham group discussed the problem in 1963:

> The 'Appeal for Amnesty' in Spain is a Communist front today. . . . However, their information is up-to-date and accurate and the work they are doing is good. There is no reason why Amnesty should not work with them, but we must not get involved with them. . . . The fact that we work with Communist parties in the West is in our favour when dealing with Iron Curtain countries and must be emphasized.

Amnesty members began to congratulate themselves for their even-handedness when governments of every ideological variety accused them of being tools or agents of the enemy in the Cold War. The organization responded by continually insisting on its humanitarian, apolitical character and built its reputation for objectivity, accuracy and neutrality on the work of the Threes, which took up cases from the First, Second and Third Worlds.

This is not to say that the organization transcended the Cold War or achieved perfect impartiality. Nor did Amnesty's determination to remain neutral keep intelligence services on all sides from trying to use or co-opt the organization. Amnesty proclaimed it would not accept any funds from governments, but it was often difficult to ascertain the ultimate source of much-needed funds. Such dilemmas would become more troublesome as the organization became more effective.

WHATEVER WORKS

Recognizing that the Threes were having difficulties in working on cases, in early 1962 Benenson returned to the model of Justice and the ICJ by sending several of his colleagues abroad on rescue missions. Blom-Cooper went to Ghana to obtain information about government opponents who had been detained three years before. MacBride went to Prague to plead for the release of Archbishop Beran and other prisoners. Vincent went to Portugal to ask after five physicians who were imprisoned. An Indian lawyer, Prem Khera, went to East Germany to investigate the disappearance of a trade unionist and a forester. None of these missions, except possibly Vincent's, seems to have resulted in releases in the short term.

The organization was careful not to claim credit when governments did let prisoners go:

> But we can note certain coincidences—such as, following Amnesty's conference on 'Personal Freedom in the Emergent Countries,' the Sudan Government proclaimed an amnesty for former ministerial detainees, or following Neville Vincent's trip to Portugal, three doctors were released. There have been sufficient coincidences such as these to make us feel that, at least, our efforts have been a contributory cause to these releases.

The first annual report also reported "general or partial amnesties" in a dozen countries and the release of "a number of individual prisoners, on whose behalf Amnesty has intervened."

The report insisted that the Appeal's most important achievement was

> that without it peoples and Governments would today be *less aware* of how narrow are the boundaries of freedom in at least two-thirds of the world; more people would be languishing forgotten behind prison bars; fewer people would be so actively concerned with promoting the basic human freedoms of opinion, religion and of expression; the Universal Declaration of Human Rights would be mouldering in the pigeonholes.

Amnesty's pioneers perceived that the international human rights movement was more than just Amnesty, but that the organization could play a crucial, timely role in shaping, directing and mobilizing it.

WHY THERE? WHY THEN?

Andrew Blane and Priscilla Ellsworth, who interviewed seventeen Amnesty pioneers, asked them why they thought the organization had emerged in Britain in 1961. Benenson replied, "The birth of Amnesty coincided with the brief thaw that we had in the Cold War, and without it I don't think we'd have got anywhere." He could not imagine the organization starting in the United States "because at that time America was . . . one of the major combatants [in the Cold War], and this was essentially a neutralist initiative. This was an idea to try and find a balance between the two major powers and seek to bring about a third force in the world."

Blane suggested that perhaps the presence of political exiles in Britain had had something to do with its appearance there, but Benenson could not see his point. Yet some of Amnesty's founding members were refugees who threw themselves into the work out of a sense of personal identification with the victims of government persecution.

Louis Blom-Cooper had a different interpretation:

> People were looking round for something other than simply the everyday activities of life. And political prisoners [were] a cause people could easily attach themselves [to] in order to assuage their consciences. And of course one was reading more and more about the sort of horror stories, I mean particularly coming out of places like Spain and Portugal, very close to home. It wasn't just these very remote places where one reckoned one always recognized there would always be persecution, like the Soviet Union.

He traced the British interest in human rights back to the mid-Nineteenth Century, when the idea of political asylum may have originated.

Sean MacBride pointed to British concern over apartheid in South Africa as a reason for the Appeal's popularity in 1961. He believed Amnesty had survived because greater literacy and education created a more informed public and increased the effectiveness of public pressure. The media brought Amnesty's message "into people's lives, into their homes, into the places where they work," he said.

Tom Sargant agreed with MacBride: "I think South Africa aroused British consciences in a most extraordinary way. [But now] we're all punch-drunk with horrors."

Neville Vincent said, "Amnesty, the idea, I think was infectious to the young."

David Astor pointed to "a strong tradition [in Britain] of trying to rescue people. . . . Amnesty isn't so much an extraordinary idea as an extraordinary accomplishment . . . [a] very simple idea, and therefore amazing that it actually works." And, he said, "The idea is beautiful."

SUFFICIENT CONDITIONS FOR SUCCESS

In July 1962 founding members from Britain and other countries met in Belgium and formally established Amnesty International as a permanent, international organization. Many factors enabled Amnesty to make the transition from a one-year campaign to an established entity:

1. International human rights covenants provided the basis of the organization's mission and gave it very great legitimacy.

2. "The idea was beautiful": Amnesty proclaimed itself a humanitarian, not a political, organization that focused on the relief of human suffering. It was a "sudden movement of the heart which is linking men and women of goodwill across the barriers of this divided world," the Threes document said.

3. Benenson and his colleagues had practical experience in civil liberties and humanitarian work, as well as carefully refined political ideals and, in some cases, religious convictions that supported their activism.

4. Benenson was a classic charismatic leader around whom people of many types could rally. His religious conversion during a serious illness seems to have reanimated him and made him a more effective and creative innovator. He also had excellent contacts among powerful sectors of British society, his professional community and international organizations.

5. Precursor organizations, from the International Committee for Political Prisoners and the ACLU to Justice and the International Commission of Jurists, provided models or patterns of action that Amnesty's pioneers followed or adopted.

6. An increasing number of people (especially educated women) in Britain and other countries had free time to volunteer and disposable income to donate to a compelling new cause.

7. Though some of the pioneers were members of Britain's political and intellectual elite, many were social outsiders, unconventional and unafraid to take risks. They were Jews, Catholics, Quakers and other dissenting Protestants, German refugees, housewives, working-class people—all on the margins of British public life. (Even Eric Baker was stigmatized early in life as an adopted child, a status that "wasn't respectable in those days at all," according to his wife.) They created an accepting alternative community in which they could thrive and through which they could be socially useful.

8. A friendly newspaper editor gave the campaign prime space to make the greatest possible impact. The organization continued to receive positive coverage, free publicity and considerable help from sympathetic journalists.

9. The press regularly reported stories about political prisoners throughout the world, providing relatively reliable information that the organization could pass along to its volunteers.

10. Local groups and staff had an improvisatory and enthusiastic spirit, took bold initiatives and worked hard. They were capable, energetic and dedicated. The organization showed itself to be dynamic, exciting and effective in its early stages.

11. The central office sought the opinions of its members and responded positively to their demands by broadening its activities, increasing its support and encouraging their activism. The pioneers tried to create a democratic form of governance.

12. Socioeconomic and political conditions in a number of other countries made the growth of an international movement feasible. Amnesty's pioneers had the foresight to foster this development.

SOMETHING OLD, SOMETHING NEW

Despite its creation myth, Amnesty International did not spring full-blown from Peter Benenson's brow. The Appeal for Amnesty grew, not only from his brilliant inspiration, but also from the hard work and active collaboration of many others. All together, they built such a firm foundation that when Benenson's health failed in the mid-1960s and he left the organization, it survived his departure and continued growing.

Amnesty was the culmination of a tradition. Two centuries of campaigns, in many places by many thousands of people, provided the foundations on which its members built the organization. The human rights movement already existed but was undefined, waiting for the catalytic action that Amnesty provided.

The creation of Amnesty also marks a turning point in the history of human rights: It opened up new areas, new strategies and new constituencies. As a result grassroots groups around the world became active and visible. Amnesty's offspring—the complex, dynamic, international movement for human rights—sprouted in its shade and then sent out seeds of its own. Over the past forty years, this movement has burgeoned, divided and multiplied. Amnesty continues to flower, now in the midst of a forest of organizations.

Rural and urban activists march together, holding seedpods, in support of land reform, Trindade, Goiás, Brazil, 1986.

Chapter 10

HUMAN RIGHTS CAMPAIGNING SINCE 1961

There are enough staid people in the world holding things as they are. We need no more of them. What we do need is people caught by the truth that no one is free when anyone is bound. That is not an easy idea to have get a hold on you. It has to be applied person by person, not just in the pious generalities of the resolutions good people pass when they gather for a moment and separate without effective action. –Allan Knight Chalmers

W hen Amnesty International emerged in the 1960s, few international human rights organizations existed. The term "human rights" was not even in common usage. Amnesty did not attain overnight success, though some versions of its creation myth give the impression of instant viability. For more than a decade it struggled to survive. But it was putting down roots and sending out shoots.

A human rights activist of a later generation, Mariclaire Acosta, remarked:

My whole human rights perspective, everything comes from Amnesty. It seems like all of these first- and second-generation Amnesty International people are like a little mafia. We all knew each other and loved each other dearly. And now we are spread all over the world doing other human rights work. . . . I think Amnesty was wonderful, because it really trained a whole set of people all over the world to become conscious of human rights. . . . It was like a star that exploded.

Acosta and other activists founded the Mexican Academy for Human Rights in 1984. They did not make a carbon copy of Amnesty but responded to national realities. Keck and Sikkink observe: "The academy focused attention of human rights issues in Mexico, trained human rights practitioners and fostered research and education. Its founders explicitly designed the academy as an academic institution rather than an activist group, hoping to provide a forum for the human rights debate in Mexico without confronting the government on specific issues."

In contrast, Amnesty developed as a membership organization, and in this sense it was rather unusual—almost unique. Most other international human rights organizations do not have rank-and-file members. They may publish reports and organize campaigns, but they do not answer to constituents or hold international assemblies where members make policy for the organization. In addition, volunteer activists play a distinctive and vital role in doing Amnesty's work. These characteristics set Amnesty somewhat apart from other nongovernmental organizations (NGOs) that have evolved over the past half-century.

EARLY DAYS

Scholars agree that the first international NGOs emerged after World War II, though some, such as the Women's International League for Peace and Freedom and the Fellowship of Reconciliation, developed during and after World War I. The early organizations grew up around the League of Nations and later the United Nations, representing very broad (and vaguely defined) sectors of what came to be called "civil society." They and other organizations sent representatives to intergovernmental bodies and lobbied on behalf of various groups and causes. For example, Ida Wells-Barnett tried to attend the Versailles peace conference in 1919 as a representative of American black organizations seeking an international declaration on racial equality.

To its credit, the League of Nations promulgated a number of human rights treaties, including the Declaration of the Rights of the Child (1924) and the International Convention on the Abolition of Slavery and the Slave Trade (1926). Another initiative to create human rights instruments was what Paul Lauren described as a "vigorous and large-scale campaign" by the author H.G. Wells in 1940. Wells, who was then president of Pen International, drafted a Declaration of Rights and distributed a series of articles, "The Rights of Man," to forty-eight countries.

During the late 1940s, 1950s and 1960s, NGO representatives participated in the drafting of the Universal Declaration of Human Rights and other international covenants. Several NGOs sought consultative status at the United Nations so they could at least observe proceedings. Similarly, Amnesty obtained consultative status and set up offices near the U.N. in New York and Geneva.

In 1947 the United Nations Human Rights Commission ruled that it had no authority to deal with human rights complaints by individuals or groups. Consequently, NGOs were forced to find other ways to denounce human rights violations by U.N. member states. They tried to use the international press to expose these violations to the world. Finally, in the mid-

1960s, the Human Rights Commission changed its policy and began accepting individual complaints. Over time, various U.N. working groups also started receiving specific cases. According to William Korey, Amnesty has always been a "principal supplier of documentation" to these bodies, but many other organizations also have filed complaints.

U.N. member nations must respond to such complaints because seventy-five percent of them have signed the seven major human rights agreements (on civil and political rights, racial and ethnic discrimination, discrimination against women, torture, rights of the child, antiapartheid, and genocide). The NGOs that bring complaints to the U.N. also pressure laggard governments to sign these agreements. For example, American NGOs lobbied the U.S. government to sign and ratify the principal treaties from 1964 to 1988, when the U.S. Senate finally began ratifying four of them: the International Covenant on Civil and Political Rights, the International Convention on the Elimination of All Forms of Racial Discrimination, the Protocol Relating to the Status of Refugees, and the Convention against Torture and Other Cruel, Inhuman or Degrading Treatment or Punishment. The U.S. still has not ratified the International Covenant on Economic, Social and Cultural Rights, the Convention on the Elimination of All Forms of Discrimination against Women or the U.N. Convention on the Rights of the Child. The U.S. and Somalia, which has no government, are the only two U.N. member states that have not ratified the children's convention.

NGOs have pressured the U.N. Human Rights Commission to work on specific issues, such as torture, "disappearances" and extrajudicial executions, and to send special rapporteurs to investigate violations in certain countries. "The basic truth . . . was that without NGOs, the entire human rights implementation system at the United Nations would come to a halt," Korey observes.

In 1968, Sean MacBride told an NGO meeting commemorating the twentieth anniversary of the Universal Declaration that governments were conspiring to evade and avoid their responsibilities to protect human rights under the U.N. Charter. Also during this period, several U.N. member states (led by the Soviet Union) waged campaigns to expel NGOs or limit their activities. The NGOs fought back, but they realized in the process that they would have to diversify their activities and do more work outside the United Nations.

Again, Amnesty provided a model for other organizations to follow. It involved the general public in human rights work, focused on cases of specific individuals rather than abstract ideas, worked on a limited range of violations, took on cases in the First, Second and Third worlds and strove for accuracy and impartiality. The Nobel Peace Prize that Amnesty won in 1977 acknowledged the effectiveness of these approaches and gave the organization unprecedented credibility.

EXPANSION OF THE HUMAN RIGHTS MOVEMENT

The number of human rights NGOs increased markedly from the late 1970s onwards. There were diverse reasons—political, economic and social—for this development. As the Cold War continued, many countries came under the control of dictatorships supported by one or another of the superpowers. On the other hand, the United States explicitly supported human rights in its foreign policy from 1976-80, and the Soviet Union backed national liberation struggles. Growing numbers of men and women in developing countries became literate, joined social movements and gained access to alternative sources of information.

Meanwhile, the "oil shocks" of the 1970s had severe consequences for countries that had hoped to attain prosperity by borrowing from multilateral lending institutions and private banks. The widespread suffering that resulted pushed many people and groups into political activity, which unstable or authoritarian governments brutally quashed. Thus local and national human rights groups grew out of people's firsthand experience of repression.

Estela Barnes de Carlotto, of the Grandmothers of the Plaza de Mayo, recalled:

> When they kidnapped my daughter, I didn't know anything about Amnesty International or the Inter-American Commission on Human Rights or the United Nations. We began to learn about these organizations through people in Argentina that had an international vision. . . . We didn't send letters directly to these places because we knew that they wouldn't arrive if they were addressed to Amnesty International, so we always took advantage when someone traveled abroad to send letters.

As thousands of the military government's opponents kept "disappearing" in Argentina, their mothers and grandmothers kept appearing once a week in the Plaza de Mayo in Buenos Aires, carrying signs with photos of their missing family members. Under terrible pressure, ordinary people were spontaneously creating human rights organizations to defend themselves and their loved ones.

In the mid-1970s, Amnesty invented a new form of action, called the Urgent Action Appeal (UA), to respond to increasing numbers of cases that required immediate attention. The first UA concerned a professor at the University of São Paulo, Brazil, who had been arrested without warning and taken to a secret location. An Amnesty researcher collected information about him as quickly as she could and sent it to members in various countries, asking them to telegraph Brazilian government officials and inquire about the professor's whereabouts. Within a few days, the professor was released. He celebrated the twentieth anniversary of his rescue in the mid-1990s.

Other NGOs followed Amnesty's example and set up urgent action networks that saved many from torture and death. In the mid-1990s about twenty-five international NGOs were coordinating such networks. They included SOS Torture, Lawyers Committee for Human Rights, Physicians for Human Rights, Survival International and the Arab Organization for Human Rights.

Thanks to improved communication technology, professional organizations in the North also began receiving urgent requests for help from their colleagues in the South and East as they became targets of government repression. Several set up human rights programs or committees to respond to these calls and educate their members. The American Anthropological Association, the Latin American Studies Association and the American Association for the Advancement of Science were among them.

The AAAS pioneered efforts to apply the forensic sciences to human rights cases. In 1984, its human rights program coordinator received a request for help from an Argentine activist in the United States. The result was a program, spearheaded by anthropologist Clyde Snow, to train forensic anthropologists to carry out exhumations of the "disappeared" and massacre victims in Argentina, Guatemala, Bosnia and other countries. The evidence they uncovered was presented to national and international tribunals, which brought some of those responsible to justice.

NGOs of many types sprang up in the 1980s. They focused on issues that Amnesty's limited mandate did not cover at the time. These included children's rights, racial and ethnic minorities, women's rights, indigenous rights, war crimes, slavery and forced labor, religious persecution, prison conditions, reparations and reconciliation, particular countries such as Tibet, Nicaragua, South Africa and many others.

Women's organizations have become especially active and vibrant. At U.N. conferences and other international gatherings, they have developed networks through which they organize campaigns, raise funds, train leaders and launch initiatives benefiting millions of women. Activists of diverse views, cultures and backgrounds found an issue of common concern, violence against women, and brought it to international attention from the 1980s on.

THE SHAPE OF ORGANIZATIONAL LIFE

Since the 1950s, the number of international human rights organizations has increased fivefold. Human rights groups comprise about twenty-five percent of all NGOs, according to the *Yearbook of International Organizations*, which separates them from women's rights, ethnic and group rights, and international law organizations that also could be considered to fall within the human rights category. Altogether, these types comprise forty-five percent of all international organizations.

A survey of about 150 organizations, conducted in 1996, shows how diverse and widespread human rights groups have become. Most are based in Western Europe and North America, but growing numbers are located in Asia, the Middle East and Eastern Europe. Thirty percent are in the "Global South," the developing countries, most of which are located in the Southern Hemisphere. Only twenty-five percent of those surveyed formed before 1966; half were founded after 1979, and twenty percent after 1988.

Human rights groups work in four areas: education, standard-setting, monitoring compliance with international standards, and enforcement. Southern NGOs are more likely to emphasize assisting victims of human rights abuses and to work on economic, social and cultural rights than are Northerners.

Their activities include campaigning, writing letters, organizing demonstrations and other events; educating the public, government officials and other NGOs; reporting human rights violations; lobbying; doing research and monitoring. Three-quarters reported contact with the U.N. Human Rights Commission, eighty percent with other U.N. agencies, thirty-three percent with the World Bank and twenty percent with the International Monetary Fund. Both northern and southern groups reported attending international conferences. Seventy-seven percent of northerners and ninety-two percent of southerners participated in NGO networks or coalitions.

Southern NGOs reported publishing more press releases, reports and briefings than northern groups, but the northerners were more likely to use electronic mail to disseminate information. (This statistic may have changed since 1996, as the Internet has become an instant means of communication for millions around the world.)

Of the southern organizations, 51 percent said they were local or grassroots, versus only 40 percent of northern groups. Nevertheless, southern NGOs may be more elitist in composition than northern ones. Smith *at al.* found that "southern NGOs were also slightly more likely to include elected [government] officials among their members" and were more likely to have paid, rather than volunteer, staff. Overall, they concluded, "The international human rights movement relies heavily on what are called 'insider' tactics, or activities that demand some formal access to political institutions and that typically require more resources than do 'outsider' tactics, such as public demonstrations and boycotts."

Three-quarters of the organizations have to raise funds to support themselves, through dues, sales and events. Sixty percent receive grants from foundations, and more than fifty percent receive funds from governments or intergovernmental agencies. This last statistic raises difficult questions about their independence and impartiality.

Korey warns that results of such a small survey must be read with caution, however, since

> the developing world (especially in Asia) has seen a veritable explosion in the number of NGOs; one writer . . . cited an estimate of 35,000 while acknowledging that 'it is impossible to measure a swiftly growing universe that includes neighborhood, professional, service and advocacy groups, both secular and church-based, promoting every conceivable cause.'

A THIRD WORLD PIONEER

The history of one group, the Arab Organization for Human Rights, shows how southern human rights organizations have developed over the past twenty years. Like many other NGOs, it emerged in the 1980s. Its predecessor was the Tunisian League of Human Rights, founded in 1977, which monitored political trials, investigated abuses, helped prisoners and reported on human rights issues. Amnesty groups also existed in some Arab countries in the early 1980s.

The AOHR began as several discussion groups whose members had been jailed for their political activities by Egyptian President Anwar al-Sadat and freed by his successor, Hosni Mubarak. They participated in the Tunis Conference of 1983, which published a declaration criticizing the lack of freedom in Arab countries. According to Jill Crystal, conference participants "demanded the trial or release of political prisoners, the reform of judicial systems and the abolition of secret police." They also called on their governments to implement the Universal Declaration of Human Rights.

Early activities of AOHR included publishing information in newsletters, bulletins and annual reports about the human rights situation in the Arab world. "It set up a judicial committee to receive and evaluate complaints, and then wrote to the governments for their side of the story before turning complaints over to a publicity committee in order to begin an international campaign," Crystal writes.

In 1987 the Egyptian government threatened to shut down the organization, but AOHR resisted, "filing legal challenges, publicizing its problem and manning the organization's building in shifts so that non-Egyptian members, whose arrests would be embarrassingly public, were always present," Crystal recounts. The government backed down, but the group's existence continued to be threatened by a repressive law that controlled the formation and operation of associations in Egypt.

AOHR's early members included lawyers, former parliamentarians, union leaders and professors. The organization did not accept government support but subsisted on individual contributions and membership dues. The annual budget was very modest indeed, about $150,000.

According to Crystal, the group sought support from international human rights organizations and "consciously patterned itself after Amnesty International." It received funding from the Ford Foundation, and it collaborated with NGOs such as Amideast, the ICJ, the International Committee of the Red Cross and Article Nineteen, an organization that protects and promotes freedom of expression.

By 1987, AOHR had received more than 150 cases from nineteen Arab countries. Seven governments replied to their inquiries. To commemorate the fortieth anniversary of the Universal Declaration of Human Rights in 1988, AOHR launched a campaign, its first international effort, on behalf of prisoners of conscience. AOHR joined with the Tunisian government, the Tunisian League for Human Rights, the Arab Lawyers Union and the U.N. Human Rights Commission to establish the Arab Institute for Human Rights in 1989. It trained human rights workers, disseminated information, and collaborated with press and bar associations, unions, university groups and women's and children's groups. That year AOHR also gained consultative status at the United Nations. Crystal explains:

> For the AOHR, attaining U.N. observer status was an important victory. Very few genuine NGOs exist in the Arab world, and the AOHR took its NGO status very seriously. . . . The U.N. tie gave the group a formal position from which to address Arab regimes and facilitated the formation of local groups in the member states. It also provided some protection for members, because governments were more reluctant to imprison those who might receive international publicity.

By 1990 the AOHR had board members from Palestine, Iraq, Sudan, Syria, Kuwait, Lebanon, Jordan, Morocco, Tunisia, Yemen, Libya and Algeria. It set up branches in six Arab countries and five western countries. The Egyptian branch worked on both collective and individual rights cases, protesting the treatment of political and common prisoners, repressive emergency laws and excessive use of force by the authorities. In 1991, AOHR conducted a campaign against torture in Egypt.

AOHR's approach to governments was diplomatic and conciliatory. Many of its leaders were former prisoners of conscience and government officials who "could speak the same language as those in power. Their similar social origins and political experience gave them access that other groups lacked," Crystal writes. But their proximity to government detracted from their credibility with the public. AOHR was not in the vanguard of a mass movement for human rights in the Arab countries, because no such movement existed.

For socioeconomic reasons AOHR and other Third World organizations restricted themselves to issues they could deal with effectively. Educating the general public about human rights and finding widespread support for their work within their societies were ambitious long-term endeavors from which many groups shied away. Financially precarious, defending themselves against repression, socially distant from the desperately poor and uneducated majority, they faced difficulties that First World organizations did not experience and often did not understand.

DIVERSITY AND DIVISION

Tensions inevitably arose between First and Third World human rights groups, especially in the 1990s, as hundreds of new, grassroots organizations from Africa and Asia entered the international scene for the first time. The big northern NGOs tended to receive most of the foundation funding, while the southern groups struggled along with sparse and sporadic support. Some southern organizations felt excluded from the planning of the NGO Forums at the U.N. conferences in Rio (on environment and development) Vienna (on human rights) and Beijing (on women). The issues they were most concerned about—economic, cultural and social rights—received much less attention than they wanted.

In Vienna, conflict developed between the international NGOs and the new grassroots groups. The well-established organizations, accustomed to working at the U.N., "saw the purpose of the [NGO] Forum to be one of working with governments in order to strengthen the UN human rights system by creating a North-South consensus," Korey writes. The local Third World groups "believed that the failure to expose human rights abuses in specific countries would constitute a betrayal of NGO hopes and operations." On that occasion, the newcomers won, and their victory helped determine the direction of the international human rights movement for the rest of the decade.

This is because both the big NGOs and the small local groups must work together in coalitions and networks to get anything done on the international level. The opposing forces—governments allied with global corporations—are too powerful to confront alone. The big organizations may wield influence at international conferences and agencies, but they have little direct experience of situations on the ground, where the local groups operate every day. And the local groups do not have the clout or resources to carry out their work without international moral and financial support.

Under such conditions, grassroots groups have had to show creativity and resourcefulness. Laurie Wiseberg cites an example from Tienanmen Square in 1989:

> A group of Chinese activists in Massachusetts kept a telephone line to Beijing open for 24 hours, immediately relaying the information they were receiving to the international press while simultaneously keeping activists [in China] informed . . . by sending news bulletins to fax machines in U.S. business offices all over China.

Organizations like Amnesty International receive much of the information they publish from grassroots activists, who may risk their lives to transmit it to researchers in London via fax machines and computer modems purchased with foundation grant monies.

Coordinating the activities of a broad-based, highly diverse, international movement composed of thousands of organizations is impossible. Organizations do keep in touch and learn from one another through encounters at international meetings and the U.N., ongoing contact via telephone, fax and the Internet, and through exchange of publications and other materials. According to Keck and Sikkink, these networks "are usually not one-way streets whereby activists in one country 'help' victims in another, but part of an interactive process by which people in far-flung places communicate and exchange beliefs, information, testimony, strategy and sometimes services. In the process of exchange they may change each other."

One of the main vehicles of such interchange is the international campaign, in which "core network actors mobilize others and initiate tasks of structural integration and cultural negotiation among the groups in the network. . . . they connect groups with each other, seek out resources, propose and prepare activities and conduct public relations," Keck and Sikkink write.

THE ENDURING CAMPAIGN

Campaigns mobilize diverse groups, which may include international and local NGOs, social movements, foundations, media, religious groups, trade unions, consumer organizations, intellectuals, government officials, intergovernmental organizations and legislative bodies. Keck and Sikkink believe these "advocacy networks" are innovative and significant because they enable "nontraditional international actors to mobilize information strategically to help create new issues and categories and to persuade, pressure and gain leverage over much more powerful organizations and governments."

Campaigns still use traditional strategies developed over the past two centuries, "dramatizing the situations of the victims and turning the cold facts into human stories, intended to move people to action." As ever, Keck and Sikkink observe, campaigners "mobilize shame." But now they have the capacity to bolster their moral arguments with unprecedented amounts and forms of information from unofficial and official sources to influence both international public opinion and government policy makers. They obtain this information through extensive international networks that link diverse groups and individuals.

For example, in the late 1980s a Brazilian indigenous group learned from an American anthropologist, who had studied their culture for many years, that the government was planning a series of dam projects that would flood vast areas of the Amazon forest where they lived. They asked the anthropologist to help them defend their constitutional right to their land.

Accompanied by two anthropologists who acted as interpreters, two Kayapó leaders traveled to Washington, D.C., to meet with World Bank officials who were considering lending the Brazilian government vast sums to build the dams. Anthropologists working with environmental organizations in Washington had arranged the meeting at the Bank. Information about the project that the Brazilian government kept secret in Brazil was available to the U.S. public in Washington, thanks to legislation designed to make the Bank more accountable to U.S. legislators and taxpayers. (The U.S. was the largest single donor to the World Bank at the time.) The American environmentalists ensured that the Indians obtained this information.

After meeting with Bank officials, the Indians returned to Brazil, where they were indicted, along with one of the anthropologists, under the Foreigners' Law, for involving themselves in politics. (The anthropologist was a foreigner, but the Indians clearly were not.) On the day of the hearing, Terence Turner wrote:

> Kayapó men and women danced through the streets and massed in the square before the Palace of Justice. . . . Kayapó orators unrolled the map of the Xingu dam scheme obtained from the World Bank in Washington on an easel erected in the square and explained the entire secret project in Kayapó and Portuguese for the benefit of the many Brazilian onlookers, who included reporters and TV crews.

The Brazilian government dropped the charges against the Indians, and the World Bank decided not to finance the dams. Northern environmental groups gave increasing attention to the Amazon after the success of this Kayapó campaign.

At about the same time, the Kayapó developed an alliance with the popular singer Sting, who agreed to help them pressure the Brazilian government to demarcate part of their traditional territory. Sting traveled around the world with Kayapó leaders, who met with heads of state and promoted their cause at his concerts.

Having involved himself intensively in indigenous issues for about a year, Sting decided to launch the Rainforest Foundation, whose professional staff would work with the Indians on sustainable development projects. In addition to funding these projects, the Rainforest Foundation campaigned internationally on behalf of the Kayapó and other indigenous groups, set up affiliates in several countries, sent representatives to international meetings, including the U.N. Earth Summit, and participated in coalitions and networks of environmental, indigenous and human rights organizations. It became a typical international NGO, funded by private donations and foundation grants, based in the North but sponsoring projects in the South, exchanging information and collaborating with other groups, and participating in human rights campaigns.

A very different kind of NGO is the Quixote Center, founded as a "peace and justice organization" in a suburb of Washington, D.C., by progressive Catholic religious and lay people in the mid-1970s. The Center became well-known for sending large amounts of humanitarian aid to Nicaragua in the early 1980s, when the U.S. government was trying to overthrow the Sandinistas. It has undertaken campaigns against the death penalty in the U.S., on behalf of Catholic activists silenced or excommunicated after expressing dissenting opinions, and for democratization and grassroots development in Nicaragua and Haiti. The Center specializes in causes that other NGOs regard as lost or hopeless, and it often works directly with grassroots organizations in the U.S. and other countries. It raises funds from thousands of individual donors and religious communities via a sophisticated, very efficient, direct-mail operation. Like the Rainforest Foundation, the Quixote Center participates in NGO networks that frequently collaborate in human rights campaigns. Center staff members often may be found walking picket lines, marching in the streets or helping coordinate demonstrations and other actions in Washington, D.C.

THIN AIR

The Rainforest Foundation, the Quixote Center and other international NGOs of the early Twenty-First Century operate in a milieu that only a few of their precursors would recognize. They comprise an independent bloc or sector with powerful constituencies and significant leverage in international affairs. Some carry on "quiet diplomacy" with nation states and intergovernmental organizations. For example, just three human rights professionals, from Human Rights Watch, the Lawyers Committee for Human Rights and AIUSA, successfully lobbied the U.S. State Department to support the establishment of the U.N. High Commissioner post in 1993. With U.S. encouragement, the U.N. announced creation of the post at the Vienna human rights conference that year.

The big international NGOs use sophisticated public relations techniques to influence international elites via their allies in the media. They also keep in touch with grassroots groups. Through varied strategies, they have become important political actors on the international stage. In the Eighteenth and Nineteenth Century, such a role was restricted to very few figures, such as Thomas Clarkson or Victor Hugo. As recently as the 1950s, someone like Sean MacBride could operate in this empyrean realm, but few others could enter. Now hundreds of organizations and thousands of individuals occupy this rarified international space.

In recent years the Nobel Peace Prize committee has recognized international NGOs that work in the intergovernmental realm. In 1996 the prize was awarded to two activists, Bishop Carlos Ximenes Belo and José Ramos Horta, who worked with international NGOs and governments for the independence of East Timor. The International Campaign to Ban Landmines, a coalition of more than 800 international NGOs—human rights organizations, children's groups, development organizations, refugee and humanitarian relief organizations and medical organizations—received the prize in 1997.

SALT OF THE EARTH

But what about the people on the ground? Lauren describes them as

> the people on the front line who dodge bullets, who speak out against brutality and tyranny, who search for the 'disappeared,' who write on behalf of the imprisoned and tortured, who try to defend the exploited and repressed, who seek to stop carnage and impoverishment, and who work in common ways to bring human rights to life. They also are the ones participating in a vast new field of action in which ordinary but dedicated people are constructing human rights projects, organizing practical training sessions in local communities, and sharing their knowledge with others through education now in virtually every quadrant of the globe.

These human rights defenders may be found in remote villages, urban slums, prosecutors' offices, Bible study groups, Buddhist monasteries, prisons, classrooms and a host of other places. For them, everyday life itself is a campaign. Without them, the international human rights movement would have little substance. Their courage, determination and creativity give the worldwide movement its distinctive character and its hope for a better future.

As communication among different parts of the movement improved during the 1980s and 1990s, human rights professionals had more opportunities to work directly with and be inspired by grassroots activists. On many occasions they shared successes. Sometimes, though, they had the terrible experience of witnessing the deaths of comrades on the front lines of the human rights struggle. In 1988, human rights workers and environmentalists witnessed the Brazilian rubber-tapper leader Chico Mendes being repeatedly threatened, harried from place to place and finally killed as he stepped off his back porch on the way to his backyard shower.

They had tried to prevent his death by issuing Urgent Action Appeals, giving him international awards, inviting him to spend time in safer places and pressuring the Brazilian government to provide bodyguards— all to no avail.

Also in 1988, Miguel Angel Pavon Salazar, a local director of the Committee to Defend Human Rights in Honduras, was shot to death after testifying before the Inter-American Court of Human Rights about a "disappearance" case. Another witness who had not yet testified also was killed. According to Wiseberg:

> These death squad killings occurred despite the fact that the Court earlier had sent messages to the Honduran government to take all necessary steps to protect the lives, personal integrity and possessions of those who had been called to the witness stand and had received death threats. The Court immediately called on the Honduran government to conduct a complete investigation into the murders, and . . . it ordered the government to identify those responsible and to prosecute them in accordance with Honduran law. Neither judicial nor police investigations into the assassinations, however, produced any leads or resulted in any indictments.

Killings like these happened many times in many countries in the 1980s and '90s.

PROTECTING THE DEFENDERS

In the mid-1980s, Peace Brigades International (PBI) began "accompanying" human rights defenders under threat in Guatemala. "The theory . . . is that the authorities and paramilitary forces will hesitate before trying to kill or disappear human rights activists in the presence of foreign witnesses," Wiseberg writes. PBI has accompanied activists in several countries, including El Salvador, Colombia, Haiti, Sri Lanka, East Timor and Mexico, with some success. But the program is costly, requires time-consuming training and cannot attract enough volunteer participants to accompany thousands of threatened activists for extended periods.

In response to the growing numbers of cases of activists who were being threatened, harassed, "disappeared" and killed, Amnesty and other organizations pushed for an international agreement to protect human rights defenders. In 1999 the United Nations General Assembly adopted the clumsily named Declaration on the Right and Responsibility of Individuals, Groups and Organs of Society to Promote and Protect Universally Recognized Human Rights and Fundamental Freedoms.

Article 1 declares, "Everyone has the right, individually and in association with others, to promote and to strive for the protection and realization of human rights and fundamental freedoms at the national and international levels." The state must protect and guarantee the rights of individuals "to meet or assemble peacefully; to form, join and participate in nongovernmental organizations, associations or groups; to communicate with nongovernmental or intergovernmental organizations."

Like the other human rights covenants, conventions and agreements, this one is a bravely worded document, filled with inspiring and hopeful sentiments. Whether it will amount to more than a scrap of paper remains to be seen. At least it serves as one more tool that human rights organizations can use to "mobilize shame."

THE MOVEMENT GOES ON

As it reached its fortieth anniversary in 2001, Amnesty International remained at the forefront of human rights organizations—still the largest, best-funded and most respected. But as Korey points out, its membership has remained "overwhelmingly western," despite recruitment efforts in the Global South and East. In many instances, human rights advocates have wanted to work on their own country, against Amnesty's rule, or they do not have the resources to support an Amnesty section with dues or contributions. Some have felt constrained by the centralized control of Amnesty's International Secretariat in London. Others have wanted to work on cases involving economic, social and cultural rights or collective rights, which Amnesty's mandate did not include until 2001. In western countries, Amnesty's members are aging, and young people have not replaced them. Such are the problems of a well-established, middle-aged organization.

Yet Amnesty still boasts more than one million members in seventy-seven countries, from Australia to Yemen. According to the organization's annual report, in 1999, more than 80,000 volunteers in some eighty countries participated in the Urgent Action Network, which issued almost a thousand UAs that year. Local groups worked on long-term cases of about 4,500 individuals, including prisoners of conscience and victims of other human rights violations, in 2000. That year, Regional Action Networks involving almost 1,800 local groups took on more than 200 medium-term cases. The organization also responded to emergency situations in Sierra Leone and Israel/Occupied Territories/Palestinian Authority.

In 2000 Amnesty launched a worldwide campaign against torture that featured a website, www.stoptorture.org, which gave visitors the opportunity to take immediate action via the Internet. Groups and professional networks worked on lesbian, gay, bisexual and transgender rights; military, security and police transfers; approaches to businesses and corporations, human rights education projects and refugee cases. AI local and student groups and national sections maintained more than 250 Web sites.

Amnesty's former Secretary General Pierre Sané said in a 1996 interview, "We are not a research organization; we are an action and campaigning organization." In this way Amnesty has remained true to two centuries of tradition and the intentions of its originators. But in many other ways, the organization has been transformed almost beyond recognition, from a cottage industry in two small, dark rooms in the basement of One Mitre Court to an International Secretariat with more than 300 employees in two large buildings. For some, Amnesty has lost many of its endearing original qualities and has become overgrown, unwieldy, rigid and bureaucratized. It could not prevent genocide in Rwanda or "ethnic cleansing" in the Balkans.

Nonetheless, Amnesty's members and staff save a certain number of lives every year. Anyone who has received word of an adopted prisoner's release after writing letters for years—or even sending a single telegram—knows the unparalleled joy of rescuing a stranger. That feeling and those actions keep renewing Amnesty's vibrant soul.

Amnesty International is only a part of a vast movement that has grown to maturity over the past two centuries. During that time millions of people have written letters, marched in protest, given speeches and sermons, published editorials, pamphlets and books, contributed money and time, helped slaves to freedom and dedicated themselves to advancing human rights in many other ways. They acted in isolation, in small groups or in large movements to achieve a great purpose—or just to save a life. Many knew nothing about those who had gone before. Others treasured the memory and example of the predecessors who inspired them. Past and present activists all belong to something much larger than themselves. Every time someone writes a letter about a prisoner of conscience, attends a demonstration or sends a check to a human rights organization, he or she is participating in and perpetuating a long tradition. The struggle always continues, and today's human rights campaigners comprise the next generation of ancestors.

NOTES

INTRODUCTION

1   "calamities to the end": Gifford 1996: 19.
3   "fierce legion of friends and comrades": Sacco and Vanzetti 1997: 15.
3   "mad with wounded self-importance": Porter 1977: 43.

1. THE FIRST HUMAN RIGHTS CAMPAIGNS

8   "the vastness of unfreedom": Drescher 1986: 17.
9   "disgusting and inadequate": Marshall 1956: 274.
9   "being social acceptable": Marshall 1956: 59.
9   "the provinces and London": Marshall 1956: 41.
10   "newspaper industry": Smith 1979: 68.
10   "humiliation of the pillory": Smith 1979: 79.
11   "virtuous by accident": Williamson 1974: 24.
11   "they would not burn": Williamson 1974: 150.
11   "the public imagination": Williamson 1974: 151.
11   "dispersed throughout London": Brewer 1976: 166
12   "in favour of arbitrary power": Brewer 1976: 166.
12   "may have been less": Brewer 1976: 172.
12   "fit for framing": Brewer 1976: 173.
12   "first political entrepreneur": Brewer 1976: 198.
13   "slave-grown cotton or sugar": Drescher 1986: 9.
13   "very respectable merchants' fortunes": Marshall 1956: 157.
13   "highly respectable": Porter 1970: 29.
13   "abolition tooth and nail": Marshall 1956: 158.
14   "property and individual responsibility": Davis 1975: 82.
14   "proprietorship of their persons": Hurwitz 1973: 25.
14   "guardians of the moral order": Hurwitz 1973: 18.
14   "they were entirely familiar": Temperley 1980: 337.
15   "plight of the Negroes": Bruns 1977: xx.
16   "slavery in the Eighteenth Century": Bruns 1977: 79.
16   "opinion against the institution": Bruns 1977: 139.
16   "the Coast of Africa": Jennings 1997: 23.
16   "Quaker organization for review": Jennings 1997: 23.
17   "they should do unto us": London Yearly Meeting 1783: 5-7.

17   "particular situations may admit": London Yearly Meeting 1783: 14-15.
17   "an international pressure group": Davis 1966: 329.
18   "inherent rights of mankind": Jennings 1997: 27.
18   "its kind in America": Drake 1950: 86.
18   "for a philanthropic cause": Drescher 1986: 64

2. CAMPAIGNERS AND STRATEGIES
IN THE LATE EIGHTEENTH CENTURY

21   "this new philosophy?": Fryer 1984: 211.
21   "inconsistent with republican government": Mathews 1980: 215.
21   "to slavery itself": Lascelles 1928: 38.
22   "into the streets to die": Lascelles 1928: 17.
22   "abolition of the slave trade": Lascelles 1928: 18.
22   "study of constitutional law": Lascelles 1928: 19.
22   "joy, to the shore": Shyllon 1974: 45.
23   "to be sold abroad": d'Anjou 1996: 146.
23   death of her master: *Public Ledger* 1772: 4.
23   "in the House of Lords": Lascelles 1928: 64.
23   "time, talents and substance": Shyllon 1974: 137.
24   "such enormous iniquity legal": Lascelles 1928: 72.
24   "who have only interests": Harrison 1982: 378.
24   "British West Indian slavery": Shyllon 1977: 43.
24   "man of feeling and sentiment": Shyllon 1977: 22.
24   "vituperation and vilification": Shyllon 1977: 41.
25   "explaining and advising": Shyllon 1977: 86.
26   "out of place": Myers 1996: 131.
27   "abolitionist movement in Britain": Fryer 1984: 203.
27   "happiness and freedom": Keane 1995: 43, 45.
27   "despotism and injustice": Keane 1995: xiii.
28   "taming their bellicose urges": Keane 1995: 303-04.
28   "publicly through the press": Keane 1995: 320.
28   "anti-Paine propaganda": Keane 1995: 335.
28   "prosecuted, fined or imprisoned": Keane 1995: 336.
28   "a latter-day dissident": Keane 1995: 337.
28   "but the contrary!": Keane 1995: 341.
29   "giant with one idea": Gifford 1996: 4.
30   "reservoir of public feeling": Oldfield 1995: 76.
30   "become of each one": Wilson 1990: 38.
31   "public face of abolition": Oldfield 1995: 74.
32   "most important, organization": Davis 1975: 215.
32   "we might lose all": Walvin 1986: 107.

32	"for the above purposes": Committee for Effecting the Abolition of the Slave Trade: 1.
33	"reprinting old ones": Oldfield 1995: 43-4.
33	"the committee's county agents": Oldfield 1995: 44.
34	"expanding consumer society": Oldfield 1995: 64.
34	"slave trade in 1788": Midgley 1992: 32.
35	"the context of religion": Midgley 1992: 25.
35	"calling for similar actions": Drescher 1986: 70.
36	"savage punishments": Walvin 1986: 119.
36	"climate of the period": Midgley 1992: 40.
37	"U.S., France and Brazil": Davis 1975: 450.
37	"shared vision of the future": Drescher 1982: 48.
37	"low, rich or poor": Walvin 1986: 113.
37	"working-class politics": Walvin 1986: 113.

3. NINETEENTH CENTURY ANTISLAVERY: "POWER CONCEDES NOTHING WITHOUT A DEMAND"

42	"in the Chartist Movement": Midgley 1992: 85.
42	"men in the movement": Thompson 1984: 258.
43	"strike that the century saw": Thompson 1984: 295.
43	"attempted with no success": Thompson 1984: 300.
43	"great cause of human rights": Mayer 1998: 110.
43	"I WILL BE HEARD": Stewart 1986: 46.
44	"over the lurid scene": Mayer 1998: 196.
45	"running with blood": Quarles 1969: 203.
45	"proceedings were quashed": Mayer 1998: 412.
46	"Burns onto the ship": Stewart 1986: 172.
46	"and raising funds": Von Frank 1998: 329.
47	"act on this subject": Lerner 1971: 139.
48	"town on a rail": Lerner 1971: 128.
48	"with a colored woman": Lerner 1971: 255.
48	"poverty and domestic problems": Lerner 1971: 292.
49	"make their weight felt": Lerner 1971: 270-71.
49	"sectarianism and isolation": Lerner 1971: 270.
49	"right to petition": Lerner 1971: 275.
49	"odious of all tasks": Lerner 1971: 273.
50	"anarchy and shameless vice": Yellin and Van Horne 1994: 222.
50	"designed us to occupy": Lerner 1971: 192.
50	"as bad as before": Horton 1993: 96.
50	"British rank and file": Quarles 1969: 118.
51	"causes are mutually beneficial": Rogers 1995: 93.
51	"apples in the streets": Quarles 1969: 32.

51   "these direct actions": Jezer *et al.* 1987: 30.
52   "protection from kidnappers": Quarles 1969: 150.
52   "safe from slavery": Horton 1993: 58.
53   "seaboard to the Great Lakes": Mayer 1998: 406.
53   "in the nation's experience": Mayer 1998: 495.
54   "comfort the martyr's widow": Mayer 1998: 504.
54   "attracts the eyes of Europe": Hugo 1859: 4.
54   Published opposition to cruel punishments goes back at least to 1764, when the Italian Cesare Beccharia argued against torture and the death penalty in *On Crimes and Punishments*.
55   "Southworth and Hawes": Yellin 1989: 130.
55   "with great enthusiasm": Hurwitz 1973: 91.
55   "slave-grown products": Midgley 1992: 111.
56   "their boards of directors": Rogers 1995: 25.
56   "humans of their free will": Horton 1993: 56.
56   "it never will": Zinn 1995: 179.
56   "political elite of Paris": Drescher 1986: 56.
56   "by word of mouth": Daget 1980: 67.
56   "working for the blacks": Daget 1980: 76.
57   "in favor of emancipation": Nabuco 1977: 19.
57   "a *political* movement": Nabuco 1977: 19.
57   "part of a whole": Azevedo 1995: 14.
57   "freedom and social justice": Azevedo 1995: xxi.
57   "involved in abolitionism": Conrad 1972: 143, 147.
58   "plantations in large numbers": Conrad 1972: 239.

4. THE AGE OF MASS MOVEMENTS AND THE "MARTYRS OF CHICAGO"

61   "all kinds of information": Stewart 1986: 179.
61   "while scanning their newspapers": Stewart 1986: 180.
62   "restricting individual freedom": Stewart 1986: 242.
62   "duties of citizenship": Stewart 1986: 261.
62   "to use as he pleases": Filler 1965: 193.
62   "fair share of the profits": Madison 1959: 71.
62   "power of incorporated wealth": Madison 1959: 73.
63   "entitled to all it creates": Madison 1959: 70.
63   "insolence and cruel rule": Stewart 1986: 322.
63   "the *Daily Advertiser*": Stewart 1986: 328.
63   "claim of downtrodden humanity": Stewart 1986: 333.
63   "to ask for support": Dinkin 1989: x.
64   "the canopy of heaven": Dinkin 1989: 36.

64   "for two to three hours": Dinkin 1989: 66.
65   "any means possible": Strasser 1989: 91.
65   "market as a battlefield": Strasser 1989: 93.
66   "the 'new journalism'": Stephens 1988: 210.
66   "rest of the century": Smith 1979: 116.
67   "assemble a crowd": Vlastos 1995: 246.
68   "opposing oligarchic rule": Vlastos 1995: 238.
68   "elaboration on our part": Lu 1997: 327.
68   "forces in a new campaign": Vlastos 1995: 242.
68   "signed similar petitions": Hane 1992: 120.
68   "limited rights and freedom": Hane 1992: 130.
70   "Communism is the most disgusting": Stewart 1986: 322.
70   "placards and banners": Avrich 1984: 111.
70   "the Socialist League": Avrich 1984: 111.
70   "agitate, organize, revolt": Avrich 1984: 147.
71   "opportunity to silence them": Avrich 1984: 235.
71   "found in humanity's formation": David 1963: 187.
71   "with a few bombs": David 1963: 188.
71   "successful at raising money": David 1963: 198.
71   "humanitarians of all creeds": Avrich 1984: 249.
72   "trial or the verdict": David 1963: 274.
72   "token of anarchist sympathies": Avrich 1984: 280.
72   "authority was right and effective": Smith 1995: 122.
72   "court of public opinion" (Smith 1995: 129.
72   "groups throughout the world": Avrich 1984: 286.
72   "no ordinary ability": Ashbaugh 1976: 86.
73   "about anarchism": Ashbaugh 1976: 105.
73   "upheld the Constitution": Ashbaugh 1976: 110.
73   "movement of the 1890s": Ashbaugh 1976: 117.
73   "not received impartial justice": Avrich 1984: 301.
74   "commutation of the death sentences": David 1963: 354.
74   "struggle for economic emancipation": Ashbaugh 1976: 128.
74   "piled high with petitions": Avrich 1984: 335.
74   "bringing in $250": Ashbaugh 1976: 129.
74   "America and the world": Avrich 1984: 330.
75   "have upon society": Gompers 1925: 180.
75   "indignation and protest": Avrich 1984: 409.
75   "little harm to society": Ashbaugh 1976: 187.
75   "deluged" with petitions: Avrich 1984: 419.
76   "reviled man in America": Avrich 1984: 424.
76   "rarely been equaled": David 1963: 436.
76   "they were usually right": Thomas 1983: 209.
76   "increasingly bitter confrontations": Thomas 1983: 217.

77   "Lincoln and Wendell Phillips": Thomas 1983: 278.
77   "an active anarchist": Wexler 1984: 35-36.
77   "radicalism in general": Wexler 1984: 38.
78   "black Friday of 1887": Ishill Collection, Letter of E. Goldman to J. Ishill,
       August 10, 1927, p. 1, bMS Am 1614 (54) folder 2, by permission of the
       Houghton Library, Harvard University.

5. THE WORLD OF THE 1890S: LYNCHING, GENOCIDE, INJUSTICE

82   "never be uncivilized again": Twain 1929: 247-48; his emphasis.
84   "outside the black community": McMurry 1998: 188.
84   "name of justice and humanity": McMurry 1998: 193.
85   "more publicity Wells received": McMurry 1998: 220.
85   "a stop to lynching": McMurry 1998: 223.
85   "play a lone hand": McMurry 1998: 282.
86   "continued to the end": thompson 1990: 102.
86   "in which he belongs": McMurry 1998: 280.
86   "prisoners in Illinois": McMurry 1998: 284.
86   "would have excluded Africans": McMurry 1998: 303-04.
86   "from the white mobs": McMurry 1998: 314.
86   "race who protested": McMurry 1998: 319.
87   "live in this country": McMurry 1998: 325.
87   "to which you refer": U.S. Department of Justice 1926.
87   "crimes against humanity": Hochschild 1998: 112.
88   "prodigious capacity for indignation": Hochschild 1998: 187.
88   "journalist of his time": Hochschild 1998: 187.
88   "governed with humanity": Hochschild 1998: 194.
89   "appendices and depositions": Hochschild 1998: 203.
89   "simple surgical operation": Hochschild 1998: 204.
89   "rough plan of campaign": Hochschild 1998: 206.
89   "the right to live": Hochschild 1998: 210.
89   "letters to local newspapers": Hochschild 1998: 210.
90   "it was in England": Hochschild 1998: 243.
91   "will not pass away": Hochschild 1998: 273-74.
91   "end of the earth": Hochschild 1998: 305.
92   "excluded from the nation": Halasz 1955: 123.
93   "who had made them" Dreyfus 1977: 41.
93   "search out the culprit": Cahm 1996: 33.
94   "wipe out its effects": Cahm 1996: 32.
94   "before public opinion": Brown 1995: 719.
95   "access to genuine information": Hoffman 1980: 16.
95   "almost total immunity": Cahm 1996: 17.
95   "films from public exhibition": Hoffman 1980: 157.

96	"no Dreyfus affair": Cahm 1996: 196.
96	"a coherent Dreyfusist movement": Brown 1995: 735.
96	"support of public causes": Cahm 1996: 69.
97	"dominate and exploit us": Cahm 1996: 96.
97	"rights had been violated": Cahm 1996: 85.
97	"obtained for a night": Hoffman 1980: 165.
98	"organized propaganda campaign": Hoffman 1980: 163.
98	"infinite capacity for resistance": Dreyfus 1977: 238.
98	"France which I loved": Dreyfus 1977: 240.
99	"justice, liberty and truth": Dreyfus 1977: 240.
99	"begins to be seen": Feldman 1981: 70.
99	"to visit that country": Feldman 1981: 118.
99	"social and legal superiority": Feldman 1981: 22.
99	"close of the Nineteenth Century": Feldman 1981: 11.
99	"the French flag": Cahm 1996: 177.
100	"committed by another": Cahm 1996: 180.
100	"more than three decades": Feldman 1981: 97.
100	"Alfred Dreyfus Arrested": Cahm 1996: 10.
101	"held around the country": Hoffman 1980: 26.
102	"arrested one fine morning": Kafka 1969: 3.
103	"all other things": Samuel 1966: 92.
103	"going on in that country": Samuel 1966: 253.

6. SACCO AND VANZETTI: AGONY OR TRIUMPH?

108	"other pressure targets": Ward 1983: 94
108	"out of San Quentin": Ward 1983: 279.
108	"indicted by Massachusetts authorities": Feuerlicht 1977: 88.
109	"fair trial in Massachusetts": Feuerlicht 1977: 88.
109	"interest and protest": Feuerlicht 1977: 84.
109	"difficulties and tensions mitigated": Avrich 1991: 134.
109	"radicals to be watched": Avrich 1991: 197.
110	"the other day?" Taylor 1977: 192.
110	"criminal cases": Feuerlicht 1977: 184.
111	"streets, not the courts": Feuerlicht 1977: 184.
111	"elements in the labor group": Joughin and Morgan 1978: 225.
111	"Felix and his wife": Jackson Reminiscences: 231.
111	women as "Comrade": Frankfurter and Jackson 1997: passim.
112	"treatment of the two men": Avrich 1995: 146.
112	"went the other way": Jackson Reminiscences: 22.
112	"try to find out?": Jackson Reminiscences: 114.
113	"for the defense committee": Jackson Reminiscences: 115, 157.
113	"children as they came up": Jackson Reminiscences: 152.

113   "remarkable human being": Jackson Reminiscences: 159.
113   "miscarriages of justice": Jackson Reminiscences: 154-55.
113   "charge of the case": Sinclair 1978: 513.
114   "counterproductive is debatable": Feuerlicht 1977: 191.
114   "judgment on his clients": Feuerlicht 1977: 309.
114   "if it was held": Sinclair 1978: 514.
114   "Anatole France": Joughin and Morgan 1978: 233-34.
115   "controversy or social friction": Joughin and Morgan 1978: 241.
115   "were doomed": Feuerlicht 1977: 312.
115   "review of the case": Joughin and Morgan 1978: 238.
115   "through legal processes": Jackson Reminiscences: 183.
115   "the Sacco-Vanzetti people": Jackson Reminiscences: 183.
116   "long talk with him": Jackson Reminiscences: 189.
116   "on such petitions": Jackson Reminiscences: 193.
116   "we couldn't accomplish something": Jackson Reminiscences: 194.
116   "had to be done": Jackson Reminiscences: 203-04.
116   "be the right thing": Jackson Reminiscences: 302.
117   "pleaded in our favor": Feuerlicht 1977: 332-33.
117   "according to Gardner Jackson": Feuerlicht 1977: 353.
117   "it certainly surprised me": Jackson Reminiscences: 200.
117   "office with this roll": Jackson Reminiscences: 201.
117   "honor of their country": David 1963: 5.
117   "the counter upon request": Feuerlicht 1977: 354.
117   "all over the world": Jackson Reminiscences: 236.
118   "of the Dreyfus case": David 1963: 13.
118   "leadership in Europe": Jackson 1954: 237-38.
118   "policy was, and is": Porter 1977: 18.
118   "they do us alive?": Porter 1977: 19.
118   "forces of the community": Joughin and Morgan 1978: 243.
119   "and probably since": Feuerlicht 1977: 389.
119   "resentment of the two men": Feuerlicht 1977: 391.
120   "first base with him": Jackson Reminiscences: 240.
120   "desperation and terror": Felicani 1967: 109-10.
120   "will live forever": Felicani 1967: 111.
121   "I had ever witnessed": Porter 1977: 39.
121   "the thing right up": Jackson Reminiscences: 217.
121   "perpetrators of the crime": Jackson Reminiscences: 241.
122   "were to be met": Sinclair 1978: 745
122   "the crematory chapel": Blackwell 1937: 219.
123   "take his advice": Jackson Reminiscences: 246.
123   "blinding him in one eye": Schlesinger 1965: 17.
123   "continue to walk": Mencken 1929: 6.
124   "believe it myself at all": Jackson Reminiscences: 270.

124 "threw it on the pavement": Jackson Reminiscences: 294.

125 "foreign intimidations": Ehrmann Papers: Sacco-Vanzetti Commemorative Committee press release, October 3, 1967.

125 "Commonwealth of Massachusetts": Jackson 1981: 90.

125 "justice and human understanding": Jackson 1981: 89.

126 "that has its effect": Jackson Reminiscences: 284.

127 "demand useful positive action": Joughin and Morgan 1978: 241-42.

127 "for their own purposes": Jackson Reminiscences: 256.

127 "democratic and undemocratic action": Joughin and Morgan 1978: 372.

128 "August 22. Remember": Sinclair 1978: 753.

128 "their final vindication": Ehrmann Papers.

7. THE SCOTTSBORO BOYS: "A TANGLED, UGLY CASE"

131 "A Tangled, Ugly Case": NAACP Archives: Letter of Walter White, May 3, 1931.

131 "Sacco-Vanzetti on their hands": Goodman 1994: 25.

131 "these lawyers got in": Patterson and Conrad 1950: 18.

131 "working to get us free": Norris and Washington 1979: 26.

132 "eight colored boys of Alabama": NAACP Archives: Letter of G.M. and H. Isom, received May 27, 1931.

132 "properly tried and defended": NAACP Archives: Letter of Will Alexander, September 30, 1930.

132 "convictions of the helpless boys": NAACP Archives: Letter of William White, April 23, 1931: 2.

132 "mass movement of protest": Carter 1969: 67.

133 "demanding our freedom": Norris and Washington 1979: 58.

133 "bring about revolution": Goodman 1994: 27.

133 "to the electric chair": Norris and Washington 1979: 58.

133 "'to lay off'": Carter 1969: 57.

133 "to see us free": Norris and Washington 1979: 59.

133 "they had say-so": Patterson and Conrad 1950: 32-3.

134 "stream of vituperation": Carter 1969: 62.

134 "signed with the ILD": Norris and Washington 1979: 59.

134 "by side in crusades": Carter 1969: 138.

135 "boys would have died": Goodman 1994: 84.

135 "saved all our lives": Norris and Washington 1979: 60.

135 "bosses' lynching mobs": Carter 1969: 145.

135 "humanity and justice": Carter 1969: 145.

137 "to the electric chair!": NAACP Archives: *Le Populaire*, June 22, 1932; my translation.

137 "bewhiskered and filthy": Chalmers 1951: 51.

138 "governor of Alabama": Goodman 1994: 148-49.

138 blacks on the juries: In one retrial, the judge called the lone black juror, an elderly man, "boy" and ordered him to sit outside the jury box.

138 "word, sign or writing": Carter 1969: 259.

138 "white and Negro auditors": Carter 1969: 261.

139 "kick them in the face": NAACP Archives: Letter of Roy Wilkins, March 14, 1934: 2.

140 "meddling in Alabama's affairs": Goodman 1994: 304.

140 "two 'hookwormy Magdalenes'": Carter 1969: 365-66.

140 "to a favorable solution": Chalmers Collection: Letter of Allan K. Chalmers, February 4, 1937.

141 "on to other things": Norris and Washington 1979: 190.

141 "torture of my daily life": Chalmers Collection: Letter of Haywood Patterson, June 17, 1945.

141 "to carry on alone": Chalmers Collection: Letter of Roy Wilkins, April 19, 1950.

142 "rights from then on": Patterson and Conrad 1950: 245.

142 "called the Movement": Hendrickson 2000: 14.

143 "on the governor's office": Norris and Washington 1979: 238.

143 "nine years earlier": Strasser 1999: 208.

144 "not political cases": NAACP Archives: Letter of William Pickens, May 19, 1931.

144 "cases in the newspapers": NAACP Archives: Letter of Walter White, May 13, 1931.

144 "to harm the NAACP": NAACP Archives: Letter of Walter White, May 11, 1931.

145 "trade union leaders": Howe and Coser 1974: 203.

8. THE ROSENBERGS: SACRIFICING THE SCAPEGOATS

150 "control of the globe": Sayre 1995: 253.

150 "irrational after all": Sayre 1995: 270.

151 "World War III": Sayre 1995: 254-55. For a detailed analysis of the anti-Communist crusade, see Schrecker 1998.

151 Different sources disagree on the length of time the ACLU refused to defend Communists during the 1950s.

152 "until proven guilty": Meeropol 1994: xx.

153 "won for these men": Meeropol 1994: 506.

153 "they met with success": Meeropol 1994: 507.

154 "people accused of espionage": Meeropol 1994: xviii.

154 "one voice was raised": Belfrage and Aronson 1978: 164.

154 "disadvantage of your country": Philipson 1988: 306.

154 "as good as dead": Philipson 1988: 190.

155 "articles in pamphlet form": Reuben 1999: 22.

155   "it was a frame-up": Reuben interview, August 24, 2000.
156   "effective public speaker": Radosh and Milton 1997: 326.
156   "I was the organizer": Alman interview, September 23, 2000.
156   "call for a retrial": Radosh and Milton 1997: 326.
156   Rosenbergs were "expendable": Philipson 1988: 315.
156   "at this late stage": Radosh and Milton 1997: 325.
156   "complete vindication": Meeropol 1994: 296.
157   "part of the committee": Reuben Reminiscences, March 15, 1983: Tape 2.
157   "nothing to hide": Alman interview, September 23, 2000.
157   "organize the opposition": Alman interview, September 23, 2000.
157   "in road building funds": Tye 1998: 58.
158   "religion of anti-Communism": Neville 1995: 29.
159   "Call, contact, visit, mail": Committee to Secure Justice in the Rosenberg Case [CSJRC] Records: "Report on the Midwest Conference on the Rosenberg Case, August 17, 1952": 7.
159   "canvassing with the postcard": CSJRC Records: Boston Committee to Secure Clemency in the Rosenberg Case, December 15, 1952.
159   "commuters' train to Boston": CSJRC Records: *Ibid.*
159   "not credit their participation": Meeropol 1994: 465.
159   "work in closer harmony": Meeropol 1994: 466-67.
159   "at the United Nations": Meeropol 1994: 656.
160   "support for Julius and Ethel": Radosh and Milton 1997: 329.
160   "win over to Communism": Philipson 1988: 343.
160   "spontaneous combustion": Alman interview, September 23, 2000.
161   "chairs instead of teeth": Radosh and Milton 1997: 348.
161   "for the Rosenberg case": Philipson 1988: 336.
161   "serve a political agenda": Garber and Walkowitz 1995: 173.
161   "America and abroad": Radosh and Milton 1997: 340.
161   "mommy and daddy go": Radosh and Milton 1997: 341.
162   "for intelligence work": Garber and Walkowitz 1995: 25.
162   "exhaustion and despair": Belfrage and Aronson 1978: 190.
163   "remained unusually silent": Garber and Walkowitz 1995: 208.
163   "her own family": Garber and Walkowitz 1995: 211.
164   "commuted by the President": Schneir 1983: 190.
164   "too shaky a foundation": CSJRC Records: Letter of James H. Wolfe, January 10, 1953.
164   "at this very hour": Philipson 1988: 345.
164   "time for routine duties": Root 1963: 20.
165   "confess or die": Neville 1995: 125.
165   "outside comment or help": Radosh and Milton 1997: 384.
165   "productions of modern times": Neville 1995: 125.
166   "Communist demonstration": Neville 1995: 133.

166   "London's West End": Schneir 1983: 251.
166   "no program, simply grief": Sharlitt 1989: 146.
166   "calamity": Reuben interview, September 2, 2000.
166   "line of graveside speakers": Neville 1995: 133.
166   "their progressive activity": Meeropol 1994: xi.
167   "American body politic": Belfrage and Aronson 1978: 175.
167   "for which he stands": Fiedler 1955: 45.
168   "blackmail was practiced on us": Fiedler 1955: 27.
168   "averted their heads": Neville 1995: 28, 135.
169   "turned back fascism": Alman interview, September 23, 2000.
169   "to free slaves": Raskin 1974: 27.
169   "mother and daughter": Raskin 1974: 142.
170   "thirties with the sixties": Raskin 1974: 215.
170   "withdrawn from the stores": Coover 1998: xvii.

9. AMNESTY INTERNATIONAL: MYTH AND REALITY

174   "bad as the old ones": Amnesty International [AI] Archives: Astor oral history: 14.
174   "against political imprisonment": AI Archives: Benenson oral history: 7.
175   "a hundred went in": AI Archives: Vincent oral history: 36.
175   "my way to Irkutsk": Avrich 1995: 361.
175   "Yiddish and half Russian": Avrich 1995: 374.
176   "that could help them": Lawson 1976: 140.
176   "a very strong committee": Lawson 1976: 140.
176   "irregular reports": Lawson 1976: 140.
176   "condemned to death": Avrich 1995: 426.
178   "military defenders": AI Archives: Benenson oral history: 2.
178   "American Civil Liberties Union": AI Archives: Benenson oral history: 31.
178   "enthusiastic for civil liberties": AI Archives: Benenson oral history: 4.
178   "and help me?": AI Archives: Sargant oral history: 5.
179   "all the other professions": AI Archives: Sargant oral history: 35.
179   "my daily bread, really": AI Archives: Benenson oral history: 57.
179   "to be the CIA": AI Archives: Benenson oral history: 6.
179   "to the general public": AI Archives: Benenson oral history: 6.
180   "seemed very unlikely": AI Archives: Astor oral history: 6.
180   "making himself heard": AI Archives: Astor oral history: 9.
180   "pressure on the government": AI Archives: Baker oral history: 17.
180   "restraining Peter's exuberance": AI Archives: Archer oral history: 20.
180   "labor into compartments": AI Archives: Letter of Peter Benenson.
181   "talking about something": AI Archives: Baker oral history: 37.
181   "a lot out of it": AI Archives: Benenson oral history: 65.

181   "part of the world": AI Archives: Benenson oral history: 72.

182   "offer it a platform": Benenson 1961a: 21.

182   "won for his body": *Ibid.*

183   "opinion or religion": *Ibid.*

183   "a long swim": AI Archives: Benenson oral history: 120.

183   "article surprised him": AI Archives: Archer 1984.

184   "The Pioneers": Andrew Blane points out that Peter Benenson's first collaborators considered him Amnesty's sole founder and suggests the word "pioneer" to characterize those who helped him realize his vision.

184   "people out of jail": AI Archives: MacBride oral history: 12.

184   "his own government": MacBride oral history: 28.

184   "prisoners of war": AI Archives: MacBride oral history: 21.

184   "hatred of injustice": AI Archives: Vincent oral history: 8.

184   "being so rich": AI Archives: Deeds oral history: 44.

185   "pushing me into action": AI Archives: N. Marsh oral history: 51.

185   "people in prison": AI Archives: N. Marsh oral history: 49.

185   "all very primitive": AI Archives: C. Marsh oral history: 20.

185   "all over the world": AI Archives: N. Marsh oral history: 60.

186   "prisoners and repression": AI Archives: Siviter oral history: n.p.

186   "to heal this world": AI Archives: Siviter oral history: 24.

186   "do with all this?": AI Archives: Archer: 7, 16.

187   "all these prisoners equally": AI Archives: "The Threes Groups": 1.

187   "journeys are not advisable": AI Archives: *Ibid.*: 2.

187   "leadership from the Centre": AI Archives: *Ibid.*: 3.

187   "wider international movement": AI Archives: *Ibid.*: 3.

187   "on level terms": AI Archives: Sargant oral history: 49.

187   "given to them": AI Archives: Deeds oral history: 26.

188   "central office staff": AI Archives: Minutes, Policy Executive Committee, November 14, 1961.

188   "people working for people": AI Archives: Archer oral history: 12.

188   "good luck to them": AI Archives: Letter of Keith Wood, June 24, 1963.

189   "dark cellar rooms": AI Archives: C. Marsh oral history: 22.

189   "a job to be done": AI Archives: Siviter oral history: 36.

189   "so terribly unprofessional": AI Archives: C. Marsh oral history: 18, 27.

189   "a proper organization": AI Archives: Crane oral history: 7.

189   "a dog's body": AI Archives: Carne oral history: 20.

189   "come to an end!": AI Archives: C. Marsh oral history: 82.

189   "concrete projects": AI Archives: MacBride oral history: 2.

189   "part of a volcano": AI Archives: Crane oral history: 20, 28.

190   "his ambitious scheme": AI Archives: Deeds oral history: 38-40.

190   "time of darkness": AI Archives: Vincent oral history: 17-18.

190   "going in France": AI Archives: Benenson oral history: 68.

191   "if I don't?": AI Archives: Redhouse oral history: 20.

191   "we got a prisoner": AI Archives: *Ibid.*: 23.
191   "this is what I did": AI Archives: Warner oral history: 43.
192   "prosecutor and myself": AI Archives: *Ibid.*: 8.
192   "the Third World": AI Archives: *Ibid.*: 5-6.
192   "cynicism and doubt": AI Archives: "First Notes on Organisation, 5th June 1961": 1.
193   "should continue": Benenson 1961b: 1.
193   "31st July, 1962": *Ibid.*: 4.
194   "Exactly the same thing": AI Archives: Siviter: 46-7.
194   "must be emphasized": AI Archives: Eltham Group Minutes, February 25, 1963.
195   "cause to these releases": Amnesty International 1962: 14.
195   "Amnesty has intervened": *Ibid.*
195   "mouldering in the pigeonholes": *Ibid.*
195   "we'd have got anywhere": AI Archives: Benenson oral history: 66.
196   "third force in the world": AI Archives: *Ibid.*: 241.
196   "like the Soviet Union": AI Archives: Blom-Cooper oral history: 34.
196   "places where they work": AI Archives: MacBride oral history: 49.
196   "punch-drunk with horrors": AI Archives: Sargant oral history: 54-55.
196   "infectious to the young": AI Archives: Vincent oral history: 22.
196   "The idea is beautiful": AI Archives: Astor oral history: 9, 21, 25, 33.
197   "this divided world": AI Archives: "The Threes": 2.
197   "those days at all": AI Archives: Baker oral history: 14.

10. HUMAN RIGHTS CAMPAIGNING SINCE 1961

201   "without effective action": Chalmers 1951: 242.
201   "a star that exploded": Keck and Sikkink 1998: 89.
202   "on specific issues": Keck and Sikkink 1998: 111.
202   "large-scale campaign": Lauren 1998: 151.
203   accepting individual complaints: The Optional Protocol of the Covenant on Civil and Political Rights, adopted in 1966, included a provision allowing individuals to present complaints to the Human Rights Com mission, but it took ten years to come into force.
203   "principal supplier of documentation": Korey 1998: 260.
203   "come to a halt": Korey 1998: 9.
204   "to send letters": Keck and Sikkink 1998: 93.
206   forty-five percent of all international organizations: Keck and Sikkink 1998: 11.
206   A survey of about 150 organizations: Smith *et al.* 1998.
206   "officials among their members": Smith *et al.* 1998: 405.
206   "demonstrations and boycotts": Smith *et al.* 1998: 394.
207   "every conceivable cause": Korey 1998: 2.

207   "abolition of secret police": Crystal 1994: 438.
207   "begin an international campaign": Crystal 1994: 440.
207   "were always present": Crystal 1994: 440.
208   "after Amnesty International": Crystal 1994: 444.
208   "might receive international publicity": Crystal 1994: 447.
208   "other groups lacked": Crystal 1994: 452.
209   "NGO hopes and operations": Korey 1998: 289.
210   "offices all over China": Wiseberg 1991: 533.
210   "may change each other": Keck and Sikkink 1998: 179.
210   "conduct public relations": Keck and Sikkink 1998: 6-7.
210   "organizations and governments": Keck and Sikkink 1998: 2.
210   "move people to action": Keck and Sikkink 1998: 20.
210   "mobilize shame": Keck and Sikkink 1998: 23. See also Robert Drinan's *The Mobilization of Shame*, Yale University Press, 2001.
211   "reporters and TV crews": Turner 1990: 16.
213   "quadrant of the globe": Lauren 1998: 280.
214   "resulted in any indictments": Wiseberg 1991: 536-37.
214   "presence of foreign witnesses": Wiseberg 1991: 535.
215   "intergovernmental organizations": United Nations 1999: 2.
215   "overwhelmingly western": Korey 1998: 301.
216   "action and campaigning organization": Korey 1998: 305.

BIBLIOGRAPHY

Alexander, William. 1981. *William Dean Howells. The Realist as Humanist.* New York: Burt Franklin.

Allison, Robert J., ed. 1995. *The Interesting Narrative of the Life of Olaudah Equiano, Written by Himself.* New York: St. Martin's Press.

Alman, David and Emily. 2000. Interview with the author, audio tape, September 23.

Altick, Richard. 1957. *The English Common Reader. A Social History of the Mass Reading Public 1800-1900.* Chicago: University of Chicago Press.

Amnesty International. 1961-65. Archives and Oral Histories. Amsterdam: International Institute of Social History.

_____.1961a. "Amnesty: The Threes Groups," typescript, Archives.

_____. 1961b. Minutes, Policy Executive Committee, February 25, typescript, Archives.

_____. 1961c. "First Notes on Organisation, 5th June 1961," typescript, Archives.

_____. 1961d. "The Threes," typescript, Archives.

_____. 1962. *Annual Report.* London.

_____. 1999. *Statute of Amnesty International* [1995]. London.

_____. 2001. *Report 2000.* London.

Arnold, David. 1998. "Sacco, Vanzetti Ordeal Haunts Longtime Advocate," *Boston Globe,* June 18, p. B1.

Ashbaugh, Carolyn. 1976. *Lucy Parsons, American Revolutionary.* Chicago: Charles M. Kerr Publishing Co.

Avrich, Paul. 1984. *The Haymarket Tragedy.* Princeton: Princeton University Press.

_____. 1991. *Sacco and Vanzetti, The Anarchist Background.* Princeton: Princeton University Press.

_____. 1995. *Anarchist Voices, An Oral History of Anarchism in America.* Princeton, NJ: Princeton University Press.

Azevedo, Celia M. 1995. *Abolitionism in the United States and Brazil.* New York: Garland.

Belfrage, Cedric and James Aronson. 1978. *Something to Guard. The Stormy Life of the National Guardian 1948-1967.* New York: Columbia University Press.

Benenson, Peter. 1961a. "The Forgotten Prisoners," *The Observer* [London], May 28: 21.

_____. 1961b. "Appeal for Amnesty. A report on the first 6 months," typescript, Amnesty archives.

Berlin, Ira. 1998. *Many Thousands Gone. The First Two Centuries of Slavery in North America.* Cambridge, MA: Harvard University Press.

Black, Jeremy. 1987. *The English Press in the Eighteenth Century.* London: Croom Helm.

Blackwell, Alice Stone. 1937. "Sacco-Vanzetti: The Dreyfus Case of Massachusetts," *Unity*, August 16.

Bode, Carl, ed. 1987. *The Portable Thoreau*. New York: Penguin.

Bolt, Christine and Seymour Drescher, eds. 1980. *Antislavery, Religion and Reform: Essays in Memory of Roger Anstey*. Folkstone, U.K.: Dawson.

Boston Globe. 1997. "Sacco, Vanzetti and Labor," September 1, p. A14.

_____. 1999. "Crime of the Century: Sacco and Vanzetti," November 1, 1999, p. B1.

Bracey, John, Jr., August Meier and Elliott Rudwick, eds. 1970. *Blacks in the Abolitionist Movement*. Belmont, CA: Wadsworth.

Brennan, James F. 1998. *The Reflection of the Dreyfus Affair in the European Press, 1897-1899*. New York: Peter Lang.

Brewer, John. 1976. *Party Ideology and Popular Politics at the Accession of George III*. Cambridge, U.K.: Cambridge University Press.

Brown, Frederick. 1995. *Zola, A Life*. New York: Farrar Straus Giroux.

Bruns, Roger, ed. 1977. *Am I Not a Man and a Brother. The Antislavery Crusade of Revolutionary America 1688-1788*. New York: Chelsea House.

Cahm, Eric. 1996. *The Dreyfus Affair in French Society and Politics*. London: Longmans.

Carter, Dan T. 1969. *Scottsboro. A Tragedy of the American South*. Baton Rouge: Louisiana State University Press.

Chalmers, Allan K. Collection. Boston: Boston University Library.

_____. 1951. *They Shall Be Free*. Garden City, NY: Doubleday.

Clopton, Willard. 1965. "Stormy Career Ends for Gardner Jackson," *The Washington Post*, April 18, p. B16.

Committee for Effecting the Abolition of the Slave Trade, Fair Minute Books. London: British Library, Add. Mss 21254-21256.

Committee for the Relief of the Black Poor. 1786. T1/630/1000, 1284, 1333. London: Public Records Office.

Congo Reform Association, 1906-12, pamphlets. London: Antislavery International.

Conrad, Robert. 1972. *The Destruction of Brazilian Slavery 1850-1888*. Berkeley: University of California Press.

Coover, Robert. 1998. *The Public Burning*. New York: Grove Press.

Crystal, Jill. 1994. "The Human Rights Movement in the Arab World," *Human Rights Quarterly* 16: 435-54.

Daget, Serge. 1980. "A Model of the French Abolitionist Movement and Its Varieties," in Bolt and Drescher, eds.

D'Anjou, Leo. 1996. *Social Movements and Cultural Change. The First Abolition Campaign Revisited*. New York: Aldine de Gruyter.

D'Attilio, Robert. 1999. Personal communication.

David, Henry. 1963. *History of the Haymarket Affair. A Study in the American Social-Revolutionary and Labor Movements*. New York: Collier.

Davis, David Brion. 1966. *The Problem of Slavery in Western Culture*. Ithaca, NY: Cornell University Press.

_____.1975. *The Problem of Slavery in the Age of Revolution*. Ithaca, NY: Cornell University Press.

Digby-Junger, Richard. 1996. *The Journalist as Reformer. Henry Demarest Lloyd and Wealth against Commonwealth*. Westport, CT: Greenwood Press.

Dinkin, Robert J. 1989. *Campaigning in America. A History of Election Practices*. New York: Greenwood Press.

Drake, Thomas E. 1950. *Quakers and Slavery in America*. New Haven: Yale University Press.

Drescher, Seymour. 1986. *Capitalism and Antislavery. British Mobilization in Comparative Perspective*. London: MacMillan Press.

_____ and Stanley Engerman, eds. 1998. *A Historical Guide to World Slavery*. New York: Oxford University Press.

Dreyfus, Alfred. 1977 [1901]. *Five Years of My Life. The Diary of Captain Alfred Dreyfus*. New York: Peebles Press.

_____. 1899. *Lettres d'un Innocent. The Letters of Captain Dreyfus to His Wife*. New York: Harper and Brothers.

Ehrmann, Herbert B. Papers. Cambridge, MA: Harvard Law School Library.

Feldman, Egal. 1981. *The Dreyfus Affair and the American Conscience 1895-1906*. Detroit: Wayne State University Press.

Felicani, Aldino. 1967. "Sacco-Vanzetti: A Memoir," *The Nation*, August 14: 108-112.

Feuerlicht, Roberta. 1977. *Justice Crucified. The Story of Sacco and Vanzetti*. New York: McGraw Hill.

Fiedler, Leslie A. 1955. "Afterthoughts on the Rosenbergs," *An End to Innocence. Essays on Culture and Politics*. Boston: Beacon Press.

Filler, Louis, ed. 1965. *Wendell Phillips on Civil Rights and Freedom*. New York: Hill and Wang.

Fischer, Louis, ed. 1962. *The Essential Gandhi. His Life, Work and Ideas*. New York: Vintage.

Fladelard, Betty. 1972. *Men and Brothers: Anglo-American Cooperation*. Urbana: University of Illinois Press.

Ford, Edwin H. and Edwin Emery, eds. 1954. *Highlights in the History of the American Press*. Minneapolis: University of Minnesota Press.

Frost, J. William, ed. 1980. *The Quaker Origins of Antislavery*. Norwood, MA: Norwood Editions.

Fryer, Peter. 1984. *Staying Power. The History of Black People in Britain*. London: Pluto Press.

Garber, Marjorie and Rebecca L. Walkowitz, eds. 1995. *Secret Agents. The Rosenberg Case, McCarthyism and 1950s America*. New York: Routledge.

Gay, Kathlyn and Martin. 1999. *The Encyclopedia of Political Anarchy*. Santa Barbara, CA: ABC-Clio.

Gifford, Zerbanoo. 1996. *Thomas Clarkson and the Campaign against Slavery*. London: Antislavery International.

Glenn, Robert W. 1993. *The Haymarket Affair. An Annotated Bibliography*. Westport, CT: Greenwood Press.

Goldman, Emma. Correspondence, Samuel Ishill Collection, bMS AM 1614 (54) folder 2. Cambridge, MA: Houghton Library, Harvard University.

Goodman, James. *Stories of Scottsboro*. 1994. New York: Pantheon Books.

Goodrum, Charles and Helen Dalrymple. 1990. *Advertising in America. The First 200 Years*. New York: Harry Abrams.

Halasz, Nicholas. 1955. *Captain Dreyfus. The Story of a Mass Hysteria*. New York: Simon and Schuster.

Hane, Mikiso. 1992. *Modern Japan. A Historical Survey*. Boulder, CO: Westview Press.

Hanke, Lewis. 1974. *All Mankind Is One. A Study in the Disputation between Bartolomé de Las Casas and Juan Ginés de Sepúlveda in 1550 on the Intellectual and Religious Capacity of the American Indians*. De Kalb, IL: Northern Illinois University Press.

Harrison, Brian H. 1982. *Peaceable Kingdom. Stability and Change in Modern Britain*. Oxford: Clarendon Press.

Hendrickson, Paul. 2000. "Mississippi Haunting," *The Washington Post Magazine*, February 27: 12-27.

Hochschild, Adam. 1998. *King Leopold's Ghost*. Boston: Houghton Mifflin.

Hoffman, Robert L. 1980. *More than a Trial. The Struggle over Captain Dreyfus*. New York: Free Press.

Horton, James O. 1993. *Free People of Color. Inside the African American Community*. Washington: Smithsonian Institution Press.

Howe, Irving and Lewis Coser. 1974. *The American Communist Party. A Critical History*. New York: Da Capo Press.

Hudson-Weems, Clenora. 1998. "Resurrecting Emmett Till: The Catalyst of the Modern Civil Rights Movement," *Journal of Black Studies* 29,2: 179-188.

Hugo, Victor. 1859. Letter to the Editor of the *London News*, December 12. College Park, MD: University of Maryland Library, Rare Book Collection.

Human Rights Internet. 1996. *African Directory. Human Rights Organizations in Sub-Saharan Africa*. Ottawa.

Hurwitz, Edith F. 1973. *Politics and Public Conscience. Slave Emancipation and the Abolitionist Movement in Britain*. London: Barnes and Noble.

International Committee for Political Prisoners. 1925. *Letters from Russian Prisons*. New York: Boni.

International Labor Defense. 1926-46. Records, microfilm. New York: New York Public Library, Schomburg Collection.

Jackson, Brian. 1981. *The Black Flag. A look back at the strange case of Nicola Sacco and Bartolomeo Vanzetti*. Boston: Routledge & Kegan Paul.

Jackson, Gardner. 1952-55. Reminiscences, microfiche. New York: Columbia University Oral History Collection.

Jennings, Judith. 1997. *The Business of Abolishing the British Slave Trade 1783-1807*. London: Frank Cass.

Jezer, Marty, Robert Cooner and Helen Michalowski, eds. 1987. *The Power of the People. Active Nonviolence in the United States*. Philadelphia: New Society Publishers.

Joughin, Louis and Edmund Morgan. 1978. *The Legacy of Sacco and Vanzetti*. Princeton: Princeton University Press.

Kafka, Franz. 1969. *The Trial*. New York: Vintage.

Kaplan, Judy and Linn Shapiro, eds. 1998. *Red Diapers. Growing Up in the Communist Left*. Urbana: University of Illinois Press.

Keane, John. 1995. *Tom Paine, A Political Life*. Boston: Little, Brown.

Keck, Margaret and Kathryn Sikkink. 1998. *Activists beyond Borders. Advocacy Networks in International Politics*. Ithaca, NY: Cornell University Press.

Kertzer, David. 1997. *The Kidnapping of Edgardo Mortara*. New York: Knopf.

Korey, William. 1998. *NGOs and the Universal Declaration of Human Rights: 'A Curious Grapevine.'* New York: St. Martin's Press.

Larsen, Egon. 1979. *A Flame in Barbed Wire. The Story of Amnesty International*. New York: Norton.

Lascelles, Edward C. 1969. *Granville Sharp and the Freedom of Slaves in England*. New York: Negro Universities Press.

Lauren, Paul Gordon. 1998. *The Evolution of International Human Rights: Visions Seen*. Philadelphia: University of Pennsylvania Press.

Lawson, Peggy. 1976. *Roger Baldwin, Founder of the American Civil Liberties Union*. Boston: Houghton Mifflin.

Lerner, Gerda. 1971. *The Grimké Sisters from South Carolina. Pioneers for Women's Rights and Abolition*. New York: Schocken Books.

Lindemann, Albert S. 1991. *The Jew Accused. Three Anti-Semitic Affairs (Dreyfus, Beilis, Frank) 1894-1915*. Cambridge, U.K.: Cambridge University Press.

London Yearly Meeting [Society of Friends]. 1783. *The Case of Our Fellow-Creatures, the Oppressed Africans, Respectfully Recommended to the Serious Consideration of the Legislature of Great-Britain, by the People Called Quakers*. London: James Phillips.

_____. 1764-1798. *Epistles*. Swarthmore, PA: Friends Historical Library.

Lorimer, Douglas. 1992. "Black Resistance to Slavery and Racism in Eighteenth Century England," in *Essays on the History of Blacks in Britain*, Jagdish S. Gundara and Ian Duffield, eds., 58-80. Aldershot, U.K.: Avebury.

Lu, David J. 1997. *Japan: A Documentary History*. Armonk, NY: M.E. Sharpe.

Madison, Charles A. 1959. *Critics and Crusaders. A Century of American Protest*. New York: Ungar Publishing Co. (2nd ed.).

Marshall, Dorothy. 1956. *English People in the Eighteenth Century*. London: Longmans, Green and Co.

Martin, Charles H. 1985. "The International Labor Defense and Black America," *Labor History* 26: 165-94.

Mathews, Donald. 1980. "Religion and Slavery—The Case of the American South," in Bolt and Drescher, eds.

Mayer, Henry. 1998. *All on Fire. William Lloyd Garrison and the Abolition of Slavery*. New York: St. Martin's Press.

McFeely, William. 1991. *Frederick Douglass*. New York: Norton.

McMurry, Linda. 1998. *To Keep the Waters Troubled. The Life of Ida B. Wells*. New York: Oxford University Press.

Meeropol, Michael. 1994. *The Rosenberg Letters. A Complete Edition of the Prison Correspondence of Julius and Ethel Rosenberg*. New York: Garland Publishing Company.

Meeropol, Robert and Michael. 1986. *We Are Your Sons. The Legacy of Ethel and Julius Rosenberg*. Urbana: University of Illinois Press.

Mencken, H.L. 1929. "A Sacco-Vanzetti Memorial," *Lantern*, August: 5-6.

Midgley, Clare. 1992. *Women against Slavery. The British Campaigns, 1780-1870*. London and NY: Routledge.

Moore, Richard B. Papers. New York: New York Public Library, Schomburg Collection.

Moura, Clóvis. 1979. *Sacco e Vanzetti: O Protesto Brasileiro*. São Paulo: Editora Brasil Debates.

Myers, Norma. 1996. *Reconstructing the Black Past. Blacks in Britain c. 1780-1830*. London: Frank Cass.

Nabuco, Joaquim. 1977. *Abolitionism. The Brazilian Antislavery Struggle*. Urbana: University of Illinois Press.

National Association for the Advancement of Colored People. Archives (1931-37). Washington, DC: Library of Congress.

National Committee to Secure Justice in the Rosenberg Case/Rosenberg-Sobell Committee. 1951-70. Archives, microfilm. Madison, WI: Wisconsin State Historical Society.

Neville, John F. 1995. *The Press, the Rosenbergs and the Cold War*. Westport, CT: Praeger.

Norris, Clarence and Sybil D. Washington. 1979. *The Last of the Scottsboro Boys*. New York: Putnam.

Okun, Rob A., ed. 1988. *The Rosenbergs. Collected Visions of Artists and Writers*. New York: Universe Books.

Oldfield, J.R. 1995. *Popular Politics and British Antislavery. The Mobilisation of Public Opinion against the Slave Trade 1787-1807*. Manchester, U.K.: Manchester University Press.

Ottanelli, Fraser M. 1991. *The Communist Party of the United States from the Depression to World War II*. New Brunswick, NJ: Rutgers University Press.

Patterson, Haywood and Earl Conrad. 1950. *Scottsboro Boy*. Garden City, NY: Doubleday.

Philipson, Ilene. 1988. *Ethel Rosenberg. Beyond the Myths*. New York: Franklin Watts.

Porter, Dale H. 1970. *The Abolition of the Slave Trade in England, 1784-1807*. [No city] Archon Books.

Porter, Katherine Anne. 1977. *The Never Ending Wrong*. Boston: Little Brown.

Power, Jonathan. 1981. *Amnesty International. The Human Rights Story*. New York: McGraw Hill.

Public Ledger [London]. 1772. "For the Public Ledger, To Mr. Richard Swords," 23 October: 4. London: British Library, newspaper microfilm 589.b.

Pugh, Martin. 1999. *Britain since 1789*. New York: St. Martin's Press.

Quarles, Benjamin. 1969. *Black Abolitionists*. New York: Oxford University Press.

Rabben, Linda. 1995. Review of *Private but Public: The Third Sector in Latin America*, in *Grassroots Development* 19(2): 56-7.

_____. 1998. *Unnatural Selection. The Yanomami, the Kayapó and the Onslaught of Civilisation.* London: Pluto Press/Seattle: University of Washington Press.

Radosh, Ronald and Joyce Milton. 1997. *The Rosenberg File.* New Haven: Yale University Press (2nd ed.).

Raskin, Jonah. 1974. *Out of the Whale. Growing Up in the American Left.* New York: Links.

Reuben, William A. 1983. Reminiscences, audio tape. New York: Columbia University Oral History Collection.

_____. 1999. Letter to the Editor, *New York Times Book Review,* January 24: 22.

_____. 2000. Interview with the author, audio tape, August 24; telephone, September 2.

Roberts, Stephen and Dorothy Thompson. 1998. *Images of Chartism.* Woodbridge, U.K.: Merlin Press.

Robson, Angela. 1999. "Founding Father," *C2* (January): 20. London: Amnesty International.

Rogers, William B. 1995. *"We Are All Together Now": Frederick Douglass, William Lloyd Garrison and the Prophetic Tradition.* New York: Garland.

Root, Jonathan. 1963. *The Betrayers—The Rosenberg Case—A Reappraisal of an American Crisis.* New York: Coward McCann.

Ryan, Mary P. 1999. "Civil Society as Democratic Practice: North American Cities during the Nineteenth Century," *Journal of Interdisciplinary History,* 29, 4: 559-84.

Sacco, Nicola and Bartolomeo Vanzetti. 1997. *The Letters of Sacco and Vanzetti,* Marion D. Frankfurter and Gardner Jackson, eds. New York: Penguin.

Sacco-Vanzetti Defense Committee. 1926. *Monthly Bulletin,* July, microfilm. New York: New York Public Library.

Samuel, Maurice. 1966. *Blood Accusation: The Strange History of the Beiliss Case.* New York: Knopf.

Sayre, Nora. 1995. *Previous Convictions. A Journey through the 1950s.* New Brunswick, NJ: Rutgers University Press.

Schlesinger, Arthur, Jr. 1965. "Gardner Jackson 1897-1965, " *New Republic,* May 1: 17.

Schneir, Walter and Miriam. 1983. *Invitation to an Inquest.* New York: Pantheon.

Schorow, Stephanie. 2000. "If these walls could talk: 'Voices of protest' retraces 300 years of debate at Old South Meeting House," *Boston Herald,* April 4: 45.

Schrecker, Ellen. 1998. *Many Are the Crimes. McCarthyism in America.* Boston: Little, Brown.

Schudson, Michael. 1978. *Discovering the News. A Social History of American Newspapers.* New York: Basic Books.

Schwartz, Shari, ed. 1992. *Scapegoat on Trial. The Story of Mendel Beilis.* New York: CIS Publishers.

Sharlitt, Joseph H. 1989. *Fatal Error. The Miscarriage of Justice that Sealed the Rosenbergs' Fate.* New York: Scribner's.

Shyllon, Folarin. 1974. *Black Slaves in Britain.* London: Oxford University Press.

_____.1977a. *Black People in Britain 1555-1833.* London: Oxford University Press.

_____. 1977b. *James Ramsey, The Unknown Abolitionist.* Edinburgh: Canongate.

Sinclair, Upton. 1978. *Boston.* Cambridge, MA: Robert Bentley, Inc.

Smith, Anthony. 1979. *The Newspaper. An International History.* London: Thomas and Hudson.

Smith, Carl. 1995. *Urban Disorder and the Shape of Belief.* Chicago: University of Chicago Press.

Smith, Jackie and Ron Pagnucco, with George Lopez. 1998. "Globalizing Human Rights: The Work of Transnational Human Rights NGOs in the 1990s," *Human Rights Quarterly* 20: 379-412.

Sobell, Morton. 1974. *On Doing Time.* New York: Scribner's.

Solomon, Flora, and Barnet Litvinoff. 1984. *Baku to Baker Street. The Memoirs of Flora Solomon.* London: Collins.

Soviak, Eugene. 1983. "Freedom and People's Rights Movement," in *Kodansha Encyclopedia of Japan,* Vol. 2: 333-37. Tokyo: Kodansha.

Stephens, Mitchell. 1988. *A History of News.* New York: Viking Penguin.

Stewart, James Brewer. 1986. *Wendell Phillips. Liberty's Hero.* Baton Rouge: Louisiana State University Press.

Strasser, Susan. 1989. *Satisfaction Guaranteed. The Making of the American Mass Market.* New York: Pantheon.

_____. 1999. *Waste and Want. A Social History of Trash.* New York: Henry Holt.

Taylor, Daniel A. 1977. "Report to the Governor in the Matter of Sacco and Vanzetti," in B. Jackson: 170-96.

Temperley, Howard. 1980. "Antislavery as a Form of Cultural Imperialism," in Bolt and Drescher, eds.

Thale, Mary, ed. 1983. *Selections from the Papers of the London Corresponding Society 1792-1799.* Cambridge, U.K.: Cambridge University Press.

Thomas, Hugh. 1997. *The Slave Trade.* New York: Simon and Schuster.

Thomas, John L. 1983. *Alternative America. Henry George, Edward Bellamy, Henry Demarest Lloyd and the Adversary Tradition.* Cambridge, MA: Harvard University Press.

Thompson, Dorothy. 1984. *The Chartists.* London: Temple Smith.

Thompson, Edward P. 1963. *The Making of the English Working Class.* New York: Pantheon.

Thompson, Mildred I. 1990. *Ida B. Wells-Barnett. An Exploratory Study of an American Black Woman, 1893-1930.* Brooklyn, NY: Carlson Publishing Company.

Tilly, Charles. 1982. "Britain Creates the Social Movement," in *Social Conflict and the Political Order in Modern Britain,* James E. Cronin and Jonathan Schneer, eds. New Brunswick, NJ: Rutgers University.

Tuchman, Barbara. 1966. *The Proud Tower.* New York: Ballantine.

Turley, Dana. 1991. *The Culture of English Antislavery, 1780-1860.* London & NY: Routledge.

Turner, Terence. 1990. "Role of Indigenous Peoples in the Environmental Crisis: The Case of the Brazilian Kayapó," unpublished ms.

Twain, Mark. 1929. "The United States of Lyncherdom" [1901], *Mark Twain's Works*, Vol. 29: 239-49. New York: Harper and Brothers.

_____. 1961. "King Leopold's Soliloquy," *Mark Twain: Life as I Find It*, 275-95. Garden City, NY: Hanover House.

Tye, Larry. 1998. *The Father of Spin. Edward Bernays and the Birth of Public Relations.* New York: Crown.

United Nations. 1999. *Declaration on the Rights and Responsibility of Individuals, Groups and Organs of Society to Promote and Protect Universally Recognized Human Rights and Fundamental Freedoms.* Geneva: Office of the United Nations High Commissioner for Human Rights.

United States Department of Justice. 1926-36. Scottsboro Correspondence, File No.158260-46. Suitland, MD: National Archives.

Vaux, Roberts. 1816. *Memoirs of the Lives of Benjamin Lay and Ralph Sandiford.* Philadelphia: Solomon Conrad.

Vlastos, Stephen. 1995. "Opposition Movements in Early Meiji, 1868-1885," in *The Emergence of Meiji Japan,* Marius B. Jansen, ed. Cambridge, U.K.: Cambridge University Press, 203-61.

Von Frank, Albert J. 1998. *The Trials of Anthony Burns: Freedom and Slavery in Emerson's Boston.* Cambridge: Harvard University Press.

Walker, Samuel. 1999. *In Defense of American Liberties: A History of the ACLU.* Carbondale: Southern Illinois University Press (2nd ed.).

Walvin, James. 1986. *England, Slaves and Freedom,* 1776-1838. Jackson: University Press of Mississippi.

_____, ed. 1982. *Slavery and British Society 1776-1846.* Baton Rouge: University of Louisiana Press.

Ward, Estolv Ethan. 1983. *The Gentle Dynamiter. A Biography of Tom Mooney.* Palo Alto, CA: Ramparts Press.

Wexler, Alice. 1984. *Emma Goldman. An Intimate Life.* New York: Pantheon.

_____. 1989. *Emma Goldman in Exile.* Boston: Beacon Press.

Williams, Raymond. 1961. *The Long Revolution.* Harmondsworth: Penguin.

Williamson, Audrey. 1974. *Wilkes, 'A Friend to Liberty.'* New York: Dutton.

Wilson, Ellen G. 1990. *Thomas Clarkson. A Biography.* New York: St. Martin's Press.

Wiseberg, Laurie. 1991. "Protecting Human Rights Activists and NGOs: What More Can Be Done?" *Human Rights Quarterly* 13: 525-44.

Yellin, Jean Fagan. 1989. *Women and Sisters. The Antislavery Feminists in American Culture.* New Haven: Yale University Press.

_____ and John C. Van Horne, eds. 1994. *The Abolitionist Sisterhood. Women's Political Culture in Antebellum America.* Ithaca, NY: Cornell University Press.

Zinn, Howard. 1995. *A People's History of the United States 1492-Present.* New York: HarperPerennial.

INDEX

Adams, John Quincy, President, 45, 64

Abolitionists, 14, 15, 16, 20, 31, 35-37, 43-45, 47-51, 53-58, 61

Advertising, 64-65, 119, 145, 157, 159

Age of Reason, The, 29

Alabama Board of Pardon and Parole, 141, 142, 145

Alabama Scottsboro Fair Trial Committee, 139

Alabama Supreme Court, 137

Alman, David and Emily, Rosenberg activists, 155, 156, 157, 159, 169

Altgeld, John, governor of Illinois, 75-6

American Bar Association, 99, 152

American Civil Liberties Union (ACLU), 111, 112, 151

American Federation of Labor (AFL), 74, 76

American revolution, 14

American Scottsboro Committee, 139

Am I Not a Man and a Brother, 6, 33, 40, 54

Am I Not a Woman and a Sister, 33, 40, 54

Amistad, 44

Amnesty Association (Haymarket), 74, 75

Amnesty International, xiii, xv, 4-5, 146, 173-98; conditions for success, 197-98; creation myth, 174; Jews in, 177, 179, 191, 197; library, 185, 189; mandate, 193-94, 215; pioneers, 177, 184-86, 195; precursors, 175-77; U.S. Section, 176, 190; Web sites, 215

Anarchists, 70, 71, 77

Anglicans, 21

Annis, John, slave in Britain, 25

Antiapartheid movement, 5

Anti-Semitism, 92, 95, 96, 97, 158, 162

Anti-Slavery International, 31

Anti-Slavery Reporter, 58

Anti-slave-trade campaign of 1787-92, 34-38

Appeal for Amnesty, 1961, 181-83, 189, 192, 194, 196, 198

Arendt, Hannah, philosopher, 100

Associated Negro Press, 132

Baker, Eric, 180, 181, 197

Baldwin, Roger, activist, 112, 113, 123, 124, 151

Baptists, 9, 21

Barclay, David, antislavery activist, 16

Barnum, P.T., promoter, 65

Bates, Ruby, Scottsboro victim, 131,

Beilis, Mendel, Russian defendant, 102-04, 126

Benenson Peter, 172, 174-75, 179, 181, 183-84, 187-88, 190-198

Benezet, Anthony, antislavery campaigner, 16, 18, 21, 29

Berkman, Alexander, anarchist, 77, 107, 109

Billings, Warren, union member, 107, 133

Black Society, 23

Blackstone, William, lawyer, 22

Blane, Andrew, oral historian, 195, 196, 231

Bloch, Emanuel, Rosenberg attorney, 154, 156, 159, 162, 165, 166

Brodsky, Joseph, Scottsboro attorney, 131, 133

Blom-Cooper, Louis, AI pioneer, 179, 195, 196

Blum, Léon, French politician, 94, 137

Boston Committee to Secure Clemency in the Rosenberg Case, 159

Boston Globe, The, 112

Boston Herald, The, 115, 119

Boston Public Library, 122

Boycotts, 31

Brazilian Antislavery Society, 57

Brazilian Underground Railroad, 57 136, 137

British Anti-Slavery Society, 31, 41, 88

Brodsky, Joseph, Scottsboro attorney, 131, 133

Brown, John, abolitionist, 52, 53-4, 62, 169

Burns, Anthony, escaped slave, 46, 47, 61

Casas, Bartolomé de las, indigenous peoples' defender, 7

Casement, Roger, diplomat, 88, 89, 91

Cause célèbre, 2, 5, 54, 66, 69, 167, 171, 193

Central Intelligence Agency (CIA), 162, 179

Chalmers, Allan Knight, Scottsboro activist, 139, 140, 141, 143, 145, 146, 201

Chappell, James, editor, 140

Chartism, 42-3, 69, 82

Cinque, slave leader, 44, 54

Civil Disobedience, 58

Civilitá Cattolica, 92

Civil War (U.S.), 62, 65

Clarkson, Thomas, 1, 2, 5, 16, 22, 25, 29-31, 32, 33, 34, 54, 58, 143, 213

Coleridge, Samuel Taylor, poet, 29

Cold War, 149, 170, 173, 194, 195, 204

Comité Catholique pour la Defense du Droit, 97

Committee for Effecting Abolition of the Slave Trade (London committee), 4, 29, 31, 32, 34, 35

Common Sense, 27

Communist Party (U.S.), 110, 118, 123, 131, 133, 134, 135, 143, 144, 153, 154, 155, 156, 160

Congo, 87-91

Congo Reform Association (CRA), 89, 90, 91

Conan-Doyle, Arthur, author, 90

Congress of Industrial Organizations (CIO), 123

Convention on the Rights of the Child, 203

Convention against Torture, 203

Convention on Women, 203

Coover, Robert, author, 170

Craft, William and Ellen, escaped slave orators, 45, 50

Crane, Peggy, AI pioneer, 189

Crimes against humanity, 87, 173

Cuguano, Ottobah, freed slave in Britain, 26

Darrow, Clarence, attorney, 75, 77, 132

Debs, Eugene V., Socialist leader, 63, 77, 109, 133, 153

Declaration of Independence (U.S.), 14, 77

Declaration of the Rights of the Child (1924), 202

Declaration on Right and Responsibility . . . , 214

Death House Letters, 161, 162, 169

Death penalty, xi, 5, 54, 155, 156, 168, 169, 180, 212

Deeds, Marlys, AI pioneer, 177, 184, 187, 190

Deists, 21

Demane, Henry, slave in Britain, 26

Demonstrations, 42, 117, 121, 126, 137, 138, 160, 163, 166, 212

Devil's Island, 93, 94, 98

Dillwyn, William, anti-slave-trade campaigner, 16, 18

Dissenters, 9, 21, 36, 37, 55

Doctorow, E.L., author, 170

Dohrn, Bernardine, terrorist, 169

Donovan, Mary, Sacco-Vanzetti activist, 115, 127

Dos Passos, John, author, 115, 117, 124, 128

Douglas, William, U.S. Supreme Court justice, 165

Douglass, Frederick, antislavery activist, 43, 45, 50, 51, 52, 53, 54, 56, 58, 83

Dreyfus Alfred, French army officer, 80, 91-102, 104, 114, 117, 119, 126, 136, 163, 168, 176, 193

Dreyfus, Mathieu, campaigner, 93, 95

Du Bois, W.E.B., author, 151, 155, 166

Dukakis, Michael, governor of Massachusetts, 125

Ehrmann, Herbert, Saccro-Vanzetti attorney, 118, 124

Eight-hour workday, 62, 69

Einstein, Albert, physicist, 120, 133, 163

Eisenhower, Dwight D., President, 151, 161, 164

Election campaigns, 63-4

Ellsworth, Priscilla, oral historian, 195

Emerson, Ralph Waldo, philosopher, 46

Emma Lazarus Federation, 163

Engels, Frederich, 66

Equiano, Olaudah, antislavery campaigner, 20, 25-6

Esterhazy, Major, Dreyfus affair culprit, 94, 101

Eton, British private school, 177

Ettor, Joseph, and Arturo Giovanitti, anarchists, 108

European Declaration of Human Rights, 184

Evans, Elizabeth Glendower, philanthropist, 111

Farmer, Fyke, attorney, 165

Federal Bureau of Investigation (FBI), 109, 150, 151, 170

Felicani, Aldino, anarchist, 110, 112, 113, 114, 116, 119, 120, 121, 127

Ferguson, Adam, economist, 14

Fiedler, Leslie, author, 167

Fielden, Samuel, anarchist, 71

"Fierce legion of friends," xii, 3, 175

Forgotten prisoners, 174, 182, 183

Forten, James, abolitionist, 51

France, Anatole, author, 89, 95, 97, 114, 120

Frankfurter, Felix, U.S. Supreme Court justice, 107, 111, 112, 113, 117, 119, 122, 128

Franklin, Benjamin, abolitionist, 15, 16, 33

French Revolution, 28

Fugitive Slave Act, 45, 47, 52, 61

Gag rule, 44, 45, 49

Gandhi, Mohandas, activist, 58, 104

Garland, Charles, philanthropist, 113

Garrison, William Lloyd, abolitionist, 43-5, 47, 48, 50, 51, 53, 55, 58

George, Henry, economist, 63, 84

Goldman, Emma, anarchist, 4, 69, 77-8, 107, 109, 176

Gompers, Samuel, labor leader, 73, 74, 77

Grandmothers of the Plaza de Mayo, 204

Great Chain of Being, 9, 13

Green, Samuel, abolitionist, 52

Green, William, black abolitionist, 26

Greenglass, David, Rosenberg case defendant, 152

Grimké sisters, abolitionists, 47-9, 53, 55; Grimké, Angelina, 48; Grimké, Sarah, 50

Habeas corpus, 26

Hall, Grover, editor, 140

Hardy, Thomas (reformer), 37

Harper's Ferry, 53

Harris, John and Alice, missionaries, 89, 90

Haymarket Affair, 2, 4, 60, 63, 69, 70-78, 81, 101, 108, 110, 168, 193

Hearst, William Randolph, publisher, 66

Henry, Col., French military officer, 98

Herndon, Angelo, black Communist, 136

Herzl, Theodor, Zionist, 100

Heyrick, Elizabeth, Quaker abolitionist, 55

Hill, Joe, labor leader, 109, 153

Hoover, J. Edgar, FBI director, 109, 158

House of Commons (Britain), 11, 13, 35, 42

House Un-American Activities Committee, 150

Howard League for Penal Reform, 179, 184

Howells, William Dean, 73, 77, 82

Hugo, Victor, author, 54, 82, 213

Human rights defenders, 213-14

Intellectuals, 8, 10, 14, 21, 27, 46, 53, 57, 67, 69, 76, 81, 82, 96, 97, 100, 101, 102, 104, 109, 115, 117, 118, 119, 123, 135, 136, 144, 155, 170, 183, 210

Interesting Narrative of the Life of Olaudah Equiano, 25, 26
Inter-American Commission on Human Rights, 204
Inter-American Court on Human Rights, 214
Internal Security Act of 1950 (McCarran Act), 150, 164
International Committee for Political Prisoners, 176, 196
International Committee of Jurists (ICJ), 176, 178, 184, 195, 196, 208
International Convention on the Abolition of Slavery (1926), 202
International Convention on the Elimination of All Forms of Racial Discrimination, 203
International Covenant on Civil and Political Rights, 173, 203
International Covenant on Economic, Social and Cultural Rights, 203
International human rights movement, 198, 206
International Labor Defense (ILD), 118, 131-34, 136-39, 143-47
International Refugee Year, 174, 179

"J'Accuse," 96, 97, 99, 101, 117
Jackson, Gardner, Sacco-Vanzetti activist, 111, 112-13, 115-24, 126-8. 151
Jews, 93, 94, 162
Jiyu minken undo (Japanese People's Rights Movement), 67-9
Justice (legal organization), 179, 184, 195

Kaufman, Irving, Rosenberg case judge, 154, 158
Kayapó, 211-12
"King Leopold's Soliloquy," 82, 87, 90
Knights of Labor, 74, 76
Korean War, 150, 152, 153, 154, 167, 168, 173
Ku Klux Klan, 126, 135

Labor movement, 62, 69-70
Labour Party (Britain), 177, 178, 184
La Croix, 100
Latimer, George, escaped slave, 44-5, 51

Lay, Benjamin, abolitionist, 15
Lazare, Bernard, critic, 94-5
Leadbeater, Mary, poet, 34
League of Nations, 202
Leopold, King of the Belgians, 87, 88, 90
L'esprit des Lois, 14
Letters of Sacco and Vanzetti, 124
Letter writing, 5, 41, 81, 135, 164
Lewis, Thomas, slave in Britain, 22
Liberator, The, 43, 44, 47, 55
Liebowitz, Samuel, Scottsboro case lawyer, 137, 139, 140
Ligue de la Patrie Française (League of the French Homeland), 97
Ligue des Droits de l'Homme (League of the Rights of Man), 97, 137, 176
Livingston, William, abolitionist, 16
Lloyd, Henry Demarest, author, 63, 73, 75, 76, 77
Local groups, 5, 32, 33, 35, 44, 49, 89, 186-7, 198, 208, 209, 215
Locke, John, philosopher, 13, 14, 18
London Meeting for Sufferings, 16, 29, 55
London Times, 89, 99, 103
London Yearly Meeting, 15, 17
Los Angeles Rosenberg Committee, 158, 165
Lovejoy, Elijah, editor, 51, 61
Lynching, 82-7
Lyons, Eugene, journalist, 111, 113, 124, 162

MacBride, Sean, 184, 187, 189, 195, 196, 203
Manchester, 35
Mansfield, Lord, jurist, 22-3
Marsh, Christel, AI pioneer, 185, 189, 191
Marsh, Norman, AI pioneer, 185, 187
Martyrs of Chicago, 61, 75, 78
McCarthy, Joseph, U.S. senator, 151
McHenry, William, escaped slave, 45
Meeropol, Michael, 152, 153, 159, 161, 165, 166, 169, 170
Meeropol, Robert, 161, 165, 166, 169, 170
Meiji restoration, 67
Meikeljohn, Alexander, educator, 112, 113

Mendes, Chico, labor leader, 213-4

Methodists, 9

Mexican Academy for Human Rights, 201

Mill, John Stuart, 24, 67

Millay, Edna St. Vincent, poet, 115, 119, 124, 128

Montesquieu, Baron de, philosopher, 14, 18, 57, 68

Mooney, Tom, prisoner, 107-8, 110, 123, 124, 126, 133, 136, 153

Moore, Fred, Sacco-Vanzetti attorney, 111, 113, 114

More, Hannah, poet, 34

Morel, E.D., Congo activist, 88-91, 104

Morison, Samuel, historian, 111, 115

Mott, Lucrecia, 47

Musmanno, Michael, judge, 124, 125

Nabuco, Joaquim, Brazilian abolitionist, 57, 58

National Association for the Advancement of Colored People (NAACP), 85, 87, 132-134, 139, 142-5, 147, 150, 151

National Committee to Reopen the Rosenberg Case, 170

National Committee to Secure Justice in the Rosenberg Case, 155, 171

National Council of Civil Liberties (Britain), 178

National Guardian, The, 155, 157, 162, 165

New England Civil Liberties Committee, 111

Newspapers, 9-10, 12-13, 34, 65, 132, 154, 166, 168

New York Times, The, xii, 99, 103, 119, 139, 140, 142, 162, 163, 170

New York Vigilance Committee, 52

Nixon, Richard, 170

Nobel Peace Prize (see also Amnesty International), 213

Nongovernmental organizations (NGOs), 202, 203, 205, 206, 207, 209, 210, 212

Norris, Clarence, Scottsboro defendant, 131, 132, 133, 134, 140, 141, 142, 143, 145, 146

North Briton, The, 11

Oxford University, 177

Paine, Thomas, revolutionary, 14, 16, 27, 29, 36

Pamphlets, 3, 10, 12, 14, 16, 17, 24, 31, 33, 34, 36, 44, 49, 55, 64, 70, 72, 73, 74, 83, 85, 87, 90, 100, 101, 117, 158

Parliament (Britain), 13, 16, 17, 23, 31, 35, 42, 91, 177

Parsons, Albert, anarchist, 70, 71, 72, 74, 75

Parsons, Lucy, anarchist, 70, 72-3, 74, 75

Parks, Rosa, activist, 142, 147

Patterson, Haywood, Scottsboro defendant, 131, 133, 134, 141

Pavon Salazar, Miguel Angel, human rights defender, 214

Peace Brigades International (PBI), 214

Pennsylvania Hall, 48, 54

Persecution '61, 181

Petitions, 16, 35, 44, 45, 81, 116, 117

Philadelphia Vigilance Committee, 52

Phillips, James, publisher, 25, 29, 30

Phillips, Wendell, public speaker, 61-63, 70, 77

Picquart, Georges, French military officer, 94, 101

Pitt, William, politician, 25

Political prisoners, 146, 173-6, 178-81, 184, 185, 196, 198, 207

Pope, Alexander, poet, 9

Pope Leo XIII, 58

Katherine Anne Porter, author, 3-4, 118, 119, 120

Presbyterians, 9

Price, Victoria, Scottsboro victim, 131, 139, 143

Priestley, Joseph, scientist, 29, 31

Prisoners of conscience, 182, 193

Protocol Relating to the Status of Refugees, 203

Public Ledger, 23

Pulitzer, Joseph, publisher, 66

Quakers (Religious Society of Friends), 8, 9, 14, 15, 16, 17, 18, 21, 26, 29, 32, 34, 45, 47, 89, 180, 197

Quixote Center, xi, 212

Radio, 131, 143, 145, 157

Rainforest Foundation, 211-12

Ramsey, James, antislavery campaigner, 14, 24-5

Raskin, Jonah, activist, 169

Redhouse, Diana, AI pioneer, 191

Religion, 55

Remond, Charles, black abolitionist, 50

Rerum Novarum, 58

Reuben, William, journalist, 155, 156, 157, 165, 166, 170

Rights of Man, The. 28, 36

Robeson, Paul, actor/singer, 151, 160

Rosenberg, Ethel and Julius, 2, 148-170

Rosenberg Fund for Children, 166

Rosenberg-Sobell Committee, 171

Rush, Benjamin, abolitionist, 16

Sacco, Nicola, 109, 115, 121, 122, 125, 133

Sacco, Rosa, 120

Sacco-Vanzetti case, 2, 78, 106, 107-28, 136, 146, 153, 168; Sacco-Vanzetti Defense Committee, 4, 110, 116; Sacco-Vanzetti Memorial Committee, 121

St. Martin in the Fields Church (London), 174, 190

Sargant, Tom, activist, 178, 187, 196

Saypol, Irving (Rosenberg prosecutor), 158

Schlesinger, Arthur, Jr., historian, 123

Schlesinger, Arthur, Sr., historian, 115, 124

Scottsboro Boys, 4, 131-147, 153, 193; Scottsboro Boy, 141; Scottsboro Defense Committee, 130, 141, 147

Seditious Societies Act, 36

Shahn, Ben, artist, 124, 131

Shanu, Hezekiah, businessman, 89

Sharp, Granville, 16, 21-24, 25, 26, 29, 32

Shavelson, Clara Lemlich, 163

Shields, Art, journalist, 111

Sims, Thomas, escaped slave, 45, 61

Sinclair, Upton, author, 113, 114, 121, 124, 128

Siviter, Keith, AI pioneer, 186, 189

Sjöblom, E.V., missionary, 88

Slavery, 1, 2, 14, 15, 20, 21, 24, 26, 27, 30, 42

Slave ship diagram, 33

Slave trade, 8, 12, 15, 16, 17, 18, 23, 30, 31, 41

Smith Act, 150, 153, 156

Smith, Adam, economist, 14

Snow, Clyde, forensic anthropologist, 205

Sobell, Helen, 155, 171

Sobell, Morton, Rosenberg defendant, 148, 152, 154, 170

Social Gospel, 63, 76

Société des Amis des Noirs, 30

Société Française pour l'Abolition de l'Esclavage, 56

Society for the Relief of Free Negroes, 16

Society of Labour Lawyers, 178, 184

Solomon, Flora and Harold, 177

Somerset, James, slave in Britain, 23

Sons of Africa, 26

Spanish Civil War, 77, 177

Spanish Prisoners Defense Committee, 178

Speed, Mrs. Craik and Jane, Scottsboro activists, 138

Stewart, Maria, 47

Sting, singer, 211

Strategies, 21, 41, 81, 158, 159

Strong, Jonathan, slave in Britain, 22

Tappan, Arthur, abolitionist, 44, 48

Tappan, Lewis, abolitionist, 44

Television, 157

Thayer, Webster, Sacco-Vanzetti judge, 110

Thomas, Norman, Socialist leader, 139, 144

Thompson, William G., Sacco-Vanzetti attorney, 113, 114

Thomson, James, poet, 8

Thoreau, Henry David, author, 46-7, 53, 58, 104

Thoughts on Slavery, 21

Threes, 186-88, 193-95, 197

Till, Emmett, murder victim, 142

Torture, 1, 5, 25, 46, 94, 103, 141, 142, 179, 194, 203, 208

Trades Union Congress (TUC), 177

Trarieux, Ludovic, activist, 97, 176

Truth, Sojourner, activist, 18, 50, 54, 55

Two Acts, the, 36

Tubman, Harriet, activist, 52
Twain, Mark, author, 82, 87, 89, 90

Uncle Tom's Cabin, 52
Underground Railroad, 51-3
Union Square, 122, 166
Unitarians, 9, 34
United Nations, 179, 202, 204, 208; United Nations Human Rights Commission, 202, 203, 206, 208; United Nations conferences, 209
"United States of Lyncherdom," 82
Universal Declaration of Human Rights, 173, 182, 190, 193, 195, 202, 207
Urey, Harold, physicist, 163
Urgent Action Appeal (UA), 204, 214, 215
U.S. Congress, 150
U.S. Justice Department, 4, 87
U.S. Supreme Court, 74, 136, 138, 139, 160, 165

Vanzetti, Bartolomeo, 3, 109, 113, 115, 121, 122, 125, 133
Vanzetti, Luigia, 120, 164
Vatican, 103, 164
Vincent, Neville, AI pioneer, 184, 187, 190, 195, 196
Volunteers, 159, 160, 179, 198, 202, 215

Walker, David, black abolitionist, 53
Wallace, George, governor of Alabama, 142
Wallace, Henry, presidential candidate, 151, 153
Warner, Dorothy, AI pioneer, 191-2
Washington Post, The, 71, 84, 142, 164
"Weatherman" movement, 169
Wedgwood, Josiah, anti-slave-trade campaigner, 6, 33
Weld, Theodore, abolitionist, 48, 49, 53, 54
Wells, H.G., author, 102, 119, 120, 202
Wells-Barnett, Ida, 83-87, 104, 202
Wesley, John, clergyman, 14, 17, 21
Whipper, William, black philanthropist, 51, 52
White Swan, 181
White, Walter, activist, 132, 144, 145

Wilberforce, William, politician, 25, 31, 34, 35, 36, 89, 143
Wilkes, John, politician, 11-12, 32
Wilkins, Roy, activist, 139, 141
Wilson, Woodrow, President, 107
Wolf, Lucien, activist, 103, 104
Women, 16, 27, 34-5, 37, 41-43, 47-52, 61, 62, 72, 83, 85, 88, 111, 163, 192, 197, 203, 205, 208, 209
Wood, Keith, AI pioneer, 188
Woods, Joseph, activist, 18
Woolman, John, Quaker preacher, 14, 15
World Bank, 206, 211
World's Columbian Exhibition, 84

Zong, 25

The publication of this book was made possible by the generosity of the following individuals and organizations:

Anonymous
George N. Appell
Christopher Avery
Megan Biesele/Kalahari Peoples Fund
Thelma Boeder
Linda Borst
Peter B. Collins
Bill D'Antonio
East Bay Community Foundation (Ted Nace Fund)
Priscilla & Whitney Ellsworth
Maureen Fiedler, SL
William Friedlander
Friends Committee on National Legislation (Education Fund)
John Garrison
Earlene & Kent Hawley
Kevin Healy
Adam Hochschild
Tom Holloway
Mary E. Hunt
Glenn Marcus
Steven M. McAllister
Lucia Ann McSpadden
The Quixote Center
Robert and Jeanne Rabben
David Rabin
Joseph Rozansky
Dr. William F. Schulz
Amelia Simpson
Sisters of St. Francis (Tiffin, Ohio)
Leif Skoogfors
Special Initiatives Fund of Amnesty International USA
Shirley Tung
Terence S. Turner & Jane Fajans
Patti Whaley
Paul Woodhull

Thanks to all for moral and financial support.

*Please support human rights
and help save lives.*

JOIN AMNESTY INTERNATIONAL.

Amnesty International (AI) is a worldwide movement of people who campaign for human rights. AI's work is based on careful research and on the standards agreed by the international community. AI is independent of any government, political ideology, economic interest or religion. It does not support or oppose any government or political system, nor does it support or oppose the views of the victims whose rights it seeks to protect. It is concerned solely with the impartial protection of human rights.

AI mobilizes volunteer activists—people who give freely of their time and energy in solidarity with the victims of human rights violations. There are more than 1 million AI members and subscribers in over 140 countries and territories. AI members come from many different backgrounds, with widely different political and religious beliefs, united by a determination to work for a world where everyone enjoys human rights. (*Amnesty International Report 2001,* pp. 1, 279.)

For more information, go to www.amnestyusa.org

ABOUT THE QUIXOTE CENTER

The Quixote Center is an international justice and peace center located in Brentwood, Maryland, near Washington, D.C. The Center's projects include:

Catholics Speak Out - encourages Catholics to challenge the leaders and members of the Roman Catholic Church on ecclesial justice and reform issues and provides resources to assist them.

Priests for Equality - works for gender equality and prepares and publishes inclusive language Scriptures and liturgical materials.

Noisy Contemplation - promotes prayer for busy people who struggle for justice.

Faith Matters - a weekly interfaith radio talk show that addresses the key religious issues of our times.

Haiti Reborn - offers literacy and reforestation assistance and solidarity to the people of Haiti.

Quest for Peace - works for economic justice for Nicaraguans, sends material aid and funds grassroots development projects in Nicaragua.

Nicaraguan Cultural Alliance - supports Nicaraguan artists and promotes their work through sales of fine art products.

Equal Justice USA - works to abolish the death penalty and, through its Moratorium Now! campaign, strives to bring about a moratorium on executions.

Books to Prisoners - a subproject of Equal Justice, provides reading material to prisoners to encourage the development of literacy.

25th Anniversary for the Quixote Center 2001

PO Box 5206, Hyattsville, MD 20782 • tel: 301-699-0042 • fax: 301-864-2182
quixote@quixote.org • www.quixote.org